Mencius
Mencius

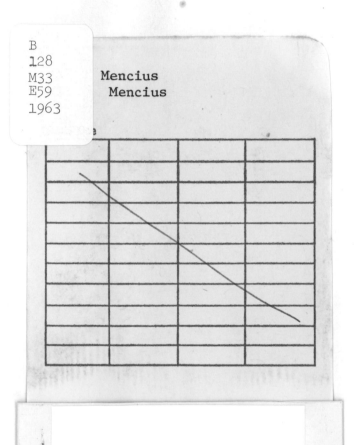

MENCIUS

MENCIUS

𝄞𝄞𝄞𝄞𝄞𝄞𝄞𝄞𝄞𝄞𝄞𝄞𝄞𝄞𝄞𝄞𝄞𝄞𝄞𝄞𝄞𝄞𝄞𝄞𝄞𝄞𝄞𝄞𝄞𝄞𝄞

A new translation
arranged and annotated for
the general reader

by
W.A.C.H. DOBSON

𝄞𝄞𝄞𝄞𝄞𝄞𝄞𝄞𝄞𝄞𝄞𝄞𝄞𝄞𝄞𝄞𝄞𝄞𝄞𝄞𝄞𝄞𝄞𝄞𝄞𝄞𝄞𝄞𝄞𝄞𝄞

University of Toronto Press

UNESCO COLLECTION OF REPRESENTATIVE
WORKS — CHINESE SERIES

This book has been accepted in the Chinese
Translations Series of the United Nations
Educational, Scientific, and Cultural Organi-
zation (UNESCO)

To

ARTHUR WALEY

who "held up one corner"

Analects VII.8

PREFACE

I HAVE BEEN READING the *Works of Mencius* with university students now, for nearly twenty years. The *Works* are the text with which most students begin their initiation into Classical Chinese. In the process, I must have read some passages hundreds of times. I have analysed the language of the text in minute detail for a work of technical scholarship. Despite this, I have never failed to derive pleasure from *Mencius* as a work of literature, and something of this pleasure I have tried to convey to my pupils. It is with the hope that this pleasure might be shared with a wider audience that this translation has been made. Mr. Arthur Waley, most successful of translators from the Chinese, first introduced me to the delights of Chinese literature and has been a kind friend ever since. This book is, with permission, dedicated to him in deference and gratitude.

W.A.C.H.D.

CONTENTS

INTRODUCTION

IF A PHILOSOPHER IS to be judged by the measure of the influence that his works have exercised, then Mencius is one of the world's important philosophers. He was born a century after the death of Confucius (c. 551-479 B.C.) and was to live to see the birth of Hsün Tzu (c. 340-245 B.C.). Confucius, Mencius, and Hsün Tzu are the founding fathers of the philosophy known as Confucianism. All have left records of their teachings. Of them those of Mencius are the most lucid and readable.

The *Works* of the earlier fathers of Confucianism lack the form and shape that the orderly presentation of ideas takes in later Chinese philosophical writing. Confucius' *Analects* are short sentence- or paragraph-length sayings of the Master, illustrative anecdotes, maxims, and the like. They were recorded by his pupils. Their purpose, it seems clear, was to provide "key texts" for the novice when being initiated by a Master into the teachings of the school. They were almost certainly intended to be committed to memory. The *Works of Mencius* follows the pattern of the *Analects*, though the paragraphs are extended and the treatment is fuller. There is not, as yet, any perceptible attempt at arrangement by topic or sequence. The reader—who is not directly addressed in *Mencius*—is, as it were, invited to eavesdrop on the conversations of a Master and his pupils ranging at random across the entire spectrum of Mencius' thought. The reader must piece together for himself, from allusion, parable, anecdote, and maxim, an ordered statement of Mencius' philosophy. It was Hsün Tzu who, some fifty years later, left his philosophy in a literary form susceptible to arrangement by subject under chapter headings. Hsün Tzu addresses the reader directly. The indirect appeal to the reader in Mencius, to my mind, gives the *Works* a freshness and intimacy which the impersonal, though much more tidy, treatment of Hsün Tzu lacks.

The *Works of Mencius* received canonical recognition in the twelfth century. But previously, in the first century A.D., the Imperial Court had designated "Masters of Learning" to devote themselves exclusively to its study. There are many commentaries on the *Works*.

It was among the first of the books studied in traditional China in the education of a gentleman. It contains the quintessence of Confucian thought. And since Confucianism has enjoyed official patronage throughout much of Imperial Chinese history, Confucian thought has been a pre-eminent influence in the moulding of the Chinese ethos.

Mencius, whose Chinese name is Meng K'o, is referred to in deference as Meng Tzu or Master Meng. He was born c. 390 B.C., in the little principality of Tsou. Tsou lies to the south of Lu, the city-state on the south of the Shantung peninsula which was the birth-place of Confucius. He died c. 305 B.C. and was thus a contemporary of Aristotle. Mencius has long been revered as a Sage, was canonized by Imperial decree, and stands second only in esteem to Confucius. Hagiography has provided a great deal of detail about him, but it is often contradictory. Very little is known about him from early or reliable sources. Even his dates are uncertain. The death of his parents is mentioned in the *Works* but we know nothing about them or about his antecedents. It is possible that his family was a cadet branch of the noble Meng-sun family of Lu. Certain it is, however, that he was educated in the manner common at the time for the sons of the aristo-cracy. He is thoroughly familiar with those mainstays of the classical curriculum—the *Book of Songs*, and the *Book of Documents*.[1] He quotes frequently from the works of Confucius, and it is likely that he studied with one of the Confucian schools. Tradition improbably makes him a pupil of Tzu-szu, the grandson of Confucius.

There is an engaging though apocryphal story of Mencius' child-hood. Mencius' family lived in the vicinity of a cemetery. His mother, noticing that he was playing among the graves imitating funeral directors and feeling that this was no place in which to bring up a son,

[1] For these works the reader cannot do better than to turn, in the first instance, to *The Analects of Confucius* by Arthur Waley (London, 1938). Here he will find, not only an admirable trans-lation of this Confucian classic, but a wealth of information on Confucianism in its earliest stages, much of which is invaluable in understanding *Mencius*. For the *Book of Songs* the reader might like to compare the translations of Arthur Waley, *The Book of Songs* (London, 1937) with those of Bernhard Karlgren, *The Book of Odes* (Stockholm, 1950). For the *Book of Documents* the reader should first see Waley, *Analects* (p. 51). Karlgren's *The Book of Documents* (Stockholm, 1950) gives a text and translation of certain chapters only. In my *Early Archaic Chinese* (Toronto, 1962) five chapters are translated together with some bronze inscriptions of the period. The standard translation of the Confucian Canon is that of James Legge, *The Chinese Classics* (5 vols., Oxford, 1893). In Legge the *Book of Songs* appears as *The Book of Odes* (vol. 4), the *Book of Documents* as *The Classic of History* (vol. 3). Legge also has a translation of the *Analects* and of *Mencius* (vol. 1). References to these Works in footnotes are to Waley for *Analects* and *Songs* and to Karlgren for *Documents*, unless otherwise stated, but the translations offered of citations are my own.

moved into the neighbourhood of the market. Here the child began playing at shopkeepers, pretending to be weighing merchandise. His mother thought that this, too, was no place in which to bring up a son and moved close to a school. Here the child amused himself at mimicking the "bowings and scrapings" of Court life, and its ceremonial. On seeing this, Mencius' mother felt that she had found, at last, the proper neighbourhood in which to raise her son.[2]

Mencius, like Confucius before him, was a teacher. And like Confucius he aspired ultimately to hold office in the courts of the city-states. As tutor to the sons of gentlemen he taught the *Book of Songs* and the *Book of Documents*. The *Songs* are an anthology of dynastic hymns and secular songs, and the *Documents* are a collection of papers from the state archives mainly, though not exclusively, from western Chou (11th—8th cent. B.C.). The philosophy later to be known as Confucianism grew in the exegesis of these documents of antiquity. They were thought to portray an ideal state of society, a halcyon era, from which the China of the day, it was supposed, had seriously declined. The Confucian plea was essentially for a restoration to this past condition. Confucians protested that their teachings contained no innovation. In reality, by "scriptural interpretation" and by investing old words with new meanings, they created, upon supposedly ancient authority, a theory of the state and of Ideal Government, and a code of ethical behaviour, which they believed should inform the state and guide the prince. It was such ideas that they imparted to their pupils. Both Confucius and Mencius sought a prince who might, under their tutelage, usher in a Confucian state. Confucius and Mencius shared in common the disappointing experience of failing to find such a prince, though Mencius, in a brief term as Minister of the State of Ch'i, thought for a time that he had found one.

Confucianism remained for the first few centuries of its existence a local and obscure movement. It was not until after the establishment of the Empire (at the close of the second century B.C.) that it came into its own.

Mencius' notions about classical antiquity differ markedly from those we gain from archaeological research today. In his time, legends

---

[2] This story, of which several accounts are found (the *Lieh-nü Chuan* is the earliest), later became a popular exemplary tale. The "three moves" are proverbial for motherly devotion and duty.

circulated about the founder heroes Yao, Shun, and Yü. Yü is the hero of a sort of Flood legend, in which he is depicted as draining the marshes and directing the courses of rivers, thereby making the north China plains habitable. Later these heroes and others were organized into "dynasties." Historians have for long been familiar with the dictum "the earlier the projection, the later the source." In Mencius' time, however, Yao, Shun, and Yü had simply been gathered into the pantheon of Ideal Kings. Of dynastic times, Mencius knew, from his literary sources, of the Hsia, Shang, and early Chou dynasties. His heroes of these epochs were the dynastic founders, the Sage Kings, and particularly King Wen and King Wu of the Chou House. His cautionary figures are the debased kings, the last of their lines, who lost the imperial succession for their houses. Of these Chieh, the last and "bad" King of Hsia, and Chou, the "bad" King of Shang, have names which have become proverbial for dissoluteness.

The early Chou kings had appealed to a doctrine they called "receiving the Mandate of Heaven." The Mandate (*ming*) was a charge given to fief-holders. Heaven conferred its Mandate, so the Chous alleged, upon one designated by Heaven as its Son (*T'ien-tzu*). The Son of Heaven, as the viceroy of the deity upon earth, enfeoffed his subjects and vassals in their turn with "charges." This Mandate, it was further alleged, was not held in perpetuity, but upon lease. It was surrendered when the incumbent "lost virtue" and brought down upon his head "the punishment of Heaven." Such "punishment," the Chous said, Heaven had charged them to bring down upon Shang, and Heaven, they averred, had placed thereafter the Mandate of Heaven in their hands.

The Chous ruled as an Imperial House, directly in their own domain, and indirectly through delegation to feudatories, and by vassalage over otherwise independent states, over the whole of the north and central China plain. They ruled in this way for some four hundred years. The central power, however, weakened, and the Feudal Lords, many of whom had ties of blood with the royal family, became independent, setting themselves up as kings and paying but ritual duties to the Imperial House. At first these city-states conducted interstate relations and sought to compose their quarrels through a confederacy, in which the participating states chose one of their number as Paramount Prince. By the time of Mencius, however, the period of the Paramountcy had spent its course, and near anarchy reigned among the princes. The Confucians saw in the signs of the times marks of the displeasure of Heaven—a time to look for the emergence of the Sage King in whom Heaven would reinvest its Mandate and restore once again the virtues and good order of the classical ages.

The architect of the doctrine of the Mandate of Heaven was probably the Duke of Chou, brother and Prime Minister to King Wu of the Chou Dynasty and for a time regent to King Wu's successor King Ch'eng, who came to the throne as a minor. In the Confucian view, Sage Kings arose with the assistance of such Sage Ministers. The disciples of both Confucius and Mencius saw in their masters the possibility of playing just such a role, and regarded them as portents that the Sage King, whose emergence was long overdue, might soon appear.

It was in their study of the documents of antiquity that the Confucians found authority for many of the ethical, political, and economic ideas which they themselves propounded. If scriptural authority were to be found for original ideas, however, these writings had to be interpreted allegorically, and new connotations given to old words. Thus *te* ("virtue") had, for Mencius, much of our modern meaning of virtue, but in his sources it had no ethical connotation at all. It was rather "power-fraught" (compare Latin *virtus*), a quality known to anthropologists as "mana." Mencius speaks much of *Jen* and *Yi*. *Jen* had properly the meaning of "the attributes of a man, manly, masculine," but in the Mencian interpretation it becomes "humane." *Yi* ("justice") stems from a word meaning "custom." *Wang*, the normal word for a king, becomes for Mencius an Ideal King, a king in more than name. *Li*, a word denoting simply a rite, acquires a generic sense for the code of decorum of the Confucian gentleman. Because of these private interpretations, and the tendency in Mencius to cite ancient authority, it is, at times, difficult to see the relevance of a clinching quotation, if read in its original context. The method, however, is not unfamiliar to us since the words of the Bible are interpreted and cited in support of the most contradictory of notions.

In the standard editions of the *Works*, apart from a division into books and paragraphs, there is little perceptible attempt at arrangement by topic or sequence. This shapelessness makes it difficult for an occidental reader to gain readily a coherent picture of Mencius and

B

his teaching. Although the *Works* translated here are given in their entirety, the parts have been rearranged in a sequence which, it is hoped, will make them more meaningful.[3] Those parts which describe Mencius in his audiences with the princes have been gathered together in the first chapter, under the title "Mencius at Court." This gives some notion of Mencius as a statesman. Mencius' encounters with political rivals and public functionaries, and the statements made about his retirement from public life, are collected in chapter II. The renunciation of political ambition marks a crisis in Mencius' life, and this chapter gives some idea of its causes and effect. In the third chapter, the more intimate conversations of Mencius with his disciples are brought together. Here, a picture is given of Mencius as a teacher. The polemical portions of the *Works* have been placed in chapter IV. Mencius had rival philosophies to contend with, and here they are examined and discussed. Mencius' comments on the events of his day are gathered together in chapter V. A number of paragraphs occur throughout the book, some long some short, which do not specifically relate either to Mencius' public life, to his disciples, or to his rivals. Where these can be assembled into groupings which relate to Mencius' teaching, they are placed in chapter VI. Maxims, epithets, and the remainder are put in chapter VII.

To one familiar with the text, the very process of rearranging its parts in this fashion throws new light on *Mencius*. It reveals, for example, some notable omissions. Though Mencius several times mentions the two prevailing philosophies of his time, the utilitarianism of Micius and the hedonism of Yang Chu, and though he attacks utilitarianism directly, not hesitating to mention Micians by name, he nowhere identifies a single hedonist. Now a great deal is known about Micius. There is a considerable *Work* of the school which has survived. But little is known about Yang Chu's philosophy. The principal source, though a fragmentary one, is the *Lü-shih Ch'un-ch'iu*. Yet Mencius in his Court utterances is full of attacks on luxury and pleasure, though Confucian teaching is not characterized by any strong ascetic tendency. Presumably these thoughts are prompted by the very prevalence in high quarters of the philosophy he is so reluctant to name. Does this not suggest that in its cautionary references, *Mencius*

---

[3] If anyone wishes to consult the original, or other translations which follow the order of the original, he can do so with the help of the Finding List on p. 209 ff.

offers further material for a study of hedonism in the fourth century
B.C.?

Again, one of the institutions of great interest to the historian of
philosophy in ancient China is the Chi-hsia Academy, founded in the
State of Ch'i by King Hsüan. To this Academy, King Hsüan invited
the most prominent thinkers of his day. We know the names of a
number of them. Mencius was at the Court of Ch'i at this time, but
nowhere is the Academy mentioned, and only one of its members is
mentioned by name. Yet the text contains a number of hidden allusions
to "men of ability," to "sinecures" and the like, without specifically
mentioning the incumbents by name. It seems fairly clear that Mencius
and his followers were not so well established that they could dispense
with caution and discretion in referring to the powerful and influential
of their place and time.

In later Confucian hagiography, both Confucius and Mencius are
represented as having been considerable figures in their day, Confucius being referred to as an "uncrowned king." Modern scholarship
has already shown how slender are these claims to worldly success in
the case of Confucius. It seems likely that this will prove to be the case
with Mencius, too. Despite his brief, and unsuccessful, term of office
in Ch'i, the *Works* are surprisingly silent on the major interstate
political issues of the day. For, although the major area of political
conflict lay in the relations of the powerful states of Ch'in, Ch'u, and
Ch'i, Mencius does not betray very great familiarity with happen-
ings outside of Ch'i and its immediate neighbourhood.

This suggests that even with the rank of minister (and King Hsüan
is known to have given high-sounding titles to philosophers who
diverted him), Mencius was not admitted to the inner councils of the
Court, and remained, as he began, an obscure teacher with a teaching
that was out of joint with the times.

As to the translation itself, I have tried to render an Archaic Chinese
original in a modern and unadorned prose. Its purpose is to assist the
general reader, otherwise unfamiliar with Chinese authors, to understand what *Mencius* is about. I have not tried to capture the "flavour"
of the original language, or striven for effect to imitate the
idiosyncrasies of Chinese word order. I have not hesitated to paraphrase freely, where more conventional translation would require a
long apparatus of explanation. A practised reader of ·Chinese texts

can accommodate himself to a plethora of Chinese proper names. The general reader finds them easily confused. Proper names are often expanded in this translation with an identifying epithet, which, though not in the original, does help a reader around this difficulty. Throughout, the aim has been to place before the general reader as clear an account as I find possible of the *Works* of this important philosopher, without encumbering the text with the footnotes and technical apparatus which the specialist quite properly demands.

Most educated Westerners are familiar with the thinkers and prophets who inform the Western spirit. But they are less familiar with the thinkers who have shaped the major Oriental civilizations. The heirs of these ancient civilizations are now once again in the ascendant. We must understand the ways and thoughts that condition their conduct. *Mencius*, I think, provides an admirable insight into one of the streams of thought of the Chinese. Indeed the perceptive reader might well find that some ideas that he thought were new and alien in the new China have familiar echoes in the *Works of Mencius*.

MENCIUS

Chapter One

ⅢⅢⅢⅢⅢⅢⅢⅢⅢⅢⅢⅢⅢⅢⅢⅢⅢⅢⅢⅢⅢⅢⅢⅢⅢⅢⅢⅢⅢⅢⅢⅢⅢⅢⅢⅢ

MENCIUS AT COURT

In the fourth century B.C., north and central China was divided into a series of city-states (kuo). Originally the Feudatories of the Chou House, they had become independent, and their rulers called themselves kings. Certain of them had by conquest and annexation become quite large. Others, though small, by sheltering under the aegis of a "major state" retained a precarious independence. The movement towards aggrandizement was centred largely in the states of Ch'in and erstwhile Tsin, Ch'u, and Ch'i. To the courts of these ambitious princes the philosophers of the time came, offering theories of government and seeking preferment. Mencius, however, is not known to have travelled very far beyond the Shantung peninsula, and the Courts in which he sought employment, the major state of Ch'i and the states of Wei, T'eng, and Lu, are all contained within a radius of some hundred and fifty miles.

Mencius believed that Heaven would raise up among the princes an Ideal King, who would unite the city-states once again and bring peace to the world. Such kings had been vouchsafed by Heaven before. There was T'ang the Successful, founder of the Shang Dynasty (c. 16th cent. B.C.), and King Wu, the first ruler of the Chou Dynasty (11th cent. B.C.).[1] These halcyon reigns recurred in cycles, and, as Mencius observed, the recurrence was belated in his day. Five hundred years was the normal span. Seven hundred years had already elapsed.[2] This, it seemed to him, was only further reason to hope that the day was at hand. In the interim, Heaven raised up men "famous in their generation"[3] (of which Confucius was one) to keep alive the Kingly Ideal. Mencius further believed that Heaven would appoint a mentor and minister for the Ideal King, who would play a role comparable to that of the Duke of Chou, the premier of King Wu. This role Mencius persuaded himself might be his own, for, as he says, "with the exception of myself, who is there to be Heaven's instrument?"[4]

[1] See Introduction to 6.43 and to 6.52.   [2] See 2.14 and also 3.3.   [3] 2.14.   [4] 2.14.

3

Mencius' highest expectations came from King Hsüan of Ch'i at whose Court he became minister for a time. King Hsüan he felt could be the Ideal King if only he would.[5] He expected less of King Hui of Liang. This king hoped to unite the world by force, a notion repulsive to Mencius. In despair of these kings, Mencius thought that even the ruler of the petty principality of T'eng was not without promise, for "One could rule as a True King with a Kingdom a hundred miles square,"[6] though this hope he does not seem to have seriously entertained for long. A major crisis in Mencius' career, and a significant stage in the development of his thought, arrived when, finally despairing of the princes, he came to the realization that "Heaven does not intend at this time to bring peace to the world,"[7] that the expected king was not to appear, and that the role he hoped he himself might play was not to be his. He resigned from office and returned home, there to gather round him his disciples and to keep alive, if only in the hearts of men, the Kingly Ideal.

When Mencius left Ch'i, one of his numerous critics observed: "If Mencius did not know that the King of Ch'i would not become another T'ang or an Wu, it shewed his lack of perception."[8] To such realism Mencius replied with the simplicity of the dévot: "The King has, after all, all that is needed to become great. If he had availed himself fully of my services, not only the people of Ch'i but all the world would now be at peace."[9]

AT THE COURT OF KING HSÜAN OF CH'I

Ch'i, which occupied the northern part of the modern Shantung peninsula, was a prosperous and anciently established state. It was one of the original Feudatories at the foundation of the Chou Dynasty.[10] It had numbered among its rulers names famed in history. In the seventh century, B.C. there had been Duke Huan and his minister, Kuan Chung.[11] They were credited with establishing state monopolies on salt, which came from the salt-flats of the coast of the Gulf of Chihli, and on iron, which came into use some time in the seventh century, but which by the fifth was a major item in city-state economy. A book purporting to contain the economic theories of Kuan Chung shelters under his name. Stories of Duke Ching of Ch'i and of his notable minister, Yen Tzu, in the sixth century, were still quoted in the fourth.[12]

[5] 1.5; see also 3.28.   [6] 1.20.   [7] 2.14.   [8] 2.16.   [9] 2.16.   [10] See Introduction to 6.52.
[11] See Introduction to 6.70.   [12] See 1.2.

King Hsüan (reigned 319-301 B.C.) himself lived in considerable luxury; his pleasure palaces and parks were bywords. But he was a patron of learning. To the Chi-hsia Academy, which he established, came many of the thinkers of his day.[13] It was to a luxurious and sophisticated court that Mencius brought his simple gospel of the Ideal King, the Ideal Minister, and the restoration of classical virtues.

I.I. TRUE PRINCES AND WORTHY KINGS

King Hsüan of Ch'i asked: "Is it true that King T'ang banished Chieh, and that King Wu slew Chou?" Mencius replied: "Yes, it says so in the *Records*."[14] The King said: "But properly speaking, may a subject slay his prince?" Mencius replied: "A man who despoils Humanity I call a robber; a man who despoils Justice, a ruffian.[15] Robbers and ruffians are mere commoners. I was aware that that commoner Chou was slain, but unaware that a prince was slain."   (1B.8)

Chieh and Chou were the last kings of the Hsia and Shang Dynasties respectively. Their names are proverbial for depravity. In the Confucian view they had surrendered their claims as princes, since Heaven withdraws its Mandate from the wicked. Though a subject may not slay his prince Heaven may commission one upon whom its Mandate is to fall to remove the prince from whom the Mandate is to be withdrawn. The State of Ch'i had lost four of its kings by assassination in the previous 150 years.

I.2

King Hsüan of Ch'i received Mencius in audience at the Snow Palace. The King said: "Did the Worthy Kings,[16] of whom you speak, have pleasure palaces such as these?" Mencius replied: "Yes, they did, though their subjects, if they had had no part in them, would have condemned their rulers for it. It is, of course, wrong to condemn one's superiors, but, too, it is wrong for a prince to fail to share his pleasures with his people. The prince who takes pleasure in those things that give his people pleasure will find that the people approve of his pleasures. Conversely, the prince who is saddened by those things

---

[13] See Introduction to 4.17.
[15] See Introduction to chapter VI.

[14] See Additional Notes, 1.28, note 109.
[16] Cf. 1.24.

that sadden his people will find that his people are saddened by the things that sadden him. No prince who has made mankind's pleasures and pains his own pleasures and pains has failed to attain the Princely Ideal.

"A former ruler of this state, Duke Ching,[17] once inquired of his Prime Minister, Yen Tzu: 'I want to inspect Ch'uan-fu and Chao-wu, and then, proceeding southward along the sea coast, to return by way of Lang-yeh.[18] What preparations should I make to ensure that this tour will be comparable to those taken by the Kings of antiquity?' To which Yen Tzu replied: 'An excellent question indeed! In antiquity an Emperor's visit to a Feudal Lord was called *hsün-shou*, that is, he inspected (*hsün*) the states under his care (*shou*). A Feudal Lord's visit to the Court of an Emperor was called *shu-chih*, that is, he made a report (*shu*) upon his feudal duty (*chih*). These things had a purpose. In the spring, the sowings came under review, so that the shortages (of seed) might be made up, and in the autumn the harvest was inspected, so that help might be sent where the yield was deficient.[19] A Hsia proverb says: 'If the king does not visit us in the spring, how can we receive favour? If he does not visit us in the autumn, how can we be helped?' Among the feudal lords of those days, the spring and autumn tours were the invariable rule. But today, things are very different. Princes travel accompanied by large armies and vast stores of food, though the hungry are not fed, nor are the weary given relief. The people avert their eyes and curse among themselves. They turn to evil. The officials batten upon the people; food and drink flow like water, ebb and flow, waste and disappear.[20] The Kings of antiquity had no pleasures or state visits involving such profligate waste. Let such, then, be the form your state visit takes." Duke Ching was pleased, and made great preparations throughout the state (for the relief of the needy) and went to live in a small hut in the outskirts of the capital.[21] Duke Ching also summoned the Master of Music and bade him compose a piece on the theme 'Princes and subjects share their pleasures'. No doubt the pieces *Chih-shao* and *Chia-shao* are

[17] See Additional Notes.
[18] Places in the north Shantung peninsula.
[19] This same passage appears in 6.70 in a different context.
[20] See Additional Notes.
[21] The act of one in mourning (cf. 1.28). The Duke is thought thus to have shown his compassion for the people's suffering.

works of the sort, for the lyrics contain the lines 'Is it wrong to please our prince? To please him is to love him'."

(1B.4)

It is more likely that the visits to the fields by the Kings of antiquity had to do with fertility rites, performed at sowing and harvest, but the events and records of antiquity are interpreted in the light of contemporary moral ideals, thus giving to solutions for current economic problems the sanction of scriptural precedent.

1.3. ON LUXURY

King Hsüan of Ch'i asked, "It is said that King Wen[22] had a hunting park seventy miles square; is this true?" Mencius replied, "Yes, it says so in the *Records*."[23] The King said, "Was the park really as large as that?" Mencius replied, "Large?—his people would have thought it small!" The King said, "But I have a park only forty miles square, and my people, it seems, think it too large—why is this?" Mencius replied, "The hunting park of King Wen was seventy miles square, but those who wished to trap small game or gather straw and kindling were allowed to enter it. King Wen shared it with his people so that with justification they thought it too small. But when I first arrived at the frontiers of your Majesty's State, and inquired as to the prohibitions that were in force here (for then only would I have presumed to proceed further) I was told that within the vicinity of the capital there was a hunting park some forty miles square in which anyone caught hunting deer was treated as though he were guilty of murder. This forty square miles constitutes a trap for the unwary within the state. If the people think it too large (a trap), they are, after all, quite right."

(1B.2)

1.4

Chuang Pao,[24] on being received by Mencius, told him that he, Chuang Pao, had had an audience with the King. The King, he said,

---

[22] Father of King Wu, founder of the Chou Dynasty (11th cent. B.C.), to whose policies King Wu's success was attributed (3.28). See Introduction to 6.43 and to 6.52.
[23] See Additional Notes, 1.28, note 109.   [24] A citizen of Ch'i.

had spoken of his love for music,[25] at which Chuang Pao had been at
a loss to know what to say. Chuang Pao asked Mencius, "What could
I have said about 'love of music'?" Mencius replied, "If the King's
love for music were profound, then Ch'i would be close (to the
Princely Ideal)."

On a later occasion, in audience with the King, Mencius said,
"Your Majesty has been speaking to Chuang Pao about your love
for music. Is that so?" The King's expression changed.[26] He said,
"I am not the sort of person who finds pleasure in the music of the
former kings. I only like today's popular music." Mencius said, "If
only your Majesty's love of music were profound, then Ch'i would be
close to an Ideal Kingdom! The music of today is like the music of
antiquity (in this respect)." The King said, "Can you explain this to
me?" Mencius replied, "Which is the more pleasurable, to enjoy
music alone, or to share it with others?" The King answered, "With
others." Mencius said, "Which is the more pleasurable, to enjoy
music with a few, or with many?" The King replied, "With many."
"Then," said Mencius, "let me tell you about music. Suppose, your
Majesty, that music is being played here, and the sound of the gongs
and drums and the notes of the flutes and pipes are heard by the people.
Suppose that they beat their heads and furrowed their brows, saying
to each other, "If our King is so fond of music, how is it that he allows
us to sink to such extremities? Father and son do not see each other;
brothers, wives, and children are separated!'[27]   Or suppose your
Majesty is hunting. The noise of your horses and chariots, and the
glitter of your banners are seen and heard by the people. Suppose
they beat their heads and furrowed their brows, saying to each other,
'If our King is so fond of hunting, how is it that he allows *us* to sink
to such extremities!'[28] If the people reacted in this way it would be
for no other reason than that your Majesty was not sharing his pleasures with them. But if the contrary were the case, if on hearing music
they felt happy and with delighted expressions turned to each other
and said, 'The King must be in excellent spirits, or otherwise he would
not be listening to music!' Or if, on hearing the sounds and sights of
the hunt, they felt happy and with pleased expressions turned to

---

[25] The words for "music" and "pleasure/to enjoy" are identical. This makes possible a play
on words that is lost in translation.
[26] See Additional Notes.   [27] See Additional Notes.   [28] See Additional Notes.

each other and said, 'The King must be in excellent health, or otherwise he would be unable to hunt.' If this were so, it would be for no other reason than that he shared his pleasures with his people. If your Majesty shared his music with the people, then he would be a Prince indeed."

(1B.1)

Foreign Relations

Relations among the city-states, after the decline of the power of the Imperial Court in the eighth century, had been regulated by a confederacy, in which the principal states chose from among their number a Paramount Prince. In the councils of the confederacy, such points of difference as arose were settled, where possible, by arbitration. The Paramountcy had declined in its turn, and in King Hsüan's time a period of near chaos in interstate relations prevailed. King Hsüan, in the incident which follows, asks Mencius about a predecessor of his, Duke Huan of Ch'i, and about Duke Wen of Tsin (both 7th cent. B.C.), the two most famous of the Paramount Princes. As Mencius observes, his school has no teaching upon the subject of the Paramountcy. Confucius lived under the Paramountcy, a system which he regarded with extreme disfavour. The Paramount Princes, in the Mencian view, were the antithesis of the Worthy Kings of antiquity.[29]

1.5

King Hsüan of Ch'i asked, "Might I ask for your views on the affairs of Duke Huan of Ch'i and Duke Wen of Tsin?" Mencius replied, "The followers of Confucius would not speak of those matters, and so those of us who succeed them have nothing to say on the subject. I know nothing about it. But since I lack the means of answering you, may I speak of True Kingship?" The King replied, "(Yes, you may.) What kind of 'virtue' should I possess, to be a True King?" Mencius replied, "Be a King by protecting your people—such a King is irresistible." The King asked, "Could one such as I be such a King?" Mencius replied, "You could." The King said, "How do you know that I could?" Mencius replied, "Hu Ho told me that your Majesty was sitting at the upper end of the audience chamber, and an ox was

[29] See Introduction to 6.70.

being led across the lower end. On seeing the ox, your Majesty asked where it was being taken, and was told that it was to be used in sacrifice at the dedication of a bell. Your Majesty ordered the release of the ox, observing that you could not bear to see it shuddering like a criminal being lead to the execution yard. On being asked if the ceremony of dedicating the bell was to be dispensed with, you replied that that was impossible, but that a sheep should be used instead. I was told this, though I do not know if it is true." The King replied, "It is quite true." Mencius continued, "A mind such as your Majesty displayed on that occasion is adequate for True Kingship. Though the people thought it was meanness on your Majesty's part, I know, to the contrary, that it was kindness." The King replied, "It is quite true that the people thought me mean, but though we refer to Ch'i as 'small and narrow' [i.e., poor][30] we would hardly grudge one ox. No, it was because I could not bear to see its suffering that I ordered its release and used a sheep instead." Mencius replied, "Your Majesty should not be surprised that the people thought you mean, for you exchanged a larger thing for a smaller, and how could they know your true motives? But since it was kindness on your Majesty's part, how could you discriminate between an ox and a sheep?" The King smiled and asked, "What were my motives? It was not that I grudged the price of an ox and used a sheep instead because it was cheaper, but even so the people did think me mean?" Mencius replied, "Do not grieve yourself on that account; this is the way of humanity. You saw the ox suffer but did not see the sheep. A gentleman who has seen an animal alive cannot bear to see it killed, and if he hears its death cry cannot bear to eat its flesh. It is for this reason that gentlemen avoid kitchens." The King was delighted with this answer and said, "When in the *Book of Songs*[31] it says, 'What others are thinking, I can divine,' it describes you, Sir. It was precisely as you describe it, though on thinking it over later, I could not recall my state of mind at the time. But when you spoke just now, what you said struck a familiar chord. In what way then, is this heart of mine, compatible with that of a True King?" Mencius replied, "Suppose someone reported to you that he was strong enough to lift three hundred pounds[32] but could not lift a feather, or that his eyesight was keen enough to see

---

[30] See Additional Notes. [31] Cf. *Songs*, 298 (Karlgren, *Odes*, 198).
[32] In 3.47 weight-lifting of this magnitude is spoken of as though it were perfectly feasible.

the tip of a hair from the new fur in autumn, but could not make out a wagon-load of faggots, would you allow that to be the case?" The King said, "No." Mencius replied, "Then how can you allow that you have kindness for an animal, but not enough kindness to reach out to your people? Failing to lift a feather, or being unable to see a wagon-load of faggots, is a matter of failing to use the strength or sight that you have. Similarly, the people's failure to obtain from you the protection they should get is a matter of your failing to exercise the kindness you already possess. And so, your Majesty's failing to be a True King is because you would not, not because you could not." The King said, "What really is the difference between 'would not' and 'could not'?" Mencius replied, "If you said you could not tuck Mount T'ai under your arm, and jump over the North Sea with it, that would really be a case of could not. If you said that you could not crack an old man's joints[33] for him, it would really be a case of 'would not' rather than 'could not'. And so your Majesty's failing to be a True King is not in the 'tucking Mount T'ai under the arm and jumping over the North Sea' class of things; it is in the 'cracking joints' class of things. If you treat your own elders as they properly should be treated, so that the example set reaches to the elders of others, and if you behave towards those younger than yourself as properly you should, so that the example set reaches to the younger of others, then you could twist the world around in the palm of your hand. In the *Book of Songs*[34] it says,

> A model to his own wife,
> His example affected his brothers,
> And so good order prevailed in his House and State.

The application of this in the present circumstances is simply this: Your Majesty should extend the mind you possess to these other things. Thus, if you extend your natural kindness this will be quite sufficient to protect the whole world. But if you fail to extend it (further than to animals) it will be insufficient even to protect your own wife and children. The reason that the men of antiquity so far excelled those of the present day lies merely in this—they were adept in extending and applying that which they basically were. How can

[33] I.e., pull out the knucklebones and so forth, when stiff.
[34] Cf. *Songs*, 245.

your Majesty now allow that you have kindness enough for an animal, but the efficacy of which fails to reach to your people? It is only by weighing that we know a thing's weight; it is only by measuring that we know its length. This is true of all things, but most true of the things of the heart. I beg that your Majesty would weigh up these things in your mind. However, your Majesty is even now mobilizing an army, intimidating your knights and servants, and arousing resentment among the Feudal Powers. Are you happy in your mind about these things?"

The King said, "No, how can such things give me pleasure? I seek by these means to gain the thing I desire so much." Mencius said, "Might I enquire what it is the King desires so much?" The King smiled but gave no answer. Mencius said, "It surely cannot be that you have not enough sweet things for your taste, light and warm (furs) for your body, colours to greet your eyes or music to delight your ears, or enough courtiers and courtesans to wait upon you? Your subjects are quite able to supply these for you. It surely cannot be for such things that you desire." The King said, "No, it is not for such things." Mencius said, "In that case I know what it is you desire so much. It is to increase your territory, to summon the princes of Ch'in and Ch'u to your Court, to rule over the central states, and to impose vassalage upon the barbarians of the four quarters. If the means you adopt are those you now propose, if the aims you intend to pursue are those at present in your mind, then you are like a man who climbs a tree to catch fish." The King said, "Is it as serious as that?" Mencius replied, "It is more serious than that. For in climbing a tree to fish, though you may not catch any fish, no further harm is done. But if you carry out your intentions with any seriousness of purpose, the most grievous harm will follow." The King said, "May I hear you further on this?" Mencius replied, "Suppose Tsou [a minor principality] and Ch'u [the major state to the south of Ch'i] go to war, which do you think would win?" The King said, "I think Ch'u would win." Mencius said, "Quite so; the small most assuredly cannot defeat the great, the few the many, or the weak the powerful. Within the world there are nine areas each of one thousand square miles, of which Ch'i comprises but one. What difference is there in expecting one of them to subjugate the other eight, and in expecting Tsou to defeat Ch'u? This is contrary to the basic nature of things. But if your

Majesty would engage in true government, displaying Humanity, then state servants throughout the world would seek employment in your Court, farmers seek to farm in your territory, merchants seek to set up their warehouses in your markets, and travellers seek to travel on your highways. Every discontented subject in the world would plead his cause in your Court. Under such circumstances who could prevent them?"[35]

The King replied, "I am not clever. I could never myself attain to this. Please strengthen my resolve and instruct me clearly, for though I am dull, I should like to try this." Mencius replied, "It is only a knight that can maintain a constant mind in default of a constant livelihood. The common people are of an inconstant mind because they lack a constant livelihood. And with inconstancy of mind, there is nothing evil that they will not do. But when they fall foul of the law they are pursued and punished. This is setting traps for the people. When has a Humane man occupied the throne and set traps for the people?[36] For this reason an enlightened prince provides for his people's livelihood, ensuring that they have sufficient on the one hand to nurture their aged, and on the other to feed adequately their wives and children. In prosperous years they are always well fed, and in the lean years they escape from starvation. Under such conditions they can be driven to goodness, for they will respond to the lightest touch. But today, conditions in the state are altogether otherwise. The people are kept at subsistence level; what leisure have they to cultivate good manners[37] and notions of the fitting? If your Majesty continues in this fashion, you will be running counter to the basic nature of things. Let the five-acre homesteads be planted with mulberry trees, and then those of fifty years of age and above might wear silk. Let the breeding of fowls, pigs, and dogs proceed in due season, and then those of seventy years of age and above might eat meat. On the hundred-acre estates do not impress the people at the times of sowing and reaping, and then large households need not starve. Take care as to the teaching in the schools. Let the curriculum be augmented with the Justice of filial piety, and fraternal duty, and then the grey-haired ones

---

[35] It is a Confucian axiom that Humane government is irresistible, and that its *virtus* undermines princes who are evily disposed, since it subverts their subjects. Thus one opposes force with virtue.

[36] In 1.32 Mencius is credited with saying this to the Duke of T'eng.

[37] See Additional Notes.

C

should not have to carry heavy loads on the roads. There has never been a state where the elderly had silk to wear and meat to eat and the common people were neither starving nor cold, and the king was other than a True King."[38]

(1A.7)

1.6

King Hsüan of Ch'i said, "Have you anything to say about the conduct of relations with neighbouring states?" Mencius replied, "Yes. Among rulers of major states, it is only a Humane Prince who would render service to a minor state. It was because they were Humane that King T'ang rendered service to Ko, and King Wen rendered service to the K'un tribes. Among the rulers of minor states, it is only a prudent prince who would render service to the ruler of a major state. It was because they were prudent that King T'ai rendered service to the Hsün Yü, and Kou Chien [King of Yüeh] rendered service to the King of Wu.[39] When major states serve minor states it is pleasing to Heaven. When minor states serve major states it shows reverence for Heaven. It is he who pleases Heaven that will protect the whole world, and he who reveres Heaven that will retain his own state. As it says in the *Book of Songs*,[40]

> We fear the wrath of Heaven,
> And doing so, will protect our state."

The King said, "Splendid words indeed! but I have a failing. I have a perverse fondness for feats of fearlessness."[41] Mencius replied, "Would that your Majesty were not so fond of these trivial acts of fearlessness. To take up a sword, look fierce and cry 'Who dares match himself against me?' is the fearlessness of an ill-bred man, one who merely matches himself against another. Would that your Majesty loved fearlessness of a larger order. As it says in the *Book of Songs*,[42]

[38] See Additional Notes.

[39] T'ang is T'ang the Successful, founder of the Shang Dynasty. The service he rendered to the Lord of Ko is described in 3.15. For King Wen, see 1.3. We know nothing about his service to the K'un tribes. For King T'ai, see Introduction to 6.52. His story is told in 1.29 and 1.31. Kou Chien, King of Yüeh, was held hostage by the King of Wu from 496 to 490 B.C.

[40] Cf. *Songs*, 220.

[41] See Additional Notes.

[42] Cf. *Songs*, 243.

The King blazed in anger
And mobilized his armies.
To halt the foe he marched on Chü.
Chou's well-being was thereby ensured.
He matched up to the world's expectations.

The fearlessness of King Wen was of this magnitude. Once aroused in anger he brought peace to the world. In the *Book of Documents*[43] King Wu is quoted as saying, 'Heaven has condescended to the common people, creating princes and leaders for them, saying that they are the helpers of God most High, thus placing a mark upon them throughout the world. Whether they are guilty or innocent, let the onus fall upon me. Who dares override the will of the common people?' If only one man went astray, King Wu took the blame upon himself. King Wu, too, once aroused, brought peace to the world. May your Majesty, too, once aroused, bring peace to the world. The people then would only fear that the King were not addicted to feats of fearlessness."

(1B.3)

I.7. IDEAL MINISTERS

King Hsüan of Ch'i asked about the functions of ministers. Mencius said, "What kind of ministers do you mean?" The King said, "Are there different kinds?" Mencius replied, "Yes! There are those appointed from among members of the Royal House and those from families not so connected." The King said, "Tell me about those of the members of the Royal House." Mencius replied, "When their prince is in grave error, their duty is to warn him, and, if this happens repeatedly and he disregards them, then they should change the incumbent of the throne." On this, the King looked displeased, and his manner changed.[44] Mencius said, "Your Majesty should not be surprised at my answer. If you ask me, your servant, a question, I cannot but answer honestly." The King resumed his former manner and asked about the duties of those ministers not of the Royal House. Mencius answered, "When the prince is in grave error their duty is to warn him, and, if this should happen repeatedly and he disregards them, they should resign."

(5B.9)

---

[43] *Documents*; see Legge V.I.i.7.   [44] See Additional Notes, 1.4, note 26.

1.8

Mencius had told King Hsüan of Ch'i that when a prince regards his ministers as his hands and feet, his ministers look upon him as their heart and belly; but when a prince regards his ministers as his horses and hounds,[45] they look upon him as upon any other person; but when a prince regards his ministers as so much ground or grass to be trampled upon, they look upon him as a robber and an enemy.[46] The King said, "According to protocol,[47] a minister, upon leaving the service of a state, should wear mourning for the prince he has lately served. How should I conduct myself, that such mourning might be worn for me?" Mencius replied, "You should act upon the minister's advice, so that its fructifying dews fall upon the people; then, when for sufficient cause he must take his leave, you should send an escort to conduct him as far as the state frontier and apprise beforehand the state to which he is going. It is only after three years, when he still has not returned, that the lands and villages alloted to him for salary should revert to the state. This is what is called 'according the threefold courtesy.' If you treat a minister in this way he will wear mourning upon taking leave of you. But if today a minister's advice is not acted upon, so that its fructifying dews do not fall upon the people, and, having sufficient cause, he leaves, then princes try to detain him by force or make difficulties for him wherever he goes. On the very day he leaves, his lands and villages revert to the state. This is what I call the behaviour of a robber and an enemy. And for a robber and an enemy, what mourning is prescribed?"

(4B.3)

1.9

Prince Tien, son of King Hsüan, asked, "What are the duties of a knight?" Mencius replied, "To exalt his ideals." The Prince said, "What does that mean?" Mencius replied, "It means to exalt Justice and Humanity—nothing more. The murder of a single innocent man is contrary to Humanity. Taking things to which one has no right is contrary to Justice. Where is the knight to be found? Wherever Humanity is present. What road does he travel? The road that leads

---

[45] See Additional Notes, 3.17, note 60.
[46] Cf. 1.1.   [47] See Additional Notes, 1.5, note 37.

to Justice. In dwelling in Humanity and in the pursuit of Justice the
duties of the great man are fulfilled."

(7A.33)

I.10

Mencius was on his way to the capital of Ch'i from Fan[48] when,
some way away, he saw the King of Ch'i's son. Sighing deeply, he said,
"How the air of a man changes with his surroundings![49] It is much
as the body alters with the food it eats.[50] What a great difference
surroundings make! But then we are all, are we not, some man's son?
The house, the horse and carriage, and the dress of the King's son
is not much different from that of any other man, but that he should
look the way he does is brought about by his surroundings. How
much more, then, the air of a man who occupies the broad mansion
of the world.[51]

"When the Prince of Lu went to Sung, he called out at the Tieh-tse
Gate, but the gate-keeper said that he did not believe it was the Prince,
though he wondered why the voice sounded so much like that of the
Prince. His mistake arose because he was seeing the Prince in surroundings no different from his own."

(7A.36)

I.11

Mencius was received in audience by King Hsüan of Ch'i. Mencius
said, "When I speak of an old-established city-state, I do not mean one
in which the trees have grown tall, but one served by officials in whose
families offices have been held hereditarily. Your Majesty has no
intimate ministers. Those appointed to office yesterday are no longer
here today." The King said, "How can I know when men lack talent
and so avoid appointing them in the first place?" Mencius replied,
"Rulers should appoint men of talents[52] only when they have no
alternative [i.e., when no candidates offer from among the hereditary
houses], for they are thereby placing the lowly born above the nobly

[48] A city in Ch'i.
[49] Literally "the place where he is or lives," but we should say in such contexts, "his surroundings, his environment."
[50] Cf. 3.47, where a man's height is attributed to his diet.
[51] Cf. 5.1.   [52] See Additional Notes.

born, and outsiders above their own kinsfolk. A ruler cannot be too careful here. When your courtiers say a man is talented, that is not enough. When your ministers say he is talented, it is still not enough. But when all agree that he is talented, then examine him carefully. If you yourself see talent in him, then engage him. But though your courtiers say a man will not do, take no notice. Though your ministers say he will not do, still take no notice. But if everyone says he will not do, examine him carefully, and if you yourself find reason to suppose that he will not do, then dismiss him from office. Similarly, when courtiers demand that a man be put to death, do not listen to them. When ministers demand that he be put to death, do not listen to them. But if everyone demands that he be put to death, then examine him carefully, and if you see a case for putting him to death, do so. This is what is meant by the saying 'the whole state put him to death.' By conducting affairs in this way, you will become in fact the 'parent of the people.' "[53]

(1B.7)

1.12

Mencius said to King Hsüan of Ch'i, "Suppose one of your ministers had gone on a journey to Ch'u,[54] leaving his wife and children with a friend, and upon returning found his family starving, what do you think he should do?" The King said, "He should cut off all relations with that friend." Mencius said, "Suppose now that the Leader of the Knights[55] had no control over the knights, then what would you do?" The King said, "I should dismiss him." Mencius said, "Suppose now the kingdom to be ill-governed, what then should be done?" The King turned to his courtiers and spoke of other things.

(1B.6)

1.13

Mencius was received in audience by King Hsüan of Ch'i. Mencius

[53] See Additional Notes.

[54] Ch'u, the major state in the central Yangtse region to the south of Ch'i, is referred to by early Confucian writers, most of whom came from the Shantung peninsula, as a sort of *ultima Thule*. See also 1.37, 4.14, and 6.33.

[55] A sort of Earl Marshal, responsible for discipline among the knights. Cf. 1.18 and 2.2.

said, "When your Majesty is building a large palace, it is the Master Craftsman that you commission to procure the great trees, and when he does so your Majesty is pleased, knowing him to be a master of his craft. But supposing one of the carpenters, in dressing the lumber, trimmed it too small; then you would be angry, feeling that the man was not up to his job. Again, suppose you had a piece of uncut jade. Even though it were worth 10,000 *yih*,[56] you would still entrust it to a skilled jade-worker to cut and polish. But if your Majesty were to say to the jade-worker, 'Forget all you know for the time being and do as I say,' what would happen to the jade? Upon reaching maturity, a man wants to practise the skills he learned as a youth. Governing states is just such a skill. If your Majesty tells me to forget all that I have been taught and to do as you say, is that any different from telling the jade-worker how to work jade?"

(1B.9; lines rearranged)

1.14. ANCIENT PRECEDENTS

King Hsüan of Ch'i said, "Everyone tells me to destroy the old *Ming T'ang*.[57] Should I do so or not?" Mencius replied, "The *Ming T'ang* pertains to kingship. If your Majesty wishes to pursue the policies of the Princely Ideal you should not destroy it." The King said, "May I hear about the policies of the Princely Ideal?" Mencius replied, "In antiquity, when King Wen[58] governed at Ch'i, the people farmed on the nine and one system[59] and the officials enjoyed hereditary tenure. At the state borders, merchandise was inspected but not taxed. No prohibitions were placed on the use of marshes and bridges. The families of criminals were not involved in the punishment of the criminal.[60] Four classes of indigents, who had no one to speak for them, were officially recognized: the elderly man with no wife, the elderly woman with no husband, the elderly who had no children to support them, and the young who had no parents. They were called *kuan*, *kua*, *tu*, and *ku* respectively. In King Wen's ordinances, and in his Humanity, these four classes received prior attention. The *Book of Songs*[61] says,

---

[56] See Additional Notes, 2.10, note 26.
[57] See Additional Notes.   [58] See 1.3.   [59] See Additional Notes.
[60] Sentence at this time was often passed on whole families for the guilt of a single member.
[61] Cf. *Songs*, 292 (Karlgren, *Odes*, 192).

> Lucky are the rich
> But pity the neglected ones."

The King said, "That is well said!" Mencius said, "If your Majesty applauds such things, then why not put them into practice?" The King said, "I have a failing, I like my wealth." Mencius replied, "In antiquity, Liu the Duke[62] liked his wealth too. As it says in the *Book of Songs*,[63]

> He gathered, he stored
> In bags and sacks tied up
> He put dried foods.
> Thus his stores were plentiful.
> He laid out bows, arrows
> Shields and daggers
> Halberd and battle-axe
> And then the expedition began.

Thus not only those who accompanied him on his expeditions, but those who remained behind, had ample provision. Indeed it was not until such provision was made that he set out on an expedition. No difficulty lies in your being fond of wealth if it is shared with the people." The King said, "But I have a further failing. I am fond of women." Mencius replied, "In antiquity, King T'ai, too, liked women, and he was in love with his wife. As the *Book of Songs*[64] says,

> Ku-kung T'an-fu
> At break of day was driving his horses
> Along the west bank.
> Coming to the foot of Mount Ch'i
> He met the Lady Chiang.
> Together they chose the site.

In those days there were no frustrated women at home or unattached men wandering abroad. If you, Sir, like your women, then see to it that the common people are so placed as to do so too. The difficulty does not lie in a fondness for women."

(1B.5)

---

[62] Liu the Duke was a legendary ancestor of the Chou Royal House. See Introduction to 6.52.
[63] Cf. *Songs*, 239.
[64] Cf. *Songs*, 240.

The Yen Affair

*Ch'i attacked the State of Yen in the north-west in the autumn of 315 B.C.
K'uang Chang, the friend of Mencius whom we meet again in 3.5 and
4.15, led the Ch'i armies. The King and the Heir Apparent of Yen were
both killed. Mencius is thought to have left Ch'i altogether in 312 B.C. He
had made up his mind to tender his resignation earlier, but did not do so
because of the "General Mobilisation" (2.17). It is clear that by the time
of the Yen Affair Mencius' influence at Court was slight. But the Yen
Affair is given much prominence in the Works.*

1.15

Ch'i had attacked Yen and overcome its armies. King Hsüan of Ch'i
said to Mencius, "Some say I should now occupy Yen, but others say
not. When a major state attacks another and overthrows its armies
within fifty days, it suggests something more than a mere triumph of
human force![65] If I do not occupy Yen I may have Heaven's displeasure to contend with, but if I do occupy it, what then?"[66] Mencius
replied, "If by your occupying it the populace of Yen would approve,
then do so. There are precedents for this in antiquity. King Wu is an
example. But if the populace would disapprove then you should not
occupy it. There are precedents too for this. King Wen is an example.
When a major power attacks another and its armies are greeted by the
people with gifts of food, it is for no other reason than that they are
fleeing from 'fire and flood.'[67] But if, on the other hand, the people
see in the invading armies something hotter than fire, more menacing
than flood, they will revert once again to their former allegiance."

(1B.10)

1.16

Ch'i, having attacked Yen, had occupied it. The Feudal Powers were
considering ways and means of coming to the relief of Yen. King
Hsüan of Ch'i said, "Many of the Feudal Powers are preparing to

---

[65] I.e., it presages supernatural intervention.
[66] See Additional Notes.
[67] I.e., from tyranny, and thus demonstrating against their own ruler.

attack me. How should I deal with them?" Mencius said, "I have heard of one with a state of but seventy miles square controlling the whole world. This was T'ang the Successful. But I have not heard of one who, as the ruler of a state of a thousand miles square, had occasion to fear any man. The *Book of Documents*[68] says,

> The punitive wars of T'ang began in Ko,
> The whole world was in sympathy with his cause.
> As his campaign progressed in the east, the tribes
> Of the west resented it.
> As he continued southward, the tribes of the north
> Resented it.
> They said, 'Why does he not free us first?'

The common people looked to T'ang, as in a drought they look for clouds. Among the people, merchants continued their business, farmers carried on with their farming. T'ang punished their rulers, but had compassion on the people. He was, to them, as rain falling in due season. The people were overjoyed. The *Book of Documents*[69] says,

> We await our king,
> When he comes, all will be restored.

Now the Prince of Yen was a tyrant.[70] Your Majesty set out and punished him. Yen's people thought you were saving them from 'fire and flood.' They welcomed your armies with gifts of food. If now you slay the King of Yen's family, bind his younger relatives in chains, destroy his Ancestral Temples, and remove his family treasures, how can you expect the people's approval? The world may fear the might of Ch'i, but if Ch'i continues to extend its territories and fails to follow Humane policies, this will indeed raise up the armed forces of the rest of the world to resist you. Your Majesty should issue orders at once, ordering the return of the captives and the cessation of looting. Confer with the people of Yen. Appoint for them a successor to the throne and then evacuate the state. All this talk of the relief of Yen will then cease."

(1B.11)

---

[68] Cf. Legge, IV, II, 6.
[69] Cf. Legge, IV, II, 6.
[70] Cf. Additional Notes, 7.20, note 4.

I.17

At the time of the Yen Rebellion the King of Ch'i said, "I feel very badly about Mencius." Ch'en Chia[71] said, "Your Majesty should not worry himself about that. Who is the more Humane, the more wise, your Majesty or the Duke of Chou?"[72] The King said, "What a thing to ask!" Ch'en Chia continued, "The Duke of Chou appointed Kuan-shu as an overseer to keep an eye on the Yin people.[73] But Kuan-shu joined the Yin people and rebelled. If the Duke of Chou appointed him knowing that he would rebel, he was the opposite of Humane. But if he appointed him not knowing that he would rebel, then he was the opposite of wise. Even the Duke of Chou could not be perfectly Humane and perfectly wise; how much less can your Majesty be expected to be? I beg of you, allow me to see Mencius and get this matter clear."

Ch'en Chia saw Mencius and asked him, "What kind of person was the Duke of Chou?" "A Sage of antiquity," replied Mencius. "He appointed Kuan-shu an overseer of the Yin people and Kuan-shu then joined them and rebelled. Is that so?" Mencius agreed that it was. Ch'en Chia continued, "Did the Duke of Chou appoint him knowing that he would rebel?" Mencius said, "He did not know." "In that case," said Ch'en Chia, "even a Sage might err?" Mencius replied, "The Duke of Chou was a younger brother, Kuan-shu an older brother. The Duke of Chou's error was therefore a pardonable one! The gentleman of antiquity, on committing an error, mended his ways. Gentlemen today, on committing an error, persist in it. In antiquity a gentlemen's faults were like an eclipse, plain for all to see. And as at the eclipse, men look for the emergence of the newly formed sun, so with the gentleman who had erred, all looked for his emergence as a reformed man. Today, gentlemen not only persist in error, but attempt to excuse it."

(2B.9)

I.18

Shen T'ung,[74] acting on his own initiative, asked Mencius, "Should the State of Yen be attacked?" Mencius said, "It should. Tzu-k'uai

---

[71] Of whom nothing further is known.   [72] See Introduction to 6.52.
[73] At the Chou conquest in the eleventh century B.C.
[74] Of. whom nothing further is known.

ought not to have handed Yen over to another, and Tzu-chih ought not to have accepted it from Tzu-k'uai.[75] Suppose now there were an officer here whom you found pleasing and suppose without informing the King, on your own initiative, you transferred your title and salary to him, and further, suppose that the officer, without authority for doing so, passed on the title to his own son. Would you think that proper? And is this any different from the problem of Yen?"

Ch'i attacked Yen. Mencius was asked, "Did you advise that we attack Yen?" Mencius replied, "Quite the contrary. Shen T'ung asked me if Yen should be attacked and I said I thought it should. So Ch'i went and attacked Yen. Had he asked me 'Who should attack Yen', I would have answered, 'He who is appointed by Heaven to do so.' Suppose that a man had committed a murder and I had been asked if he should be executed I would have said that he should. But if I had been asked who should execute him I would have said, 'the Leader of the Knights.'[76] In the case of the recent attack, it was a matter of one Yen attacking another Yen, and that surely is something I would not have advised."

(2B.8)

I.19. THE TROUBLE WITH KING HSÜAN

Mencius said, "It is not surprising that the King does not act wisely. No one can raise even the most easily grown plant if it lies in the warm sun for one day and then is left in the chill shade for ten! The King receives me but seldom and the audience is no sooner concluded than a 'chill shade' is ushered in. Though I may have planted some grain of wisdom, what is likely to happen to it afterwards? To be good at chess is a minor accomplishment, but even so it can only be acquired with undivided attention and persistence. Take Ch'iu, the chess-master. He is the best player in the kingdom. Suppose two pupils take lessons from him. The one puts his whole mind to the task, persists, giving the master his undivided attention, while the other is pre-occupied by the thought that at any moment a goose may fly overhead and he must snatch up his bow, grab an arrow, and shoot. Though fellow pupils of the same master, the second will be no match at chess

---

[75] See Additional Notes.   [76] See I.12.

for the first. Why is this? Because the first is any more clever? Not really!"

(6A.9)

AT THE COURT OF THE KINGS OF LIANG

During the sixth century, Tsin, a major state which a century earlier had held the Paramountcy under Duke Wen, had fallen into the hands of an oligarchy, the Six Hsiang. In the middle of the fifth century they had split up Tsin into Han, Wei, and Chao. In 403, the House of Chou recognized them and gave them the title and status of Feudal Lords. It was to Wei, whose princes called themselves after the name of their capital city, Liang, that Mencius came, to find that, as with Ch'i, the memories of the Paramountcy still fascinated its princes more than "the Way of the Former Kings." Liang, however, as King Hui (reigned 370-319 B.C.) explains, is under heavy pressure from Ch'i, Ch'u, and Ch'in and had suffered loss at their hands. Even so, its princes were imbued with the idea of "uniting the world once again."[77]

I.20. PAST GLORIES

King Hui of Liang said, "No state, at one time, was greater than Tsin, and that, Sir, you know full well. But in my time we have been defeated by Ch'i in the east; my oldest son died in that campaign. We have lost seven hundred miles of territory to Ch'in in the west. Ch'u has humiliated us to the south.[78] I feel the disgrace of this keenly, and hope before I die to expunge this disgrace in one fell swoop. What should I do to bring this about?" Mencius replied, "One could rule as a True King with a kingdom a hundred miles square.[79] If the people saw your policies to be Humane, if you were to lighten the penal code, reduce taxes, encourage intensive ploughing and clearing of waste land, then the able bodied would have leisure to cultivate filial and fraternal duty, loyalty, and trust. On the one hand they could serve the elders of their families, and on the other serve their seniors

---

[77] But not under the legitimate Chou House. Han and Chao had divided the Imperial domain into two parts in 367 B.C., making the Imperial House even more impotent.

[78] See Additional Notes.

[79] What Mencius really thought of King Hui's territorial losses he expresses privately to his disciple Kung-sun Ch'ou (see 1.25).

in the state. They could oppose the stout mail and sharp weapons of Ch'in and Ch'u with sharpened sticks. Those great states deprive their people of labour in the farming seasons so that they can neither sow nor reap in season to feed their families. Parents freeze and starve to death. Brothers, wives, and children are separated.[80] Those princes ensnare their people. If the King were to set out and punish them, who would dare oppose him? For this reason it is said, 'None can oppose the man of Humanity.' Let not your Majesty doubt this."

(1A.5)

1.21. HUMANITY AND JUSTICE

Mencius was received in audience by King Hui of Liang. The King said, "Aged Sir! You have come, with no thought for so long a journey, to see me. You have, no doubt, some teaching by which I might profit my state?" Mencius replied, "Why must your Majesty use that word 'profit'?[81] There is after all just Humanity and Justice, nothing more. If your Majesty asks 'How can I profit my state?' your nobles will ask 'How can we profit our estates?' and knights and commoners will ask 'How can we profit ourselves?' All ranks in society will be competing for profits. Such would undermine the state. In a 'ten-thousand-chariot state' [a major state][82] he who slew his prince might gain a 'thousand-chariot estate' [a large estate], and in a 'thousand-chariot state' he who slew his prince might gain a 'hundred-chariot estate.' A thousand in ten thousand, a hundred in a thousand is no small profit. If indeed you put profit first and relegate justice to a minor place, no one will be happy unless they are forever grabbing something. There has never been a Humane man abandoned by his kin. There has never been a Just man who turned his back upon his prince. The king should speak of Justice and Humanity; why must he speak about profit?"

(1A.1)

Mencius here sums up his teaching in the words "Humanity" and "Justice." These words will occur frequently throughout the Works *(see 6.1.i). What*

---

[80] See Additional Notes, 1.4, note 27.

[81] "Profit" was a keyword of the Utilitarians, but anathema to Mencius; see 4.4.

[82] In theory, a state capable in feudal duty of mobilizing a thousand chariots of war, but the figures are conventional and indicate nothing more than relative size.

he means by "Humanity" is never precisely defined, but it is exemplified throughout the Works. It has something of the love which parents have naturally for their children. It has something of the compassion which a man of sensitivity feels when seeing an innocent animal slaughtered.

By "Justice" Mencius meant the fulfilment of obligation. The princes were under an obligation to see that their subjects were adequately provided for, and subjects had a duty to see that princes were loyally obeyed, within a system of understood obligations.

Thus "Justice" is the fulfilment of obligation and "Humanity" the sentiment that motivates its fulfilment.

I.22. A MANPOWER SHORTAGE

King Hui of Liang said, "As far as governing my state is concerned, I do devote my entire mind to it. When calamity strikes in the region of Ho-nui I transfer people to Ho-tung[83] and send supplies of grain to Ho-nui. If calamity strikes in Ho-tung, I reverse the proceedings. Yet if you were to examine the governments of neighbouring states, you would not find a prince so devoted as I. But the population of those states does not decrease, and my own population does not increase. Why is this?"[84] Mencius replied, "Your Majesty is fond of war. Allow me to answer you with an illustration drawn from warfare. The drums have sounded the advance[85] and weapons are engaged, when the troops abandon their armour on the field and, trailing their weapons, flee. Some run a hundred paces and some run fifty. If those who ran fifty paces mocked those who ran a hundred for being cowards, what would you think?" The King said, "They should not, for they too ran, though they did not run so far." Mencius replied, "If the King understood the purport of this, then he would not expect his population to increase. Do not disregard the farmer's seasons, and food will be more than enough. Forbid the use of fine-meshed nets, and fish and turtles will be more than enough. Take wood from the forests at prescribed times only and there will be material enough and to spare. With a sufficiency of grain, of fish, and

[83] The Yellow River, which at this period reached the sea in the region of modern Tientsin, entered the State of Liang at the west flowing eastward, and then turned abruptly north, forming two regions in Wei, Ho-nui and Ho-tung.

[84] Cf. I.5, note 35.

[85] And, in the warfare of this period, the bells sound the retreat.

of material, the people would live without anxiety. This is the first principle of Princely Government. Let the five-acre homesteads be planted with mulberry trees, and those of fifty years of age and above might wear silk. Let the breeding of fowls, pigs, and dogs proceed in its seasons, and then those of seventy years of age, and above might eat meat. On the hundred-acre estates, do not impress the people at the times of sowing and reaping, and then large households need not starve. Take care as to the teaching in the schools; let the curriculum be augmented with the Justice of filial piety and fraternal duty, and then the grey-haired ones would not be carrying heavy loads on the roads. There has never been a state where the elderly had silk to wear and meat to eat and the common people were neither starving nor cold where the king was other than a True King. In the good years your dogs and your swine are fed upon men's food. You do not store your grain for the lean years. On your highways there are starving men at large. You do not issue the grain for their relief.[86] When your people die, you say, 'It is not my fault, it was a bad harvest.' How does that differ from killing a man by stabbing him and saying, 'It was not my fault, it was the knife'? If the king did not lay the blame on bad harvests, then the world's populations would come to him."

(1A.3)

In his concern for the "livelihood of the common people" Mencius has much to say to the princes about their extravagent palaces and the disproportionate amount of forest and marsh set aside for the pleasures of the chase. In the exactions of forced labour by the princes, the people were deprived of a "time to reap and a time to sow." In the enclosing of land for hunting preserves, the time-honoured rights of the people to trap fish and game and to gather kindling had been denied them. There is much talk of "starving peoples on the roads" seeking, one supposes, to escape from the harsh exactions of venal princes. The princes in their turn show concern "that their populations do not increase," an ancient way of referring to a manpower shortage. In these conditions Mencius is to argue that wealth itself is not wrong, but is to be shared by the commonalty. The Micians will carry this further and make a virtue of frugality and ascetic living.

[86] As was done in Ch'i; see 2.12.

1.23

King Hui of Liang said, "I would like you to teach me. You may dispense with formality." Mencius replied, "Is there any difference between killing a man with a knife and with a club?" The King said, "No difference at all." Mencius said, "Is there any difference between killing a man with a knife and with (faulty) governmental policies?" The King replied "No difference at all." Mencius said "Yet in your kitchen you have tender meat, in your stables well-fed horses, though the people's faces are pinched with hunger, and the starving roam the countryside. This is a policy of 'governing animals and eating men.'[87] Animals eat their own kind, and human beings despise them for doing so. He who aspires to be a parent of the people yet whose policies get no further than 'governing animals and eating men' brings hatred upon his person. Confucius said, 'When grave-images were first made, what grievous results followed.[88] As the images were made in human form the practice has arisen of using human beings!' If this is deplorable what can be said of the prince who puts his subjects to death by starving them!"

(1A.4)

1.24. ON LUXURY

Mencius was received in audience by King Hui of Liang. The King was standing at a pool, looking at the geese and deer. He said, "Did the Worthy Kings of whom you speak enjoy these things?" Mencius replied, "It is only when one is worthy that one really enjoys them. The unworthy, though they may possess these things, do not enjoy them. In the *Book of Songs*[89] it says,

> He planned and worked on the Spirit Tower
> Planned it and built it.
> The people set to work.
> No time limit was set.
> They built it unurged,
> Coming to work, as a son to help his father.

[87] A reversal of the expected "governing men and eating animals." This passage also occurs in 5.5, and in 3.3 where it is attributed by Mencius to Kung-ming Yi.

[88] Cases had occurred of immuring a prince's wives and concubines with him at his death, rather than with token grave-figures, with which at this time he had been buried. Confucians, who were authorities on the precedents for burial rites, were considerably shocked at this innovation.   [89] Cf. *Songs*, 244.

D

> The King is in his Spirit Park
> Where the buck and doe lie
> The deer in fine fettle
> The white birds glisten.
> The King is at his Spirit Pool.
> Oh how the fish rise!

King Wen built a tower and a pool with the labour of his people, yet the people took pleasure in it. They called his tower the Spirit-fraught Tower, and called his pool the Spirit-fraught Pool, delighting in his having deer and fish. The men of antiquity shared their pleasures with their people, and so could really take pleasure in them. The *Declaration of T'ang*[91] says,

> If today, for whatever reason, we perish,
> I will perish with you.

The people wanted to perish with him. Though one may possess towers, pools, and animals and birds of the chase, can one enjoy them by oneself?"

(1A.2)

1.25. THE TROUBLE WITH KING HUI

Mencius said, "King Hui of Liang is the antithesis of *jen* (Humane). The man of Humanity brings upon the things he hates, the thing he loves. But the man who is not Humane brings upon the thing he loves, the thing he hates." Kung-sun Ch'ou[92] said, "What does that mean?" Mencius said, "King Hui of Liang ravished his own people for the sake of territory and went to war. When defeated, he tried again and fearing that he might not succeed he drove the son he loved to fight and his son was sacrificed.[93] This is what I mean by 'bringing upon the thing he loves, the thing he hates.'"

(7B.1)

King Hui died in 319 B.C. and was succeeded by King Hsiang. To Mencius, of whom only one interview with King Hsiang is recorded, Hsiang

---

[90] See 1.3.   [91] In the *Book of Documents*; see *Documents*, p. 20.
[92] A disciple of Mencius; see Introduction to chapter III.
[93] See 1.20.   [94] Cf. 1.10.

*was a man "bent on slaughter." Such a man would be difficult to persuade
that the power of virtue is greater than the resort to arms. Hsiang dismissed
Mencius curtly, and Mencius' hopes that the Ideal Prince would arise in
Liang were brought sharply to an end.*

1.26. THE WAY OF FORCE

Mencius was received in audience by King Hsiang of Liang. Upon
coming out, he remarked to someone, "As I looked at him, he did
not look like a prince.[94] As I approached, I saw nothing to respect
in him. Abruptly[95] he asked, 'How can the world be pacified?' To
which I replied, 'It will be pacified by being brought into unity once
again.' 'Who can unite it?' he asked, to which I replied, 'He who is
not bent on slaughtering people, he can unite it.' He asked, 'Who
would ally himself with such a person?' I answered, 'There is no one
who would not ally himself with such a person. Your Majesty understands about plants. During the seventh and eighth months it is dry.
The stalks wither. Then clouds gather in the sky, and the rains come.
The plants revive of themselves, and what can prevent them? Among
contemporary rulers, there is not one who is not bent on slaughter,
yet if there were but one who was not, the people would crane their
necks in expectation to him. It really is so. The people would turn
to such a man as surely as water flows downwards. They would come
in a flood and who could prevent them?'"

(1A.6)

AT THE COURT OF THE DUKE OF T'ENG

*The Principality of T'eng to the south of Ch'i lay on the route to the major
state of Ch'u, but as Mencius, who visited T'eng both informally and officially
in c. 323 and 321 B.C., says, "It is a long journey from Ch'i to T'eng"
(2.6). Its rulers, who called themselves "Dukes," were a collateral of the
Lu Ducal House. They maintained a precarious independence by "serving
the major states," that is, by becoming satellites in the major power politics
of Ch'i, Ch'u, Ch'in, and erstwhile Tsin in their struggle for supremacy.
Duke Wen of T'eng seems to have been kindly disposed to philosophers,
for we find him providing hospitality not only for Mencius, but also for
Hsü Hsing and his followers, and for the Agronomists, the brothers Ch'en
(see 4.14).*

[95] I.e., without the polite preliminaries that decorum prescribed.

1.27. THE POTENTIALS OF THE WAY

When Duke Wen of T'eng was Crown Prince, he was on his way to Ch'u when, on passing through Sung, he met Mencius. Mencius spoke to him about the essential goodness of human nature, referring constantly to Yao and Shun.[96] On his way back from Ch'u, the Prince saw Mencius again. Mencius said, "Does your Highness still doubt the truth of what I said? The Way is one. Ch'eng Chien[97] once said of Duke Ching of Ch'i,[98] 'He is a man; I too am a man; why should I be afraid of him?' Yen Yuan[99] said, 'Whatever kind of being Shun was, I too am that kind of being. It is a question of being willing to be so.' Kung-ming Yi[100] said, 'May King Wen be my teacher and the Duke of Chou (my exemplar). He will not lead me astray.' The state of T'eng is some fifty miles square, but it still could become an excellent state. The *Book of Documents*[101] says, 'If the drug does not cause a reaction in the patient, it will not cure the disease.' "[102]

(3A.1)

1.28. MOURNING

When Duke Ting of T'eng died, the Crown Prince said to his tutor, Jan Yu, "When I was in Sung, Mencius used to talk to me, and I have never forgotten the things he said and now, unfortunately, the 'great affair of state'[103] devolves upon me, and I want you to go and seek his advice before I undertake this duty."

Jan Yu went to Tsou[104] to see Mencius. Mencius said, "How excellent it is that the death of a parent should so stir a son to exert himself.[105] As Tseng Tzu[106] said, 'Filial piety is serving parents according to the Rites when they are alive, burying them according to the Rites when they die, and sacrificing to them according to the Rites thereafter.'[107]

---

[96] See Introduction to 6.43 and to 6.52.

[97] Said to have been one of the "tough knights"; see Additional Notes, 1.6, note 41.

[98] See Additional Notes, 1.2, note 17.

[99] The Yen Hui of the *Analects*, Confucius' favourite disciple; see Introduction to 6.73.

[100] See Additional Notes.

[101] *Documents*, Legge IV. vIII, i.8.

[102] An excellent state, like an effective drug, "causes a reaction." That is to say, the virtue of its rulers subverts the subjects of less virtuous rulers. See 1.5, note 35.

[103] The funeral of the King his father.

[104] See 1.36.

[105] Cf. *Analects*, XIX. 17.

[106] See Introduction to 6.73.

[107] See Additional Notes.

I have not myself made a study of the Rites for a Feudal Lord, but I have often heard that the three years of mourning,[108] the wearing of clothes of coarse cloth, and eating plain food were observed for all from the Son of Heaven down to the commoners, in all the three dynasties of antiquity."

Jan Yu returned and reported this to the Prince. It was decided to observe the three years of mourning. But the relatives of the Prince and the officials of state objected to this. They said, "None of the former rulers of Lu, our ancestral state, did so, and neither did our own forebears. It would be most inappropriate if your Highness reversed such a precedent. Further, the *Manual* says,[109] 'In matters of mourning and sacrifice follow the precedents set by your forebears.' We too know the source from which he should seek for guidance."[110] The Prince said to Jan Yu, "In my youth I did not give myself to study, but preferred hunting and the military arts. Now, my elders and officials do not think me adequate. I fear that I may not be able to discharge the 'great affair' as I should. Ask Mencius about this for me."

Jan Yu went to Tsou again and asked Mencius what he thought about this.

Mencius said, "What he says may be so, but he cannot seek a remedy in others. Confucius said, 'When a king dies, the ceremonies are conducted by the prime minister. The king-to-be sips gruel, his face heavily veiled, and, as he approaches the throne, he weeps. The entire Court is then moved to wail, but the prince gives the lead. What the superior wishes, the inferior must wish even more so. The power of a prince is like the wind, that of his people like the grass. When the wind blows the grass bends.'[111] This matter rests entirely with the Prince."

Jan Yu returned and reported this to the Prince. The Prince said, "He is right; it does indeed rest with me." For five months he remained in the mourner's hut, issuing no decrees. His relations and officials said, "It can properly be said that the Prince is knowledgeable." On the day of the funeral people from all parts came to witness it. The grief on their faces and their tears in the keening gave great satisfaction to the mourners.

(3A.2)

---

[108] See *Analects*, 17.21, and Waley's note.   [109] See Additional Notes.
[110] See Additional Notes.   [111] See Additional Notes.

1.29. THE NEUTRAL'S DILEMMA

Duke Wen of T'eng said to Mencius, "T'eng is a minor state. Though I make every effort to render the service I should to the major states, I never manage to rid myself of the demands they make upon me. What should I do?" Mencius replied, "In antiquity, when King T'ai[112] lived in Pin, the Ti tribes invaded his territory. He offered them furs and silk but could not get rid of them. He offered them horses and hounds but could not get rid of them. He offered them pearls and jade but still could not get rid of them. Whereupon he gathered the elders of his people together and told them, 'The Ti tribes want to take my lands. I have heard it said, a True Prince does not allow the people to be harmed by interfering with the things upon which their livelihood depends. Sirs! I am going to leave this place. It will do you less harm to have no prince (than to be deprived of your land).' He left Pin, crossed the Liang-Shan, and built his capital at the foot of Mount Ch'i and settled there. The people of Pin said, 'A man of Humanity indeed! We cannot do without him,' and so they followed after him, as crowds flock to a market. But someone has said, 'A feudal holding is held by hereditary right; it is not something which the individual can negotiate. King T'ai should have defended it with his life, and refused to desert it.' Your Majesty, and I say this with all due deference, must choose from among these two courses."

(1B.15)

1.30

Duke Wen of T'eng said to Mencius, "T'eng is a minor state. It lies between the major states of Ch'i and Ch'u. Should I serve Ch'i or serve Ch'u?" Mencius replied, "This is not the kind of advice I aspire to offer,[113] but if I were pressed, there is one thing I might say. You might deepen the moats, build up the city walls, and with your people man the defences. If at the critical moment they would remain at their posts, then that would be one course open to you."

(1B.13)

1.31

Duke Wen of T'eng said to Mencius, "Ch'i is going to fortify the

[112] See Introduction to 6.52.   [113] For Mencius' views on this sort of advice, see 5.2 and 5.3.

City of Hsüeh. This alarms me.[114] What should I do about it?"
Mencius replied, "In antiquity when King T'ai[115] lived in Pin, the
Ti tribes invaded his territory. He therefore left Pin and settled at the
foot of Mount Ch'i. It was not that he chose to move; he had no
choice. Do you, Sir, do the thing that is good. If you do so, among
the generations that will succeed you, a True King will most assuredly
arise. A prince founds his inheritance and passes it on to his successors
so that it may continue. His immediate success rests with Heaven.
What should you do about Ch'i? Do good—nothing more."

(1B.14)

1.32. PRINCELY GOVERNMENT

Duke Wen of T'eng consulted Mencius about ruling a state. Mencius
replied, "Those things which concern the common people brook no
delay. The *Book of Songs*[116] says,

> By day you must gather the rushes
> At night you must twist the twine.
> Soon we will go up to the mat-sheds,[117]
> And then we will begin to sow.

With a constant livelihood the people have a constant mind. Without
a constant livelihood the people will not have constant minds.[118]
This is the way of the common people. If the people are inconstant in
their minds, there is nothing evil that they will not do. But when they
do so they fall foul of the law and are pursued and punished. This is
setting traps for the people. When has a Humane man occupied the
throne and set traps for the people? Therefore a worthy prince will
show respect for the people, exercise restraint (in his expenditure),
and be courteous to his inferiors, setting limits upon the demands he
makes of the people. Yang Huo[119] said, 'You cannot be rich and
Humane, you cannot be Humane and rich.' (In antiquity) fifty acres
was the Hsia unit, and they exacted the *kung*. Seventy-five acres was
the Shang unit, and they exacted the *chu*. A hundred acres was the
Chou unit, and they exacted the *ch'e*. Actually each of these amounts

---

[114] See Additional Notes.   [115] See 1.29.   [116] *Songs*, 159.
[117] Living in the villages during the winter, the peasants built mat-sheds in the fields during
the sowing and harvest seasons, as they have continued to do up to modern times.
[118] A doublet, see 1.5.   [119] See Additional Notes.

to a tenth. *Ch'e* is 'to allot'; *tsu* is *chieh*, 'tribute.' Lung Tzu[120] said,
'The *chu* is the best of these land revenue systems, and the *kung* the
worst.' Under the *kung* system assessment was based on an annual
average yield. In a good year, when the harvest was plentiful, a high
assessment could be made without being oppressive, for the actual
payment was small (in comparison with the yield), but in a lean year,
which hardly paid for the fertilizer, to insist on a full tax payment,
puts the Parent of the People in the position of engaging his children
in unremitting toil. They work hard all year only to find that they
have not only no means of feeding their parents, but must borrow to
supplement their livelihood. The very old and the very young roll
dead in the gutters. What then of him who is the 'Parent of the
People'?[121]

"As far as the system of hereditary tenure of office goes, that has
long been practised in T'eng.

"In the *Book of Songs* it says[122]

> Rain falls upon the Lord's field,
> And rains on our fields too.

It is only in the *chu* system that there is a 'Lord's field.'[123] And so we
see from this, that even in Chou times it was used.[124] And then too,
for the purposes of education, *hsiang, hsü, hsüeh,* and *hsiao* [i.e., schools]
should be established. The word *hsiang* means *yang,* 'to nurture';
the word *hsü* means *she,* 'archery'; the word *hsiao* means *chiao,* 'instruction.' *Hsiao* was the Hsia term, *hsü* was the Shang term, and *hsiang*
the Chou term, while *hsüeh* is a term they all had in common. All
these places were for the purposes of making clear the rules of human
conduct.[125] When the rules of human conduct are understood among
the upper classes, family affection will appear among the people below.

"If the True Prince were to appear, he would certainly, then, take
an example from you, and thus you might become his teacher. In
the *Book of Songs*[126] it says,

> Though Chou was an old-established state,
> Its Mandate was newly conferred.

---

120 Lung Tzu occurs again in 4.12, but nothing further is known about him.
121 See Additional Notes, 1.4, note 28.
122 *Songs,* 162.   123 See Additional Notes, 1.14, note 59.
124 See Additional Notes.   125 See Additional Notes.   126 *Songs,* 241.

This speaks of King Wen. But if you, Sir, energetically pursue such policies, then your own titles to the state might be newly conferred."[127]

Later, the Duke sent one Pi Chan, to inquire further about the "well-field" system. Mencius said, "Sir, your Prince proposes to put Humane government into practice. You have been chosen and appointed to office by him. You yourself then must exert every effort. Humane government begins with land-boundaries. If these are not perfectly straight, then the well-field system becomes inequitable, and the salary system unjust. Tyrannous princes and venal officials treat land-boundaries with contempt. When the land-boundaries are straight, then the apportioning of lands and revenues can be settled at Court. T'eng's lands, though narrow and small, must have within them its gentry and its country-folk. Without the gentry there would be no one to control the country-folk. Without country-folk, there would be no one to feed the gentry. My request would be that in the country-side, the "nine and one" system be put into effect and the *chu* exacted. While within the domain proper a tenth be assessed, to be paid by the payee in kind. For all from the rank of minister (*ch'ing*) down, there must be *kuei* fields allotted. A *kuei*[128] grant is fifty acres. For the rest, twenty-five acres.

"Upon death, or at a change of residence, the country folk should not leave the district. In the districts, fields belong to a common well-field unit. In their comings and goings, let friendliness prevail among the people, and let there be co-operation in the duties of watch and ward, and mutual help in time of sickness. Then the people will live in affection and accord. A square mile divided by the well-field system should give nine hundred acres. The 'Lord's fields' are the centre ones, which leaves an allotment of one hundred acres each for eight families for their own use. All attend to the 'Lord's fields,' and not until their work is finished there may the families attend to their own allotments. This maintains the proper distinction between the gentry and the country-folk. This, Sir, is the system in broad outline. It rests with your Prince and with you yourself to adapt it to local conditions."

(3A.3)

---

[127] See Additional Notes.　　　[128] See Additional Notes.

1.33. THE TEACHER

When Mencius went to T'eng, he was given lodging in an upper room. The lodge-keeper came looking for a sandal that was being made but was unfinished and had been left on a window sill. He failed to find it. Someone asked him, "Was it 'hidden'[129] by one of his followers?" Mencius said to the lodge-keeper, "You think my followers came to steal sandals, don't you?" The lodge-keeper said, "Probably not." Mencius replied, "When I give instruction, I neither run after those who leave, nor do I rebuff those who stay. If they come with a mind to learn, then I teach them. There is nothing more to it than that."

(7B.30)

1.34

Kung-tu Tzu[130] said, "When Keng of T'eng[131] presented himself at your gate, he behaved as decorum requires that one in his position should, yet you made no response. Why was that?" Mencius replied, "I make no response to those who, when seeking answers from me, presume on their rank, their ability, their seniority, upon obligations I may have incurred, or upon former acquaintance. Such people I do not acknowledge. Keng of T'eng offended on two of these counts."

(7A.43)

AT THE COURT OF THE DUKE OF LU

The State of Lu holds a special place in Confucian hagiography as the birthplace of Confucius. For Confucius himself, Lu was, so legend held, the fief of his hero, the Duke of Chou (4.5). It was popularly supposed, therefore, to be the place par excellence *where "early Chou culture" was best preserved. But Lu too, in Mencius' time, exemplified the depths to which Chou power had sunk. Its captive dukes had been manipulated by oligarchies and deposed by commoner-dictators, and Lu was indeed within sight of its end. Lu was destroyed by Ch'u in 256 B.C.*

Most of Mencius' references to Lu are cautionary ones. A pupil of his,

---

[129] A way of suggesting, without directly saying so, that it had been stolen. Mencius in his answer uses the bald word "steal," which makes the lodge-keeper recoil from the suggestion of a direct accusation.

[130] A follower of Mencius, see 3.1 ff.

[131] The younger brother of the Duke.

who later proved a disappointment, did obtain office there (3.22), and through
his mediation Mencius attempted to see the Duke of Lu, but it is clear that
whatever hopes Mencius may have had for other princes, Lu was the state
that had rejected Confucius, and in any case "it was decreed by Heaven that
I [Mencius] should not see the Lord of Lu" (1.35).

1.35

Duke P'ing of Lu was just about to leave his palace when a courtesan
Tsang-ts'ang made a request. She said, "At other times when my
Lord is about to leave, he has always instructed his courtiers as to
where he is going. His horse and carriage are now ready to leave. If
he does not inform us, we shall not know where he has gone. May I
ask where he is going?" The Duke replied, "I am going to see
Mencius." She replied, "How is this? Is my Lord going to demean
himself by appearing before a commoner?[132] Is it because you think
him a Worthy? Decorum and Justice derive from Worthies. Yet the
funeral which Mencius gave for his mother was far more lavish than
the funeral he gave for his father whom she survived. Would that my
Lord would not go to see Mencius."[133] The Duke agreed not to go.
Yo-cheng Tzu[134] was received by the Duke and asked, "Why would
my Lord not go to see Mencius?" The Duke answered, "Someone
informed me that the funeral Mencius gave for his mother was far
more lavish than the funeral he gave for his father. I therefore did
not go to see him." Yo-cheng Tzu said, "But why not? What was
called 'lavish' derived from the fact that on the occasion of his father's
death he was a mere knight, but later, when his mother died, he was a
Great Officer. He used three tripods on the first occasion (as a knight
should) and five on the latter occasion (as a Great Officer should).
Was it because of that?" The Duke said "No. It was because of the
lavishness of the inner and outer coffin and of the shrouds." Yo-cheng
Tzu replied, "That was not a question of lavishness. His financial
circumstances had changed."

Yo-cheng Tzu saw Mencius and said, "I spoke to the Duke about
his visiting you. He would have come to see you, but one of his
courtesans, a certain Tsang-ts'ang, prevented him and so he did not

---

[132] It is usually commoners who call on princes.
[133] See Additional Notes.   [134] See 3.31.

come." Mencius replied, "Whether my way is to progress or be impeded is not within the power of man to determine. It was decreed by Heaven that I should not see the Lord of Lu; it could not be that girl of the Tsang family who prevented me."

(1B.16)

AT THE COURT OF THE DUKE OF TSOU

Tsou, like T'eng, was another of the minor principalities whose feudal rulers held precarious tenure under the shadow of the large and encroaching major states. It was exterminated in 256 B.C. It was the putative birthplace of Mencius (though Mencius buried his mother in Lu), and it was to Tsou that Mencius went on leaving public life.

1.36

There had been an incident in which the forces of Lu and Tsou had clashed. Duke Mu of Tsou said to Mencius, "Thirty-three of my officers were killed, and none of my people were prepared to die for them. Yet there are too many people to punish for this, but if I do not punish them then I shall be overlooking their witnessing the death of their superiors without attempting to go to their assistance. What should I do?" Mencius replied, "In the lean years at bad harvests, the old and feeble of my Lord's subjects roll into the gutters and ditches,[135] and the able-bodied are separated, wandering to the four quarters. Some several thousands are affected in this way. Yet your granaries are full of grain, your arsenals well-stocked, and not one of your officers reports the state of affairs to you. Being arrogant, the upper classes regard the lower classes with contempt. Tseng Tzu[136] said, 'I warn you solemnly, that which emanates from you will return to you.' Your people are now returning to you (that which emanated from you). You should not put the blame on them. If you practised Humane government, then the people would regard their superiors as their own kith and kin and would die for them."

(1B.12)

[135] See 1.4.
[136] See Introduction to 6.73.

IN THE STATE OF SUNG

Sung was the state in the vicinity of which the early Chou kings had en-
feoffed the remnant of the Shang royal family after the conquest. Shang
culture was popularly supposed to have been preserved there. But Con-
fucius, for whom the Rituals of the Shang were of interest, complained of
"a lack both of documents and of learned men there"[137] *and wondered how*
one could talk of the "Rituals of the Shang."

In Mencius' day Sung was a minor state and had been an ally of Ch'i in
several campaigns. In 328 B.C. its Duke had assumed the title of king,
which perhaps accounts for the hint by Wan Chang (3.15) and the expec-
tation by some men in Sung that the new King of Sung might be the looked-
for king indeed. Mencius is persuaded that he is "not, as you say 'putting
Humane policies into practice' "(3.15).

Mencius is not recorded as having been received by the King. This King
of Sung was its first and last. Sung was destroyed by Ch'i in 286 B.C.

1.37. IN SUNG

Mencius told Tai Pu-sheng,[138] "Your wish is that your Prince might
be good, is it not? Let me explain this matter of goodness to you.

"Suppose a Great Officer of the State of Ch'u wanted his son to
learn the Ch'i dialect. Would he appoint a Ch'i man to teach him—
or a man of Ch'u?" Tai Pu-sheng said, "Why a Ch'i man naturally!"
Mencius continued, "If a Ch'i man were teaching him, but he were
surrounded by Ch'u people shouting at him in the Ch'u dialect, even
though the pupil were beaten daily, he would never acquire the Ch'i
dialect. Now suppose such a pupil were sent to live in the Chuang-
yüeh[139] quarter of the capital of Ch'i; after a few years there, even
though he were beaten daily, he would be unable to recall his Ch'u
dialect. You, Sir, describe Hsüeh Chü-chou as a good knight, and
you suppose that, by his residing at the palace, all at the palace, old and
young, noble and meanly born, will become men like Hsüeh Chü-
chou, so that the King will not then have the companions with whom
to do evil. But suppose that all at the palace, old and young, noble and

---

[137] *Analects*, III.9.
[138] A minister of the State of Sung. His family was a branch of the Sung royal family.
[139] See Additional Notes.

meanly born, are not men like Hsüeh Chü-chou! With what companions will the King do evil! What can one Hsüeh Chü-chou do for a man like the King of Sung?"

(3B.6)

1.38

Tai Ying-chih[140] said, "It is not possible at the present time to keep taxes down to a tenth and to abolish the market-levies altogether, but could I not simply lessen taxes and await a more propitious time in the future?" Mencius replied, "What would you think of a man who robs his neighbour's hen-house every day and when being told that this was ungentlemanly says, 'Well let me rob his hen-house only once a month and await a more propitious time to reform in the future.' If you know a thing to be unjust, then stop it at once. Why wait for a more propitious time in the future?"

(3B.8)

[140] A noble of Sung, presumably of the same family, if not the same person, as Tai Pu-shêng of 1.37.

Chapter Two

꿍꿍꿍꿍꿍꿍꿍꿍꿍꿍꿍꿍꿍꿍꿍꿍꿍꿍꿍꿍꿍꿍꿍꿍꿍꿍꿍꿍꿍꿍꿍꿍꿍꿍

MENCIUS
IN PUBLIC LIFE

When Mencius became a minister in Ch'i, he felt that he, a minister after the mind of Heaven, had met a Prince upon whom the Mandate of Heaven might fall. It is clear, however, from the conversations he had with King Hsüan, that Mencius' teaching of the irresistibility of virtue, of the gentle practice of Humanity and Justice, and of the innate perfectibility of man hardly constituted advice which the princes of his day thought practical.

Mencius had, in fact, little flair for statesmanship. But, as so often with idealists, he seems to have had difficulty in recognizing this. In the glimpses we have of him in office there is a rigidity in his insistence upon punctilio and an Olympian aloofness in his bearing towards his fellow ministers that must have made him an easy prey for his many enemies and hardly endeared him to his Prince.

Impractical, however, as the King may have thought Mencius to be, he felt that his presence in the state was a "good example."[1] But this was a role far short of that which Mencius felt he was destined to play. Disillusioned, he at first declined his salary and after a time resigned his office altogether, persuaded finally that "Heaven does not intend at this time to bring peace to the world."[2] This realization appears to have had a profound effect upon Mencius. It precipitated a crisis in his life. In the Works *there are a number of references to "Mencius leaving Ch'i."*

2.1. THE KING HAS A COLD

Mencius was just leaving for the dawn session at Court when a message arrived from the King. It said, "I intended going to Court today,

---

[1] For Mencius' views on "good examples," see 1.37 and 2.13.   [2] 2.14.

but I have a cold and cannot expose myself to the wind. If you are going I wonder if I shall have an opportunity of seeing you?" Mencius replied, "Unfortunately I too am ill and cannot attend at Court."[3]

On the day following, Mencius went out to attend a funeral at the Tung-kuo family. Kung-sun Ch'ou [a disciple][4] said, "Yesterday you excused yourself on account of sickness, but today you attend a funeral. Surely either your action yesterday or today is improper?" Mencius said, "Yesterday I was ill; today I am better. Why should I not attend the funeral?"

The King sent someone to ask how Mencius was feeling. He also sent a doctor. Meng Chung-tzu [thought to be Mencius' nephew] received them. (Temporizing) he said, "Yesterday, when the King's summons came, Mencius was a little upset and could not attend at Court. This morning he was feeling a little better. He hurried to Court. I do not know whether he has arrived there yet or not!" Meng Chung-tzu then sent several people off to try to intercept Mencius and to say, "Please do not come home, but go to Court at once."

On hearing about this, Mencius felt that he had no alternative but to go to the residence of Ching Ch'ou and stay there for the night. Ching Ch'ou said, "The great obligations of a man in private life are those which bind a father and son. The great obligations of a man in public life are those which bind a prince and his minister. Kindness is the duty that binds a father and son. Respect is the duty that binds prince and minister. I have noticed the respect that the King pays to you, Sir. But I have not noticed any way in which you have shown respect for the King." Mencius said, "What a thing to say! There is not a single man in Ch'i who will speak to the King about Humanity and Justice, and this is not because they think Humanity and Justice matters too delicate to mention. No! It is because in their hearts they say, 'The King is not fit to discuss such matters with.' In speaking thus they shew the greatest possible disrespect to the King. For my part I dare not but advocate in the King's presence any but the Way of Yao and Shun.[5] In doing so, no one in Ch'i is my peer in showing respect for the King." Ching Ch'ou said, "That is not what I am saying. The *Rites* say, 'When a father calls, a son should not use the

[3] See Additional Notes. [4] See Introduction to chapter III.
[5] See Introduction to 6.43 and to 6.52.

informal "yes";[6] when a prince issues a summons, a minister must not delay, even to wait for his carriage.'[7] Yesterday you really were going to Court. It was only after the King's message arrived that, in fact, you decided not to go. It really seems that you acted contrary to the requirements of the *Rites*." Mencius said, "You surely cannot mean that! As Tseng Tzu[8] said, 'The wealth of a Tsin or a Ch'u is unattainable for a state such as ours. Let them have their wealth, we have our Humanity. Let them have their noble connections, we have our Justice. What regrets have we?' Would Tseng Tzu have said that if it were not just? This is an integral part of the Way. There are three things for which a man is honoured: rank, seniority, and virtue. Rank takes precedence at Court. Seniority takes precedence in social intercourse, but in being the support of the times, in being the chief advocate for the people, virtue takes precedence. How can I uphold rank and seniority at the expense of virtue? The prince who is to accomplish great things will always have one minister he cannot just beckon, a minister who, if he has a matter to discuss, the prince will call and see. Unless such a prince shows that he gives precedence to virtue and delights in the Way in such fashion he is not worth having to do with. T'ang was first taught by Yi Yin[9] before he appointed Yi Yin to office, and so T'ang without difficulty became an Ideal King. Duke Huan of Ch'i was first taught by Kuan Chung[10] before he appointed Kuan Chung to office, and so Duke Huan without difficulty became Paramount Prince.[11] In the world today, the states are of comparable extent and their 'virtue' is on a par. None stands clearly above the rest. Why is this? For no other reason than that rulers want to make those people ministers who will take instructions from them. They do not want ministers who will give them instruction. T'ang would not have taken the liberty of summoning Yi Yin, and Duke Huan would not have taken the liberty of summoning Kuan Chung! If even Kuan Chung could not be summoned, how much more does this apply to me who would not stoop to be a Kuan Chung!"

(2B.2)

---

[6] See Additional Notes.
[7] He should hasten on foot if necessary; see 3.18, note 67.
[8] See Introduction to 6.73.
[9] See 3.7.
[10] See Introduction to 6.70.
[11] See Introduction to 6.70.

2.2. MENCIUS AND HIS FELLOW MINISTERS

Mencius said to Ch'ih Wa, "It was because you sought an opportunity to speak your mind that you declined the governorship of Ling-ch'iu and asked for the post of Leader of the Knights.[12] Some months have passed now; have you spoken your mind yet?"

Ch'ih Wa thereupon made his protest to the King, but it was unheeded so he proferred his resignation and departed from Ch'i.

The people of Ch'i said, "Mencius could propose an admirable course of action for Ch'ih Wa—but what course he proposes for himself—nobody knows!"

Kung-tu Tzu[13] reported these remarks to Mencius. Mencius said, "I have heard it said that a man with an official function to carry out, unable to carry out that function, resigns. And that a man with a protest to make, unable to make that protest, also resigns. But I have no official function and have no protest to make. Whether I remain or retire is a matter of my own choosing."

(2B.5)

2.3

P'en Ch'eng-k'uo received an official appointment in Ch'i. Mencius said, "They will kill him." P'en Ch'eng-k'uo actually was murdered. Mencius' followers asked him, "How, Sir, did you know that he would be murdered?" Mencius replied, "He was a man with a certain amount of ability but knew nothing of the Way of the True Gentleman. He had just enough ability to get himself killed—but little more."

(7B.29)

2.4

On a visit to P'ing-lu, Mencius said to the Governor there, "If one of your spearmen failed to report for duty three times in a single day, would you get rid of him?" "I would not wait for the third time!" was the reply. Mencius said, "Yet you, Sir, have 'failed to report for duty' frequently. In the lean years when the harvest fails, several

[12] See 1.12, note 55. [13] A follower of Mencius; see 3.i ff.

thousands of the old and feeble among your people roll in the ditches and gutters, while the able-bodied wander to the four quarters (in search of food)."[14]

The Governor replied, "This is not a thing which I can do anything about!"

Mencius said, "Suppose a man is entrusted with the care of another's livestock. Surely it is his responsibility to find pasture and fodder for them? If he cannot do so, should he surrender his charge or stand by and watch them die?"

The Governor replied, "I have been remiss in my duty."

Some time later, in audience with the King, Mencius said, "I know five of the governors in the state, and of them K'ung Chü-hsin alone acknowledges his faults. In your Majesty's interests, I plead for him." The King said, "It is I who am at fault."

(2B.4)

2.5

Ch'u Tzu[15] said to Mencius, "The King has ordered that you be kept under observation to see if, in fact, you are different from other men." Mencius said, "In what way could I differ from other men? Neither Yao nor Shun[16] were any different from other men!"

(4B.32)

2.6

When Mencius was a minister in Ch'i he was sent to represent the state at the obsequies of the Court of T'eng. The King sent Wang Huan,[17] the Governor of Kai, to assist him. Wang Huan was in daily attendance upon Mencius as they travelled from Ch'i to T'eng, but Mencius never once mentioned the matter of their mission. Kung-sun Ch'ou[18] said, "The dignity of a minister of Ch'i should certainly not be slighted. But even so, it is a long journey from Ch'i to T'eng, yet you never once mentioned the matter of your mission to your assistant. Why was this?" Mencius replied, "Whether satisfactorily settled or not, the matter was closed. Why should I speak of it?"

(2B.6)

---

[14] See 1.4. [15] See 2.11. [16] See Introduction to 6.43 and to 6.25.
[17] See 2.7 note 20. [18] See Introduction to chapter III.

2.7

Kung-hang Tzu[19] was in mourning for a son. The Master of the Right[20] went to offer his condolences. On entering the main gate, some of the mourners came forward and spoke to the Master then and there, while others approached him and spoke to him after he had taken his place. Mencius did not speak to him at all, and this displeased the Master of the Right. He said, "Everyone has spoken to me except Mencius. He wants to slight me!"

On hearing of this Mencius said, "I was merely observing protocol. At Court, one may not leave one's place to speak to someone else, or break ranks to bow to another. I merely wished to observe protocol, but Tzu-ao thinks I meant to slight him. How odd this is!"

(4B.27)

2.8. MENCIUS IN MOURNING

Mencius went to Lu from Ch'i to attend his mother's funeral. On the return journey, he stopped at Ying. Ch'ung Yü[21] made a request. He said, "Unaware of my incompetence, you, Sir, charged me with the arrangements for the making of the coffin. At the time you, Sir, were preoccupied. I did not dare to question it. But now, with all due deference I would like to raise the matter with you. The wood I thought was too good."[22] Mencius replied, "In far antiquity the thickness of the inner and outer coffin was not prescribed. In middle antiquity seven inches was prescribed. From the Son of Heaven down to commoners this was so, not merely for the sake of appearance, but to satisfy a need felt deep in the heart. Not to have done so would have given no reassurance and without such materials no reassurance was possible. The ancients used such materials provided they were available, to obtain reassurance. Why should I not do so too? Furthermore, when the time of dissolution comes, to feel that the earth will not

[19] A Great Officer of Ch'i.

[20] The Master of the Right was Wang Huan, the Governor of Kai (see 2.6). Tzu-ao is his courtesy name. It was Tzu-ao who was responsible for Yo-Cheng Tzu, Mencius' disappointing pupil, coming to Ch'i—a matter which caused his old tutor grave concern (see 3.31 and 3.32).

[21] Ch'ung Yü, here entrusted by Mencius with the details of the funeral, also followed his master into retirement (see 2.14).

[22] It was not only Mencius' friends who commented on the expense of this funeral. The reader will remember that it was a matter of Court gossip in Lu (1.35).

come into proximity with the corpse is surely reassuring? I have heard that the true gentlemen would not stint where his parents were concerned for the whole world."

(2B.7)

2.9

King Hsüan of Ch'i wished to shorten the period set aside for mourning. Kung-sun Ch'ou said, "A year's mourning is at least better than none at all!" Mencius said, "That is as bad as saying 'Do it gently!' to someone twisting his older brother's arm,[23] rather than the proper course, which is to teach him filial affection and brotherly duty!"

The mother of one of the King's sons had died, and his tutor asked that he might be given a period of a few months off for mourning. Kung-sun Ch'ou[24] asked Mencius what he thought of that.

Mencius replied, "This is a case of desiring to complete the full term of mourning, but being unable to do so. Even the addition of a single day is better than none in such a case. My objection had to do with mourning that is dispensed with when there is nothing to prevent its being fully discharged."

(7A.39)

2.10. RECEIVING GIFTS

Ch'en Chin[25] said, "Once in Ch'i the king sent you a gift of a hundred *yih*[26] but you declined it. In Sung, you were presented with 70 *yih* and you accepted it. In Hsüeh, you were presented with 50 *yih* and you accepted it. If your declining a gift on one occasion was right, then your accepting it on another was wrong. Master, you must be consistent in these things." Mencius said, "I was right on each occasion. In Sung, I was about to set out on a long journey. Travelling incurs expenses. The gift was offered with the message 'for your travelling expenses.' Why should I not have accepted it? In Hsüeh I was concerned about my personal safety. The gift was offered with the message, 'Hearing of your forebodings, I send you this gift to cover the cost of

---

[23] It must be remembered that the person of an older brother was sacrosant for the younger brother, and such an act was a serious affront.
[24] See Introduction to chapter III.   [25] See 3. vi ff.   [26] See Additional Notes.

an escort.' Why should I not have accepted it? In Ch'i, on the contrary, there was no occasion for accepting a gift. To offer a gift when there is no occasion for doing so is bribery. One cannot procure a true gentleman with a bribe."

(2B.3)

2.11

When Mencius was living in Tsou, the younger brother of the Lord of Jen was temporarily in charge of Jen and sought by an exchange of gifts to approach Mencius. Mencius accepted the gift but did not reciprocate. Staying at P'ing-lu where Ch'u Tzu[27] was Assistant, the same thing happened. On a later occasion, when travelling from Tsou to Jen, he called upon the younger brother of the Lord of Jen, but when travelling from P'ing-lu to Ch'i he failed to call upon Ch'u Tzu. Wu-lu[28] his disciple, was delighted and said, "This is my chance."[29] He said to Mencius, "I suppose your calling upon Jen's younger brother and not calling upon Ch'u Tzu was because the latter was merely an Assistant?" Mencius said, "Not so. The *Book of Documents*[30] says,

> In the giving of gifts there are many formalities.
> If the formalities did not match the gift
> It would be thought of as not given because
> No thought lay behind the giving and so
> It ceases to be a gift.

Wu-lu was pleased with this answer. When asked about it Wu-lu said, "The reason for Mencius behaving as he did was because the younger brother of the Lord of Jen could not go to Tsou, but Ch'u Tzu could have gone to Mencius in P'ing-lu."

(6B.5)

2.12

There was famine in Ch'i. Ch'en Chin[31] said, "The people are hoping that you, Sir, will plead once again for a distribution of grain from the

---

[27] It was Ch'u Tzu who informed Mencius that the King was having Mencius watched; see 2.5.

[28] See 3.37.

[29] Presumably to show what an astute pupil he was.

[30] Cf. *Documents*, p. 52.

[31] See 3. vi. ff.

state granaries at T'ang[32] but perhaps you cannot do so twice." Mencius said, "To do so would be as foolhardy as was Feng Fu. This Feng Fu, a man of Tsin, was at one time skilled at taking tigers barehanded, but later he became a noted scholar. Travelling in the countryside in this latter capacity he found the inhabitants pursuing a tiger. They had the tiger cornered, but no one dared seize it. Seeing Feng Fu they hurried to greet him. Feng Fu immediately bared his arms and got down from his carriage.[33] He gained the plaudits of the peasantry, but the scholars scorned him."

(7B.23)

2.13. MENCIUS RETIRES FROM PUBLIC LIFE

When Mencius tendered his resignation from office to return home, the King came to see him and said, "Before you came to Ch'i I wanted very much to meet you but I was never able to do so. When at last we met as prince and minister at Court it gave me great pleasure. Now you are leaving us to return home. Will I have another opportunity of seeing you?" Mencius replied, "It would certainly be my wish to do so but I would not be so bold as to ask."

Later the King said to Shih Tzu,[34] "I would like to build a house for Mencius in some central position in the capital and to provide a pension of 10,000 *chung* to support him and his followers. They would set an example for our nobles and citizens to emulate. Would you not mention this to him for me?" Shih Tzu conveyed this offer to Mencius through Ch'en Tzu.[35]

When Ch'en Tzu told Mencius what Shih Tzu had said, Mencius replied, "Really this is impossible, though Shih Tzu would hardly understand. If I could be attracted by money, would an offer of 10,000 attract me when I have already declined 100,000?"

Chi-sun said, "How strange!" Tzu-shu, however, was in two minds about it. Mencius said, "Since the King charged me with the responsibilities of state, but failed to follow my counsel, I resigned my office. If now, he wants to avail himself of my own pupils, of all people,

---

[32] A Ch'i practice, begun by Duke Ching (see 1.2). It was not the practice in Liang; cf. 1.22.

[33] And presumably dealt with the tiger, though the text does not say so. In India, civil servants who shot man-eating tigers were admired, as readers of Colonel Corbett's excellent books will know. In Mencius' China, gentlemen engaged in the public service did not engage in feats of such foolhardiness; see Additional Notes, 1.6, note 41.

[34] Of whom nothing else is known.   [35] See 3.36.

then who will *not* be attracted by mere money and position. If I were put in the position of being surrounded by rank and riches I should be tempted to show favouritism in choosing among them. Traders in the markets of antiquity exchanged the goods they had to dispose of for the goods they needed, while a market official kept order among them. Then, an official of mean disposition took for himself the profits of the markets by selling his favours. Thus merchants were taxed. The practice of taxing merchants began with that low person."[36]

(2B.10)

2.14

Mencius left Ch'i, accompanied by Ch'ung Yü.[37] As they journeyed, Ch'ung Yü said, "You, Sir, seem distressed at the way things have turned out, yet on a former occasion when I spoke to you about this you said, 'A gentleman does not feel resentment against Heaven, or put the blame upon men.'" Mencius replied, "The circumstances then and now are quite different. After five hundred years, a True King should have arisen for the Chou people, and the dynasty in the meantime should have been served by men famous in their generation. Yet seven hundred years have now passed since Chou began. As a matter of simple calculation the time is overdue, though, judging from the signs of the times, it still could come about. The delay can only be because Heaven does not intend at this time to bring peace to the world. If it did, with the exception of myself, who is there to be Heaven's instrument? How can I not be distressed?"

(2B.13)

2.15

After Mencius left Ch'i, he spent several nights in Tsou. A man there, wishing on the King's behalf to detain Mencius further, came to him, sat down, and talked. Mencius lay, leaning on a head-stool dozing, and took no notice. The man was displeased and said, "I fasted and purified myself before I presumed to come before you, yet you sleep and will not listen to me. At the very least, command me not to address you any more." Mencius said, "Please be seated, and I shall

[36] See Additional Notes.   [37] See 2.8.

make this whole matter clear to you. In Duke Mu of Lu's day,[38] Tzu-szu[39] was reassured by having an attendant from the King constantly by his side. Hsieh Liu and Shen Hsiang[40] were reassured by having one of their own men constantly at the King's side. You, Sir, show concern for a man your senior but do not do so with the King's authority. This is far from treating me as Tzu-szu was treated. Now, Sir, in my disregarding you, was it a matter of your being snubbed by your senior or your presuming before your senior?"

(2B.11)

2.16

After Mencius left Ch'i, Yin Shih said of him, "If Mencius did not know that the King of Ch'i would not become another T'ang or an Wu, it showed his lack of perception. If, on the other hand, he did realize this, then he merely resigned[41] from office over a matter of salary. It is said that he travelled a thousand miles to see the King, and, not finding the King the man he sought, he left. Yet, before he left Ch'i, he spent three nights lingering in Chou and how reluctant he was to leave! His explanation seems to me most unsatisfactory."

Kao Tzu[42] told Mencius about this. Mencius said, "What does Yin Shih know of my motives? It was certainly my wish to come to Ch'i. I did indeed 'travel a thousand miles to see the King.' But it was certainly not my wish to leave. 'Not finding the King the man I sought I left' indeed, for I had no other choice. I 'spent three nights in Chou,' not lingering, the time flew all too fast. I thought the King perhaps might change, and that, if he did, he would order my return. But up to the time I left Chou, no messenger came after me. Then my mind was finally made up. I would return home. Even so, it can hardly be said of me that I deserted the King. The King has, after all, all that is needed to become great. If he had availed himself fully of my services, not only the people of Ch'i but all the world would now be at peace. It is my daily hope that the King might change. I am surely not to be

---

[38] See Introduction to 6.73.

[39] The grandson of Confucius; see Introduction to 6.73.

[40] Hsieh Liu appears again in 3.23, and in 4.18 as Tzu-liu. Shen Hsiang (475-405 B.C.) is identified by Ch'ien Mu with the Tzu-mo of 4.1; see *Hsien-Ch'in Chu-tzu Hsi-nien* (Hong Kong, 1956), p. 248.

[41] Reading *chih* as the *chih* in 2.13.   [42] See 3. v ff.

judged by these trivial people who, upon rebuking their prince and finding that the prince disregards them, get angry and, feeling anger, show it upon their faces. When they resign they petulantly put a day's hard riding between themselves and their prince, before *they* stop for the night."[43] When Yin Shih heard of this, he said, "I was indeed one of these trivial people."

(2B.12)

2.17

After Mencius had left Ch'i and when he was living in Hsiu, Kung-sun Ch'ou[44] asked, "Was it the way of the ancients to engage in the state service without remuneration?" Mencius replied, "No, but I did so because, after I had been received by the King in Ch'ung, I had made up my mind to resign from his service and, not wishing to be persuaded to the contrary, I declined my remuneration. I continued to do so, but, when the general mobilization was proclaimed,[45] I could not present a request to resign, though it was certainly not my intention to remain so long in Ch'i."

(2B.14)

[43] Suggesting that they are beyond recall and making clear that their resignation is irrevocable.
[44] See Introduction to chapter III.
[45] See Introduction to 1.15.

Chapter Three

ⓢⓢⓢⓢⓢⓢⓢⓢⓢⓢⓢⓢⓢⓢⓢⓢⓢⓢⓢⓢⓢⓢⓢⓢⓢⓢⓢⓢⓢⓢⓢⓢⓢⓢⓢⓢⓢ

MENCIUS AND
HIS DISCIPLES

Philosophers in ancient China had their adherents and followers, no less than princes, and they were known as "men of their gate." Confucius is credited with having seventy.[1] *Those of Micius are said to have run into the hundreds. But we are hard put to it to find any such numbers for Mencius.*[2] *The King of Ch'i once offered to provide an establishment for Mencius and his followers in his capital to serve as "an example to our nobles and citizens,"*[3] *but this offer was declined, and Mencius is once asked if he does not regard as gross the spectacle of "gentlemen, with dozens of carriages in their train, and hundreds of followers, going from court to court."*

In the Works *several followers are mentioned, but their names occur more to provide the occasion for a question, and very little is revealed about them.*

Of them, Kung-sun Ch'ou appears to have served Mencius the longest, and to have been his most intimate friend. Kung-tu Tzu seems to have been the "doubting Thomas" of the circle, for all the questions he asks reflect current criticism in some form or another of Mencius' teaching. With Wan Chang, the companion of his old age, Mencius is concerned mostly with questions of exegesis of the books of antiquity, and we may suppose that after his withdrawal from public life his interests became increasingly bookish. Tradition attributes the compilation of the Works *to Wan Chang and his circle, with whom Mencius spent his declining years "working on the* Book of Songs *and the* Book of Documents." *On teaching in general, Mencius has this to say:*

[1] Credited, that is, by Mencius (see 6.7). But on this, see Waley, *Analects*, Introduction, p. 19.
[2] See Additional Notes.
[3] 2.13.

55

3.1

A True Gentleman offers instruction for five reasons;

Because some, as with parched earth after timely rain, are trans-
    formed by his teaching,
Because some perfect their virtue by his teaching,
Because some develop their talents by his teaching,
Because, for some, questions are thereby answered,
And because there are some who, indirectly, glean[4] from it.

It is for these five reasons that he offers instruction.

(7A.40)

3.2

Mencius said, "There are many ways of teaching. By the very things
I do not think worth teaching, I teach a man something."

(6B.16)

KUNG-TU TZU

*We have already met Kung-tu Tzu in 1.34 and 2.2. He will appear again
in 4.10 and 4.11.*

3.3

Kung-tu Tzu said, "Outside of our circle, men say that you, Sir, simply
like to argue. May I ask what you yourself say to this?" Mencius replied,
"It surely cannot be thought that I like to argue! I do so because I have
no other recourse. It is a long time now since man first appeared upon
the earth. At times he has been well governed, but at others quite the
contrary. In the days of Yao, the waters, flowing uncontrolled, inun-
pated the central states. They became the habitation of serpents and
dragons. The people had no settling place. They dug pits in the ground
and cut out caves in the hills. As the *Book of Documents*[5] says,

The raging waters are a warning to us.

The 'raging waters' were the Flood. Yü was sent to control it. He

---

[4] As Mencius "gleaned" from Confucius' teaching; see 6.50.
[5] *Documents*, cf. Legge, II.ii.14.

dug ditches and drained off the waters into the sea. He drove out the serpents and dragons, banishing them to the marshes. The waters, flowing off the land, became the Yang-tse, the Huai, the Yellow River, and the Han. Once the dangers were removed, the wild animals harmful to man disappeared. Then man took possession of the plains and built his houses there. But once Yao and Shun were dead, the Way of the Sages fell into decline. Tyrants arose who destroyed those houses by re-flooding the plains to make fishing grounds, so that the people were homeless once more. They withdrew land from cultivation to create hunting preserves, so that the people were deprived of food and clothing. Evil words and violent deeds once again prevailed throughout the land. With the increase of hunting parks and fishing grounds the wild animals returned. By the time of King Chou of the Shang Dynasty the world had once again reverted to confusion. The Premier of King Wu, the Duke of Chou, punished the Shang ruler. For three years he had Yen under attack, killing its prince and driving the *Fei-lien* to the shores of the sea, slaying them there. Fifty states were destroyed. He flushed out the tiger and leopard, the rhinoceros and the elephant, banishing them to distant places. Everywhere the people approved. As the *Book of Documents*[6] says,

> Magnificent indeed were King Wen's policies.
> Praiseworthy indeed the ardour with which
> King Wu carried them out.
> They benefited us, their successors.
> None have gone amiss, because of their rectitude.

But the House of Chou fell into a decline, and the Way became obscured. Evil words and violent deeds once again prevailed. Instances occurred of subjects assassinating their princes and of sons slaying their fathers. Confucius feared for his times. He worked upon the *Spring and Autumn Annals*.[7] These *Annals* are concerned with the affairs of the Son of Heaven. It was because of this that Confucius said, 'If I am to gain recognition, it will be because of my work on the *Annals*. If I am to be condemned, then that too will be because of my work on the *Annals*.'[8] But no Sage King arose. The Feudatory continued in their dissolute ways, and idle scholars engaged in pointless discussions. The teachings of Yang Chu and of Micius flooded the world; indeed the whole world

---

[6] *Documents*, p. 196.   [7] See Additional Notes.   [8] See Additional Notes.

talked either like Yang Chu or like Micius. Yang Chu speaks of 'acting in my own interests' as though princes did not exist. Micius speaks of 'loving all equally' as though the family did not exist. It is only among wild animals that a state is found in which neither the prince nor the family is of any account.[9] Kung-ming Yi said,[10] 'In their [i.e., the Feudal Lords'] stables are well fed horses, in their kitchens tender meat, while the people's faces are pinched with hunger, and the starving roam the countryside. This is a policy of "governing animals and eating men." '[11]

"Yet the teachings of Yang Chu and Micius continue without cess, while the Way of Confucius is not set forth. Their pernicious doctrines mislead the people and clog the channels of Humanity and Justice. 'Governing animals and eating men' will lead in the end to man eating man. I (like Confucius before me) am fearful for the times. I unlock the door of the Way of the Former Sages and set myself against the teachings of Yang Chu and of Micius. Their licentious words, and perverse theories, ought never to have been allowed to begin. But they begin in the mind, and cause harm to the practice of things. When they begin to cause harm to the practice of things they cause harm to government. If a Sage were to emerge once more, he would not alter a single word of this protest of mine. In antiquity, once Yü had dealt with the Flood, the world found peace. Once the Duke of Chou had extended his government over the Yi and the Ti, and had driven away the ferocious beasts, the people were at ease. Once Confucius had completed his work on the *Annals*,[12] rebellious ministers and unruly sons were terror-stricken. As it says in the *Book of Songs*,[13]

> When the Ti and the Jung were smitten
> When Ching and Hsü were suppressed
> No one then dared oppose us.

Those who regard the Prince and the family as of no account, those the Duke of Chou would have smitten. I, too, wish to set aright the minds of men, to put an end to pernicious teaching, to stand opposed to wicked deeds, and to banish evil talk, and thus to continue with the work of these three Sages. It surely cannot be said that I 'like to argue.' I

[9] See Additional Notes.
[10] This passage also occurs in 1.23 but is there attributed to Mencius. For Kung-ming Yi, see Additional Notes, 1.27, note 100.
[11] See Additional Notes.   [12] See Additional Notes.   [13] *Songs*, 251.

do so because I have no other recourse. He who can confound the arguments of Yang Chu and of Micius, he it is who is a true follower of the
Sages."

(3B.9)

3.4

Kung-tu Tzu said, "We all are men, but some are great men, and some
lesser men. Why is this?" Mencius replied, "Those who are actuated by
the greater parts become great men; those who are actuated by the lesser
parts become lesser men."[14] Kung-tu Tzu said, "We are all men then,
but some are actuated by the greater parts and some by the lesser parts.
Why is this?" Mencius replied, "It is not the function of the eyes and
ears to think—objects merely impinge upon them. When those objects
interact, the ears and eyes merely transmit it. It is the function of the
mind to think, and when it does so it receives what is transmitted to
it. When it fails to think, it simply fails to receive. These functions are
imparted to us by Heaven. It is when a man sets his face primarily
towards the greater parts that the lesser parts are unable to obtrude.
It is this, nothing more, that makes him a great man."

(6A.15)

3.5

Kung-tu Tzu said, "Everyone throughout the state says that K'uang
Chang[15] is an unfilial son, and yet you, Sir, consort with him and
accord him every courtesy, Why do you do this?"

Mencius said, "There are five commonly accepted unfilial acts which
make a man unmindful of his duty to provide for his parents. These are:
to be lazy; to gamble, play chess, and be overfond of wine; to love
money or be selfishly attached to your wife and children; to pursue
selfishly the pleasures of the senses which bring disgrace upon parents;
and to brawl and do foolhardy deeds which place one's parents in
jeopardy.[16] Is K'uang Chang guilty of any of these?

"K'uang Chang once had occasion to reprove his father, and thereafter they did not see eye to eye. To reprove a man for his good is

[14] Cf. 6.29.　　　　　　　　　　[15] See Introduction to 1.15.
[16] By leaving them childless and thus unsupported in old age.

proper among friends, but between father and son reproof does the greatest harm to the feeling of kindness that should exist between them. But even so, K'uang Chang surely did not wish that the relationship of husband and wife, or of son and mother, should cease, but because he had offended his father he was denied both of these and forced to drive out his own wife and children,[17] and for the rest of his life he was denied their comfort. He felt that if he did not act in this way he would have been guilty of the most grave of crimes.[18] This, then, is the case of K'uang Chang."

(4B.30)

WAN CHANG

3.6

Wan Chang said, "Some say that when Confucius was in the State of Wei, he stayed with Yung Chü, and that in the State of Ch'i he stayed with the eunuch Chi Huan.[19] Is this true?"

Mencius said, "No. It was not so. This is the fabrication of gossips. In Wei, Confucius stayed with Yen Ch'ou-yu. Tzu-lu's wife[20] was a younger sister of the wife of Mi Tzu of Wei. Mi Tzu had said to Tzu-lu, 'Let Confucius stay with me, and then he may become a Minister of Wei.' Tzu-lu told Confucius this. Confucius said, 'It is the will of Heaven.' Confucius entered a state with due propriety and left out of regard for Justice. Whether he was offered office or not, he said, was the will of Heaven. But to stay with such men as Yung Chü or the eunuch Chi Huan would neither show a regard for Justice, nor would it be the will of Heaven. When Confucius had incurred the displeasure of the rulers of Lu and Wei, Huan, Master of the Horse in Sung,[21] attempted to intercept and kill him. He passed through Sung in disguise. At this time he was in danger. He stayed with Chen Tzu, the city gate-keeper who was a servant of Chou, the Lord of Ch'en. I have heard a man is to be judged by the company he keeps.[22]

"If Confucius had stayed with Yung Chü or the eunuch Chi, would he still be Confucius?"

(5A.8)

---

[17] To appease his father.

[18] It would have been unfilial to desert his father, a crime he felt greater than that of disposing of his wife and children.

[19] See Additional Notes.   [20] Tzu-lu was a disciple of Confucius.   [21] Cf. *Analects*, 7.22.

[22] Literally, "At home judge a man by the people to whom he acts as host, abroad by the people that play host to him."

3.7

Wan Chang said, "It is said that Yi Yin[23] first met King T'ang through his knowledge of cooking. Was this so?"

Mencius replied, "No. That was not the case. Yi Yin was farming some land in the territory of the Ruler of Hsin. He learned to appreciate the Way of Yao and Shun[24] there. Had he been offered the salary of the ruler of the world, he would have disregarded the offer if it involved anything contrary to the teachings and just principles of Yao and Shun. Had he been offered a thousand teams of harness horses, he would not have given the offer a glance. He would neither give nor receive a single straw if it involved anything contrary to the teachings or just principles of Yao and Shun. T'ang sent messengers with gifts to entreat him to come to court. With complete indifference he said, 'What could I do with these gifts? It is surely better for me to remain here among my fields, for here it was that I learned to appreciate the Way of Yao and Shun.'

"Three times, T'ang sent messengers to entreat him. His air of indifference then changed. He said, 'If they allow me to remain among my fields, I can appreciate the Way of Yao and Shun, but perhaps I might be able to make this King a Yao or a Shun, and make his people a people after the order of Yao and Shun's people? Perhaps I might see this done with my own eyes. When Heaven begat our people (Heaven ordained that) those who already know should teach those who are yet to know, and that those who are already taught should apprise those who have yet to be taught. I am one from among Heaven's people who has already been taught. I will teach these people the Way of Yao and Shun, for if I do not do so then who will?' He was concerned that while among the common people, both men and women, there were those who had never felt the life-giving beneficence of Yao and Shun, it was as though he himself had pushed them into a ditch. In this way, he took upon himself the heavy burden of the world. He went to King T'ang as a result, proposing that T'ang attack the Hsia and rescue the common people. I have never heard of one who being himself twisted was able to straighten others, and much less of one who being in disgrace himself was able to set the world aright. The Sages acted each in their own way.

[23] Yi Yin was first tutor and then minister to T'ang the Successful, founder of the Shang Dynasty. He forms one of a trinity of model ministers (see 4.18, 6.64, 3.29, and cf. 3.8).
[24] See Introduction to 6.43 and to 6.52.

F

Some stayed far away from the court while others stayed in its vicinity. Some left court while others have remained. They have been governed by the necessity to keep themselves undefiled. I have heard that Yi Yin first met T'ang on account of the teachings of Yao and Shun—but never that he did so through his knowledge of cooking! The *Teachings of Yin*[25] says, 'The punishment of Heaven (of Chieh) began with the attack on the Palace of Mu. I shall begin at Po.' "

(5A.7)

3.8

Wan Chang said, "There is a saying to the effect that virtue had declined by Yü's[26] time, because Yü failed to pass on the Empire to a worthy man, but appointed his own son instead. Is there any truth in this?"

Mencius replied, "No, it was not so. If Heaven wishes to appoint a worthy man, a worthy man is appointed. If Heaven wishes to appoint the son, the son is appointed. In antiquity Shun recommended Yü to Heaven. Seventeen years later Shun died. At the end of the three-year period of mourning Yü fled to Yang-ch'eng to avoid the sons of Shun. The people followed after him. And just as with Yao before him, the people followed not Shun's sons, but followed Yü. Yü recommended Yi to Heaven. Seven years later Yü died. After the three-year period of mourning, Yi fled to the area north of Mount Chi. But the Feudal Lords in paying homage, and those seeking arbitration in lawsuits, did not go to Yi but came to Ch'i, son of Yü. The singers of songs sang not to Yi but to Ch'i, son of Yü. They said, 'He is the son of our Lord.'

"Neither Tan Chu [a son of Yao], nor the sons of Shun were even comparable with their fathers. But Shun as the Premier of Yao and Yü as the Premier of Shun held office for a long period. They had, for a long time, been shedding the beneficence of their policies upon the people.

"Yi as the Premier of Yü held office for but a short period. He had a short time to shed the beneficence of his policies upon the people. Between Shun, Yü, and Yi a long period had elapsed. That their son's abilities were not comparable with theirs was a matter that rests with Heaven. It was not something that a man can contrive. To contrive

[25] In the *Book of Documents*, see Legge IV.iv.2.   [26] See Introduction to 6.43 and to 6.52.

what man cannot contrive, that rests with Heaven. To bring to the throne he whom no man can bring, that rests with Heaven's ordinances. One who, being a commoner, becomes the Son of Heaven, must be a man whose virtue is of the order of Shun's and Yü's and, too, he must have a Son of Heaven to propose him. It was for this reason [i.e., because no Son of Heaven was in a position to propose him] that Confucius did not become the Son of Heaven. For one who by virtue of dynastic succession becomes the Son of Heaven is only set aside by Heaven if he is a man of the order of Chieh or Chou.[27] It was for this reason [i.e., because there were heirs to the throne already] that men like Yi,[28] Yi Yin,[29] and the Duke of Chou[30] never became Son of Heaven. Yi Yin was the Premier of T'ang and through him T'ang became King of the World. When T'ang died, T'ai-ting did not succeed him, but Wai-ping did so for two years, and Chung-jen for four years. It was T'ai Chia[31] who subverted the Statutes of T'ang, for which Yi Yin banished him to T'ung. After three years of banishment, T'ai Chia mended his ways, regretting his errors, and reformed himself. While in T'ung, he lived in Humanity and shifted his position towards Justice. After three years, he was prepared to accept the admonitions of Yi Yin so that once again he returned to Po. The Duke of Chou did not succeed to the Chou Throne, just as Yi did not succeed to the Hsia Throne, or Yi Yin to the Yin Throne.

"Confucius said, 'T'ang [i.e., Yao] and Yü [Shun] abdicated their thrones to worthy men while the Lords of Hsia, Yin, and Chou were succeeded by their children, but in either case the essential Justice was observed.'"

(5A.6)

3.9

Wan Chang said, "Hsiang[32] had made it his business, day after day, to try to kill Shun, but when Shun became Son of Heaven, he merely banished Hsiang.[33] Why was this?"

Mencius replied, "He actually enfeoffed him, though some thought this was banishing him."

[27] See Introduction to 6.69.   [28] See 4.14.   [29] See 3.7, note 23.
[30] See Introduction to 6.52.   [31] An early King of Shang; cf. 3.24.
[32] Hsiang was the younger brother of Shun; see Introduction to 6.43 and to 6.52.
[33] See Additional Notes.

Wan Chang said, "Shun drove out Kung Kung to Yü-chou, banished Huan T'ou to Mount Ch'ung, slew the prince of the San Miao at San Wei, and imprisoned K'un at Mount Yü. Having punished these four offenders, the world paid him homage. It was the punishment of the Inhumane. But of all men Hsiang was the most Inhumane, yet he was enfoeffed with Yu-p'i. Why should punishment be inflicted upon the people of Yu-p'i? Does a Humane man really behave in this way? Other men were punished, but his own younger brother was enfoeffed!"

Mencius replied, "A Humane man in his dealings with a younger brother neither harbours anger nor entertains resentment against him. He loves him as his own kin. Since he is his own kin, his wish is for rank and honour for him. Since he loves him, his wish is for wealth for him. Shun enfoeffed his brother with Yu-p'i to provide rank and honour and wealth for him. For if he, being the Son of Heaven, had allowed his younger brother to remain a commoner, would that have been loving him as his own kin?"

Wan Chang said, "May I ask what you meant by saying 'some thought this was banishing him'?"

Mencius replied, "Hsiang was not able to do what he should in his state, and so the Son of Heaven sent an officer to administer it for him and to pass on its revenues to him. For this reason, it was said he had banished him. Hsiang surely ought not to have been allowed to oppress the people. Even so Shun wished constantly to see him and he was forever coming (to the capital). The phrase[34] 'He did not wait for the time of tribute-offering or excuse himself because of state business to receive the Ruler of Yu-p'i' has reference to this."

(5A.3)

3.10

Wan Chang said, " 'Yao handed over the Empire to Shun'[35]—that is so, is it not?"

Mencius said, "No! The Son of Heaven cannot 'hand over' the Empire to anyone."

Wan Chang said, "Shun gained possession of the Empire. Who, then, handed it over to him?"

Mencius replied, "Heaven did so."

---

[34] From a work now lost.　　　　[35] See Introduction to 6.43 and to 6.52.

Wan Chang said, "In doing so, was the charge given in so many words?"

Mencius said, "No. Heaven does not express itself in words. Heaven indicates its wishes through the actions and service of others."

Wan Chang said, "How is that?"

Mencius replied, "The Son of Heaven can recommend a man to Heaven, but cannot compel Heaven to give the Empire to his candidate just as a Feudal Lord can recommend a man to the Son of Heaven, but cannot compel the Son of Heaven to present him with a Feudatory, or as a noble can recommend a man to his Feudal Lord, but cannot compel his Lord to present him with a noble's rank. In antiquity, Yao having recommended Shun to Heaven, Heaven accepted him. He presented him to the people and the people accepted him. It was for this reason that I said, 'Heaven does not express itself in words. Heaven indicates its wishes through the actions and service of others.'"

Wan Chang said, "May I ask about 'recommending him to Heaven and presenting him to the people.' How was that?"

Mencius replied, "He ordered him to preside at the sacrifices, and the spirits responded favourably to his sacrifices. Thus it was that 'Heaven accepted him.' He put him in charge of affairs of state, and they were carried out well and the people were content. Thus it was that 'the people accepted him.' We may say that both Heaven and man gave the Empire to him. That is why I said, 'The Son of Heaven cannot hand over the Empire to anyone.'

"Shun was premier to Yao for twenty-eight years. This is not something that a man can contrive; it is an act of Heaven. When Yao died and the three years of mourning were over, Shun fled to the south of the Southern River to escape the sons of Yao. But the Feudal Lords who came to pay homage came not to the sons of Yao, but to Shun. Those who came for arbitration in lawsuits came not to the sons of Yao but to Shun. The singers of songs sang not to the sons of Yao but to Shun. That is why I said, 'It is an act of Heaven.' It was only after these things had happened that Shun returned to the central states, stood in the place of the Son of Heaven, and took up residence in Yao's Palace. If he had begun by driving out the sons of Yao, it would have been pure usurpation. It would not have been a case of 'Heaven handing over to him.'

In the *Book of Documents*[36] it says,

> Heaven sees as the people see
> Heaven hears as the people hear

and it is of these things that it speaks."

(5A.5)

3.11

Wan Chang said to Mencius, "In the *Book of Songs*[37] it says,

> What should we do when taking a wife?
> We must always tell our parents.

If this is really so, then Shun,[38] properly speaking, should have been the highest examplar of it, but he did not tell his parents when he took a wife—why was this?" Mencius said, "If he had done so, he would never have been able to marry. For a man and a woman to set up house together is one of the fundamental human relationships. If he had told his parents, (their refusal) would have meant that he must forego one of the fundamental human relationships, which would have been to the detriment of his parents.[39] This is why he did not tell them."

Wan Chang said, "I understand now why Shun took a wife without telling his parents, but why did the Emperor not inform Shun's parents when he gave his daughters in marriage to Shun?" Mencius replied, "The Emperor, too, knew that if he had informed them he would not have been able to give his daughters in marriage."

Wan Chang said, "We are told that Shun was sent by his parents to repair a granary. The ladder was removed. Ku Sou [his father] set fire to the granary. And, too, that Shun was sent to dig a well. He had already left the well but Ku Sou (unaware of this) filled it in again. Hsiang [his younger brother] said, 'I am the one who should gain from the plot to conceal Shun from the Ruler. May his cattle and sheep, his granary and treasuries revert to our parents but may his shield and spear be mine, may his lute and his bow be mine. May my two sisters-in-law be made to look after my own women's quarter.' Hsiang then entered Shun's palace. Shun was lying on a couch playing his lute. Hsiang said, 'I am concerned only for you, my Lord,' and he blushed. Shun said, 'Do you undertake, on my behalf, to govern these my

---

[36] *Documents*, Legge, V.i.ii.7.
[37] *Songs*, 71.
[38] See Introduction to 6.43 and to 6.52.
[39] By depriving them of descendants; see 6.18.

subjects and people?' We are told this, but I myself do not know if Shun realized that Hsiang was about to slay him—did he?"

Mencius replied, "How can he not have realized it? But when Hsiang was sad, Shun was sad. When Hsiang was pleased Shun was pleased." Wan Chang said, "Quite so, but was not Shun merely pretending to be pleased?" Mencius replied, "Not at all. Someone once sent a gift of a live fish to Tzu-ch'an of Cheng.[40] Tzu-ch'an gave the fish to his gamekeeper to be kept in the fish-pond, but the gamekeeper in fact cooked the fish and ate it. In reporting to Tzu-ch'an he said, 'When first I released it, it seemed fettered still, but after a short time it was free and swam merrily away.' Tzu-ch'an replied, 'It is in its element once again. It is in its element!' On coming out, the gamekeeper said, 'Which of you says that Tzu-ch'an is a wise man? Though I had cooked the fish and eaten it, he said "It is in its element.'"

"One might deceive a true gentleman by appearances but never entrap him in matters contrary to his principles. Hsiang came to Shun imposing on the love which an older brother should show, and therefore Shun believed him and was pleased but his pleasure was not a pretence."

(5A.2)

3.12

Wan Chang asked, "'Shun went into the fields, he wept, crying aloud to bright Heaven'—why did he 'weep and cry aloud'?" Mencius replied, "Because of the resentment occasioned by the object of his affections."[41] Wan Chang said, "But why resentment? When a son is loved by his parents, though happy he never forgets them, and when hated by his parents, though distressed he never resents them. Was Shun then resentful?" Mencius replied, "Ch'ang Hsi said to Kung-ming Kao,[42] 'You have already instructed me on the passage "Shun went into the fields" but I still do not understand the line which follows: "he wept, crying aloud to bright Heaven and to his parents."' Kung-ming Kao said, 'This is a matter which you and I do not understand.' He said this because he thought that a man whose mind was so set upon filial piety

[40] See 6.72.
[41] I.e., of his parents; see 3.11. See also Introduction to 6.43 and to 6.52.
[42] Ch'ang Hsi was a pupil of Kung-ming Kao and a contemporary of Tzu-szu (see 3.13). For Kung-ming Kao, see Introduction to 6.73.

would not be so heartless as to say, 'I exert my entire energies ploughing my family's fields but this is simply the duty of a son. The fact that my parents do not love me is beside the point.' But then Emperor Yao commanded that his own nine sons and his two daughters, his officials, his herds and flocks, and his treasuries and granaries should be placed at Shun's disposal in the draining of the fields. Many of the gentry joined Shun and the reason that they did so was because Yao proposed to share the government with Shun and eventually to transfer it to him; despite this, Shun himself, because of his parents' lack of sympathy, likened himself to a poor and homeless man. We all desire to be the object of approval by others, but it was not enough to dispel Shun's grief. We all desire the love of beautiful women but even his marriage to the two daughters of the Emperor was not enough to dispel Shun's grief. We all desire riches but though he possessed the wealth of the whole world, it was not enough to dispel Shun's grief. We all desire rank and honour but the supreme rank and honour of 'Son of Heaven' was not enough to dispel Shun's grief; neither approval, beauty, riches, nor rank were enough to dispel his grief. Only a reconciliation with his parents could have done that. When young, our parents are the object of our affections but when we become older the attraction of women's beauty gradually takes its place. When we marry and have children, then our wives and children become the objects of our affections. When we enter the service of the state, then the prince becomes the object of our affections. If we fail to obtain such service, then we burn within, but, to the man of supreme filial piety, parents are always the object of his affections and in Shun we see an example of a man of whom this was still true at the age of fifty."

(5A.1)

3.13

Wan Chang said, "Might I ask about friendship?"

Mencius replied, "True friendship does not presume upon seniority, upon rank, or upon family connections. For friendship is a relationship of virtue. It does not allow of presumption. Meng Hsien Tzu was a member of a great feudal family.[43] He was friend of five men,

---

[43] In Lu. He died in 554 B.C. His son is favourably mentioned in *Analects*, 19.18, for the meticulousness with which he observed certain details of mourning for his father.

Yo-cheng Ch'iu, Mu Chung, and three others whose names I have forgotten. It was friendship that bound Meng Hsien Tzu to them and had nothing to do with his family connections. If family connection had obtruded itself, he would have withdrawn his friendship. And this principle is not only true for members of great feudal families; it is true too for the princes of minor states. Duke Hui of P'i[44] said, 'Tzu-szu's[45] relationship to me is that of teacher; Yen Pan's, that of friend. As for Wang Hsün and Ch'ang Hsi,[46] they simply render service to me.' And, too, it is true for princes of major states. Duke P'ing of Tsin[47] was the friend of Hai T'ang. When occasion demanded, Hai T'ang entered the Duke's presence, or left it, sat with him, or ate with him. Though the food was of the plainest, he ate to the full[48] for he would not have presumed to do otherwise. But friendship stopped short here. He did not intrude upon royal prerogatives, sharing the seat of Heaven, sharing the direction of the Heavenly offices, or partaking in the eating of the Heavenly offerings. He was a worthy to be honoured among the knights, but not a worthy to be honoured among kings. Shun continued to be received in audience by the Emperor, though he was, as the Emperor's son-in-law, living in the Second Palace. Shun too entertained the Emperor. They acted as guest and host alternately. Thus an Emperor befriended a commoner. The deference paid to a superior by an inferior we call 'giving to rank what is due to rank.' The deference paid to an inferior by a superior we call 'giving honour to the worthy.' The essential principle is the same in both cases."

(5B.3)

3.14

Wan Chang said, "Some say that Po-li Hsi[49] sold himself to a cattleman of Ch'in for five sheepskins and tended his cattle so that he might meet Duke Mu of Ch'in. Is this story reliable?"

Mencius replied, "No. It is not. It is the fabrication of gossips. Po-li Hsi was a native of Yü. The State of Tsin had sought rights of passage through Yü to attack Kuo. They had offered a Ch'ui-tz'u jade and a team of Ch'ü-bred[50] horses as an inducement. Kung Chih-ch'i of Yü had protested, but Po-li Hsi (though against the proposal) did not do so. He knew that with the Duke of Yü it would be pointless. He left Yü

[44] See Additional Notes.   [45] See Introduction to 6.73.   [46] See 3.12, note 41.
[47] See Introduction to 6.70.   [48] As protocol required.   [49] See Additional Notes.
[50] Ch'ui-tz'u and Ch'ü, it is generally agreed, are place names in north-west China.

and went to Ch'in. At that time he was already seventy years old. If, at this age, he did not know that it would be a demeaning thing to seek to meet Duke Mu of Ch'in by herding cattle, could he be thought a wise man? Surely it was wise not to protest when a protest would be ineffectual? To have realized that the Duke of Yü's career was shortly ending, and to have left before the débacle, cannot but be thought wise. In time he was taken up by Ch'in. To have realized that Duke Mu was a man with whom he could associate and with whom his policies might prevail, to have become his Premier—can this not be thought of as wise? To have been Premier of Ch'in and to have brought lustre to his Prince throughout the world and to have passed into history as an example for later generations—is this something that an unworthy man could do? As to the belief that he 'sold himself to gain entrée to his Prince,' this is something that even a country bumpkin, however brash, would not do. Can we imagine a worthy doing so?"

(5A.9)

3.15

Wan Chang said, "Sung[51] is a minor state. If they propose to put Humane policies into practice, but Ch'i and Ch'u, being hostile, attack them, what could they do?"

Mencius replied, "When T'ang the Successful lived in Po, his neighbour, the Lord of Ko, being a dissolute man, had neglected his sacrifices. T'ang sent to inquire why he did so. The Lord of Ko said, 'I have no way of providing the sacrificial animals.' At this, T'ang had sheep and oxen sent to him. The Lord of Ko slew and ate them. He continued to neglect his sacrifices. T'ang sent to inquire once more why he did so. The Lord of Ko said, 'I have no way of providing the necessary grain.' At this, T'ang sent a party of able-bodied men from Po to Ko to plough his fields for him, with orders to the old and feeble to keep those men supplied with food. The Lord of Ko, leading his own people, intercepted the food carriers, taking from them their wine and rice. Those who refused to give up the food were slain. There was a boy among them carrying meat and millet. They killed him and took away his food. When the *Book of Documents* says[52]

The Lord of Ko treated the food-carriers as enemies,

---

[51] Cf. Introduction to 1.37.　　　　　　[52] *Documents;* see Legge, IV.ii.6.

it refers to this incident. It was because of the murder of this boy that T'ang attacked Ko. The whole world said, 'He did not attack them to enrich himself by conquering the world. He attacked them to avenge the parents of a commoner's boy.' When T'ang undertook his punitive campaigns, he began with Ko. He attacked eleven princes. But he aroused no enmity in the world. When he campaigned to the east the western tribes-peoples were resentful. When he campaigned to the south, the northern tribes-peoples were resentful. They said, 'Why does he not come to us first?' The common people looked upon him as in a drought they look upon rain. They continued to go to market. The work in the fields continued without change. He punished the rulers but consoled the people. As with timely rain, the people rejoiced in him.[53] The *Book of Documents* says,[54]

> We await our Lord, when he comes we will
> not be punished.

"And, too, after the Chou conquest, there were those who would not become the subjects of Chou. Chou attacked the Eastern Territories bringing peace to the people. They met him with baskets of black and yellow silks, saying, 'We have received favour from our King of Chou.' They submitted as subjects to the great City of Chou. Their princes filling baskets of black and yellow silks welcomed the princes of Chou. Their commoners with gifts of food welcomed the commoners of Chou. Chou had saved them from fire and flood[55] seizing only their oppressors. The *Book of Documents*[56] says

> The might of my arms shall be manifest when
> I cross their frontiers
> I will seize the oppressors,
> The punishment I impose will be great,
> I shall be more glorious than T'ang.

Sung is not, as you say, 'putting Humane policies into practice.' But if Sung really were to do so, then all within the four seas would raise their heads in expectation to him, hoping that Sung would become

---

[53] Mencius is quoting here or at least paraphrasing, for the same passage occurs in 1.16 with parts attributed to the *Book of Documents*.

[54] *Documents;* see Legge, IV.v.ii.5.

[55] I.e., from tyranny. The phrase is conventional, see 1.15.

[56] *Documents*, cf. Legge, V.I.ii.8.

their prince. However great Ch'i and Ch'u may be, why then should Sung fear them?"

(3B.5)

3.16

Mencius said to Wan Chang, "The good knight in the village befriends the other good knights in the village. The good knight in the state befriends other good knights in the state. The good knight in society befriends other good knights in society. But, if the good knight in society finds that there are not enough good knights to befriend, he can still have converse with the men of antiquity, chanting their songs, and reading their works.

"Can he befriend them without knowing them? He can, for he can have converse with their world. Thus he still has friends."

(5B.8)

3.17

Wan Chang said, "Why is it that a knight makes no claim upon a Feudal Lord for his support?"

Mencius replied, "It would be presumption to do so. There is an obligation in protocol for one Feudal Lord to support another when he has been deposed, but for a knight to make such a claim would be contrary to protocol."

Wan Chang said, "If a prince presents a knight with a gift of food, may be accept it?"

Mencius replied, "He may."

Wan Chang asked, "With what justice?"

Mencius replied, "It is the prince's duty to relieve distress among his people."

Wan Chang said, "Then if it is a matter of relief, he accepts it, but if it is merely a gift he does not. Why is this?"

Mencius replied, "It would be presumption to do otherwise."

Wan Chang said, "May I ask where the presumption would lie?"

Mencius replied, "Even gate-keepers and night watchmen[57] are provided for by the prince when they have regular duties, but they

---

[57] See Additional Notes.

would think it a matter of presumption if they received gifts from a prince without having regular duties to perform."

Wan Chang said, "If a knight may accept a gift (under proper circumstances), may he do so repeatedly?"

Mencius replied, "Duke Mu of Lu[58] made frequent inquiries about Tzu-szu,[59] sending him gifts of cooked meat. Tzu-szu took exception to this importunity. Finally, he motioned to the messenger to put the gift outside the main gate. He then, saluting and with deep bows, declined the gift. He said, 'Now I know what it feels like to be the kept horse or hound[60] of a prince.' No doubt this was why no further gifts were sent. A prince may take pleasure in a worthy man, but if he cannot grant him an official post, then he should not provide for his keep. And if he does not grant him an official post, can he really be said to take pleasure in him?"

Wan Chang said, "A prince ruling a state might wish to support a gentleman. May I ask under what conditions he properly may do so?"

Mencius replied, "When a prince issues an order for a gift to be made to a gentleman, the gentleman receives it with salutes and deep bows. But if, thereafter, the Granary Keeper continues to issue grain to him regularly, and the Royal Cook continues to send him gifts of meat, without a specific order in each case to do so, the gentleman is still required to salute and bow. It was this that made Tzu-szu think that gifts of this kind turned him into a serving man, continually bowing. This is not the proper way to treat a gentleman. Yao[61] ordered his nine sons and his two daughters to serve Shun. He married his two daughters to him. He placed his officials, his flocks and herds, his granaries and treasuries at Shun's disposal in his work in the fields. Later he raised him to the highest office. This is an example of what we mean when we say, 'Kings honour worthy men.' "

(5B.6)

3.18

Wan Chang said, "May I ask what principle of Justice is involved in your not seeking audience with a prince?"[62]

[58] See Introduction to 6.73.   [59] See Introduction to 6.73.   [60] See Additional Notes.
[61] See Introduction to 6.43 and 6.52.
[62] A matter which evidently irked not only Wan Chang but also Kung-sun Ch'ou (see 3.23) and Ch'en Tai (see 3.38).

Mencius replied, "Within the city, a subject is known as 'the servant of wells and markets.' In the countryside, he is known as 'the servant of growing things.' But both are commoners. Commoners who have not presented their credentials as subjects do not, as a matter of protocol, seek audiences with princes."

Wan Chang said, "Suppose a commoner is summoned to perform some service; he should perform that service, but if the prince wishes to receive him and he summons him, and the commoner fails to respond, what then?"

Mencius said, "He would be in the right in performing the service, but would not be in the right if he were received in audience; but why should the prince wish to receive him?"

Wan Chang said, "Because perhaps he is a learned man or a worthy man."

Mencius said, "Even the Son of Heaven would not summon a teacher, however learned. How much less should this be so in the case of a Feudal Lord? As to his being worthy, I have never heard of that being given as reason for summoning him. Duke Mu of Lu frequently received Tzu-szu.[63] The Duke said to him, 'In antiquity a major Feudal Lord might engage in friendship with a knight. What do you think about that?'[64] Tzu-szu was displeased at this and said, 'The men of antiquity had a saying "render service to him" but surely they had no saying "befriend him." ' In his displeasure, Tzu-szu might well have said, 'Our respective positions are those of prince and subject; how could I presume to be on terms of friendship with you? Virtue should govern your relationships with me; how can you offer me friendship?' If it was not permissible for a great Feudal Lord to seek for a knight's friendship, how much less should he beckon to him like a servant? Duke Ching of Ch'i[65] was hunting. He summoned his huntsman by signalling to him with a plumed flag. The huntsman would not come. The Duke was about to kill him. But the 'knight of stout heart ever remembers that he may end up in the gutters; the brave knight never forgets that he may lose his own head.' What lesson did Confucius draw from this? The lesson 'do not respond to summons improperly given.' "

[63] See Introduction to 6.73.

[64] I.e., "What do you think about that as a maxim?"

[65] See Additional Notes, 1.2, note 20. This story occurs again in 3.38 in a slightly different context.

Wan Chang asked, "May I ask what form of summons would be proper for a huntsman?"

Mencius replied, "A wave of the hunting cap. A commoner should be summoned with a plain flag, a knight with an embroidered flag, and a noble with a flag with a feathered plume at the mast. The huntsman would have died rather than answer a summons proper to a noble, and should a commoner answer a summons proper to a knight? How much the more so, then, should a worthy man refuse to answer a summons proper only to an unworthy man. When a prince wishes to receive a worthy man in audience, and summons him in an inappropriate manner, it is like asking a man to come into your house, and then slamming the door in his face. Justice is the path that leads to the house, protocol the gate by which we enter. It is only a gentleman who can tread this path, and enter and leave by this gate. The *Book of Songs*[66] says:

> The highways of Chou are as flat as a millstone.
> They are straight as an arrow.
> They are trodden by gentlemen,
> Commoners merely look on."

Wan Chang said, "When Confucius received his prince's summons, he set out at once, 'without waiting for his carriage.'[67] Was he then at fault for doing so?"

Mencius replied, "Confucius at the time was in office and had the duties of office to carry out. The summons was appropriate to one in such a position."

(5B.7)

3.19

Wan Chang said, "Might I ask what kind of thoughts should prompt the exchange of gifts?"

Mencius replied, "They should be thoughts of respect."

Wan Chang said, "But it is thought disrespectful to refuse a gift. Why is this?"

Mencius replied, "It is disrespectful when he who offers the gift does

---

[66] *Songs*, 284.
[67] As protocol required; see 2.1 and cf. *Analects*, 10.13.

so to pay us honour. We should not ask if the gift were come by honestly or not before accepting it. That is to show disrespect. Such gifts should not be refused."

Wan Chang said, "Suppose that one had ascertained that the gift was dishonestly come by—by some improper exaction from the people, for example. And suppose that one had mentally refused to accept it without specifically saying so. Would it be in order to refuse the gift on some other pretext?"

Mencius replied, "If the gift were given as a matter of principle, and it was accompanied with the full observance of protocol, Confucius would have accepted it."

Wan Chang said, "Suppose now a highwayman, beyond the city gate, intends to give a gift as a matter of principle, and he offers it in accordance with the requirements of protocol, could one accept his gift knowing it to be stolen?"

Mencius replied, "One could not! In the *Book of Documents*[68] it says: ... those who kill and overthrow others, who go for spoil, the men of force who have no fear of death, none of these but are detested by the people. ...

Thus without giving such people warning, they are to be killed. Yin received (the Mandate) from Hsia, Chou received it from Yin. These are examples of 'receiving, without declining.' Even today they are well-known examples. What can be said of their 'receiving a gift'?"

Wan Chang said, "The Feudatories of the present time take from the common people as a highwayman takes from his victims. How can you explain that a gentleman might accept a gift from them, providing the elegances of ceremonial accompany the giving?"

Mencius replied, "Do you, Sir, think that, if today a True King arose, he would slay all of the Feudal Lords outright? Or would he instruct them first? And then if they did not mend their ways, put them to death? You call all who take what does not belong to them thieves, but really the Feudal Lords are merely overasserting their rights.[69] When Confucius held office in the State of Lu, some men there were engaged in the 'contest for game.'[70] Confucius took part in it. If *that* were quite proper, how much more proper was his receiving gifts from princes."

[68] *Documents*, p. 41.
[70] See Additional Notes.

[69] See Additional Notes.

Wan Chang said, "Does that not mean that, when Confucius was in office, he acted contrary to the Way?"

Mencius said, "No, he acted according to the Way."

Wan Chang said, "In that case, how could he have taken part in the 'contest for game'?"

Mencius replied, "Confucius first set right the sacrificial vessels according to the inventory, and not according to the amount of (sacrificial) food available."[71]

Wan Chang said, "But why did he not resign?"

Mencius said, "He took such things as an omen, an omen sufficient to suggest that his Way might ultimately prevail, but finding that this was not so, he did in the end resign. That is why he never completed a term of three years in any office. Confucius took office when there was a chance of his Way prevailing, when properly received, and when accepting support from the Duke.[72] Under Chi Huan-tzu he took office when there was a chance of his Way prevailing, under Duke Ling of Wei he took office, being properly received, and under Duke Hsiao of Wei because that Duke supported him."[73]

(5B.4)

3.20

Wan Chang said, "When Confucius was in Ch'en he said, 'Should we not go back? Come! Our followers in Lu are headstrong and careless. They want to take office and seize their chance. Let us not forget what beginners they are!'[74] Why would the thoughts of Confucius *at that moment* turn to his headstrong followers in Lu?"

Mencius said, "Confucius had been unable to secure men who steer a middle course, and so he taught such as they. He had to choose either the headstrong or the timid. The headstrong want to take office (prematurely) and seize their chance. The timid have other limitations.[75] It was certainly not that he would not have wished for men who steer a middle course, but he could not be sure of getting them, and so his thoughts turned to those who were, for him, 'a second choice.'"

---

[71] See Additional Notes.   [72] See Additional Notes.

[73] Chi Huan-tzu was a member of the Three Huan, the oligarchy that had seized power in Lu from its dukes. On this, cf. *Analects*, 18.4.

[74] A recognizable, but differently worded, version of this passage occurs in *Analects*, 5.21.

[75] See Additional Notes.

Wan Chang said, "Might I ask what sort of person he would have called 'headstrong'?"

Mencius said, "Men such as Ch'in Chang, Tseng Hsi, and Mu P'i[76]— these Confucius thought headstrong."

Wan Chang said, "Why did he think them headstrong?"

Mencius replied, "They were men with grandiose aims. The words 'the men of antiquity' were often on their lips, but their behaviour never matched up to them. Failing headstrong men, he chose men of fastidious purity and taught them. These were the timid ones and they were his third choice. Confucius said, 'They pass my gate, but do not enter my house, but I bear no resentment against them. They are the honest villagers. But they are the thieves of true virtue.' "[77]

Wan Chang said, "Why did he call them 'honest villagers'?"

Mencius replied, "Why were they so grand in manner? Their words belied their actions, and their actions belied their words. When the words 'the men of antiquity' were on their lips, why were their actions so singular, so cold? Because men born in an age reflect the age. Good, they might have been, but they were servile and sought the favour of the age with their unction. They were the 'honest villagers.' "

Wan Chang said, "If such men were acknowledged by the whole village to be honest men, and if they consistently maintained such a position, why should Confucius call them 'thieves of true virtue'?"

Mencius replied, "Contradict them, and they would make no reply. They ran with popular opinion—were at ease in a corrupt world. Live with them, and they would appear loyal and trustworthy. Travel with them, and they would seem disinterested and pure. They offended none and thought themselves right—yet, he could not speak to them of the Way of Yao and Shun, and so Confucius called them 'thieves of virtue.'

"Confucius said, 'I dislike those who seem but are not really so. I dislike the tare for fear that it will be taken for corn, and I dislike the specious for fear that they will be taken for the just. I dislike smart talk for fear that it will be taken as trustworthy. I dislike the airs of Ch'eng for fear that they will corrupt music itself. I dislike the violet hues for fear that they will be taken for true scarlet. I dislike the "honest

---

[76] For Ch'in Chang, see note 6 to Waley, *Analects*, 9.6. Tseng Hsi was the father of Tseng Tzu; see Introduction to 6.73. Mu P'i is not otherwise known.

[77] Cf. *Analects*, 17.13. From the occurrence of the sentence there, it is surprising to find it used in a context such as this.

villagers" for fear that they will be taken for the truly virtuous. The true gentleman seeks the main thread only. When the main thread is straight, then commoners are stirred. And when they are stirred, then perversity disappears.' "[78]

(7B.37)

KUNG-SUN CH'OU

Kung-sun Ch'ou has been introduced to the reader already in 1.25 and again in 2.1, 2.6, 2.9, and 2.17.

3.21

Kung-sun Ch'ou said, "Kao Tzu says[79] the song *Hsiao-p'an*[80] is a mean man's song."

Mencius asked, "Why does he say that?"

Kung-sun Ch'ou said, "Because of its hurt tone."

Mencius replied, "How dense Master Kao is in his understanding of the *Songs*. Suppose a man is threatened by a Yueh man[81] drawing his bow. He would appeal to him, but coaxingly and with a smile. Why? Because a Yueh man is a stranger to him. But suppose he is threatened by his older brother. He would appeal to him too, but with tears of entreaty in his eyes. Why? Because his older brother is of his own kin. The hurt tone of the *Hsiao-p'an* derives from the feeling we have for our kin. This feeling is Humanity. How dense Master Kao is in his understanding of the *Songs*."

Kung-sun Ch'ou said, "How then is it that the song *K'ai-feng*[82] has no hurt tone?"

Mencius replied, "The fault of the parents in the *K'ai-feng* is but a minor one, but that in the *Hsiao-p'an* is a major one. To have shown no feeling of being hurt when the fault was so grave would only be to increase the estrangement.[83] But for a minor fault, to feel hurt is to put an obstacle in the way.[84] To increase the estrangement is an un-filial act. To place obstacles in the way is, too, an unfilial act. Confucius

---

[78] Cf. *Analects*, 15.10.   [79] See Introduction to 3.34.   [80] *Songs* (cf. Karlgren, *Odes*, 197).
[81] Men of Yueh in the Yang-tse basin were thought particularly savage by northerners.
[82] *Songs*, 78.   [83] It would have suggested a callous disregard for the parents.
[84] To reconciliation. *Chi*, "a stone obstructing a stream," is used verbally and metaphorically here.

said, 'In Shun filial piety reached perfection. At fifty he still felt for his parents.' "[85]

(6B.3)

3.22

It was proposed in the State of Lu to put Yo-cheng Tzu[86] in charge of its government. Mencius said, "When I heard about the proposal, I was so delighted I could not sleep." Kung-sun Ch'ou said, "But is he forceful enough?" Mencius replied, "No." "But is he thoughtful enough?" Mencius replied, "No." "Then is he experienced enough?" Mencius replied, "No." "Then," said Kung-sun Ch'ou, "why were you so delighted that you could not sleep?" Mencius replied, "As a man he inclines towards the good." Kung-sun Ch'ou asked, "But is that enough?" Mencius replied, "In inclining towards the good, he would be adequate to govern the whole world, much less the State of Lu! For if he really inclines towards the good, all within the four seas will report to him, regarding a journey of one thousand miles as a light matter. But if it transpires that he does not incline towards the good, then men will say 'an upstart!' 'He thinks he knows everything.' The sight and sound of an upstart will drive men a thousand miles away. When True Gentlemen stay a thousand miles away, gossip-mongers and toadies gather. Can those who associate with gossip-mongers and toadies help to govern the state?"

(6B.13)

3.23

Kung-sun Ch'ou asked, "May I ask what principle of Justice is involved in your not seeking audience with a prince?"

Mencius replied, "In antiquity it was never done unless one was in the prince's service. Tuan Kan-mu[87] jumped over a wall to avoid meeting his prince. Hsieh Liu[88] barred his door rather than admit his Prince. These two were perhaps over-scrupulous. If pressed to do so, one might call upon a prince.

"Yang Huo[89] wanted to see Confucius but feared to offend against

[85] For this, see 3.12.
[86] See introduction to 3.31.
[87] See Additional Notes.
[88] See 2.15.
[89] See Additional Notes, 1.32, note 119.

the rules of courtesy. (He knew that) 'A noble might give a gift to a gentleman but the gentleman should not receive it in his own house,' and so he went and did obeisance before Confucius' gate. He watched for a time when Confucius was not at home and sent into the house a gift of roast pig. Confucius too watched for a time when Yang Huo was out and went and did obeisance before his gate.[90] On that occasion Yang Huo made the first move and surely Confucius could have seen him (if he had not had good reason not to do so).

"Tseng Tzu said, 'Sycophants work harder than peasants in the fields in summer.'

"Tzu-liu[91] said, 'When I see the flush on the faces of those who pretend to agree when really they do not, I do not want to know them.' From such remarks we understand what it is that the true gentleman wishes to cultivate."

(3B.7)

3.24

Kung-sun Ch'ou said, "Yi Yin[92] once said, 'I cannot associate with the disobedient,' and so he banished T'ai Chia[93] to T'ung.

"The common people were delighted. T'ai Chia proved to be a worthy man and so he was freed from banishment. The common people were delighted at this, too. May I ask: Can worthy men, when they are subjects, in fact banish princes whom they think unworthy?"

Mencius replied, "With the purpose that Yi Yin had in mind they may, but to do so otherwise would be simply usurpation."[94]

(7A.31)

3.25

Kung-sun Ch'ou said, "It says in the *Book of Songs*,[95] 'He does not eat the bread of idleness,' yet gentlemen do not plough and reap but they eat all the same. How is this?"

Mencius replied, "When a gentleman takes up residence in a state, supposing that his prince employs him, he enjoys peace, wealth, honours, and rewards. If his children follow in his footsteps then filial piety,

[90] This story is given in another version in *Analects*, 17.1.
[91] A disciple of Confucius. [92] See 3.7. [93] An early king of Shang; cf. 3.8.
[94] Cf. 1.1. [95] *Songs*, 259.

brotherly duty, loyalty, and good faith are the result. What better example could one find of not eating the bread of idleness?"

(7A.32)

3.26

Kung-sun Ch'ou said, "As far as your teaching is concerned, it is lofty and admirable; indeed, it is like an ascent to Heaven—something one cannot quite attain to. Why not make it a little more attainable by daily unremitting effort?"

Mencius replied, "The Master Craftsman does not accommodate the inept workman by tampering with the measuring line. Yi the Archer[96] did not accommodate an inept pupil by changing the target or the rules. The true gentleman leads. He does not turn aside. He leaps forward as it were, placing himself squarely in the centre of the Way. Those who can, follow him."

(7A.41)

3.27

Because his father, Tseng Hsi,[97] was so fond of the northern date, his son, Tseng Tzu, could not bring himself to eat them. Kung-sun Ch'ou asked, "Which is the better eating, cooked meat or dates?"

Mencius replied, "Cooked meat, of course!"

Kung-sun Ch'ou asked, "In that case why would Tseng Tzu eat cooked meat, yet not eat dates?"

Mencius replied, "Everyone eats cooked meat, but dates are a personal taste.[98] It is the personal name we refrain from using after a man is dead, not his family name. The family name we all have in common but the personal name belongs peculiarly to the individual."

(7B.36)

3.28

Kung-sun Ch'ou asked, "If you, Master, obtained preferment in the

---

[96] See Introduction to 6.78. [97] See 3.20, note 76.

[98] A fondness for these dates was a peculiarity of his father, and so Tseng Tzu, who is esteemed in Confucianism as the exemplar of filial piety, refrained in deference to his father's memory from eating them.

State of Ch'i could we expect, once again, results such as those once obtained by Kuan Chung and Yen Tzu?"[99]

Mencius replied, "You really are a man of Ch'i. You know of none but Kuan Chung and Yen Tzu. Tseng Hsi,[100] the grandson of Confucius, was once asked who was the better man, he himself, or Tzu-lu.[101] Much embarrassed he replied, 'My grandfather had the greatest respect for Tzu-lu.' He was then asked who was the better man, he himself, or Kuan Chung. Angry and displeased he replied, 'How dare you compare me with Kuan Chung? He held his prince in his hand—such was the authority he exercised. In policy matters his way was unopposed—such was the security he enjoyed. Yet, when it came to his "glorious accomplishments," of what a mean order they were! 'How dare you compare me with such a man?' Tseng Hsi had no wish to become a Kuan Chung; would you wish that I should?" Kung-sun Ch'ou said, "Kuan Chung did, after all, make his ruler Paramount Prince and Yen Tzu brought great distinction to his prince. Do you really think they are not worth emulating?"

Mencius replied, "If it comes to that, one could make Ch'i an Ideal Kingdom as easily as turning the hand."

Kung-sun Ch'ou said, "If that is so then we, your followers, are even more perplexed. Even with such virtue as King Wen possessed, his writ had still not spread throughout the world though he lived to be a hundred. It was only after King Wu and his Premier, the Duke of Chou, had succeeded him that the writ of Chou became universally effective. You speak of an Ideal Kingdom as though it were a simple matter. Can it be that King Wen is an inadequate example to follow?"

Mencius replied, "On the contrary, his example could not be bettered. The world of his time had rendered allegiance to the Yin (Shang) Dynasty for a very long time. From T'ang the Successful through to King Wu-ting, some six to seven Worthy Kings had reigned, and, having served Yin so long, the change was not easy. King Wu-ting of the Shang kings,[102] for example, had the allegiance of rulers everywhere and possessed the whole world as though he held it in his hand. King Chou's reign was not far removed in time from that of Wu-ting. The ancient families and old customs, the prevailing influences and

---

[99] See Introduction to 6.70.

[100] Not ot be confused with the Tseng Hsi of 3.20, 3.27, and 6.13, the father of Tseng Tzu. The *Hsi* is spelled differently.

[101] A disciple of Confucius.   [102] See Introduction to 6.52.

excellences in administration still survived, and, too, King Chou had such worthy men as the Lord of Wei and his son, the Princes Pi Kan and the Lord of Chi, and Chiao Chi to assist him.[103] It was for this reason that so long a period elapsed before he lost his kingdom. Prior to this he had undisputed possession of every foot of territory and the undisputed allegiance of every single subject. King Wen (on the other hand) had but a fief of a hundred miles square—such were his difficulties. There is a popular saying in Ch'i, 'Better seize a good chance, however wise one may be; better take advantage of the weather, however well equipped the farm is.' For King Wen, things were difficult. Today in Ch'i they are easy. In the heyday of the Hsia, Yin, and Chou Dynasties, the territory never exceeded a thousand miles. Today, Ch'i alone has as much territory as they had. From one border of Ch'i to the other, the barking of dogs and crowing of cocks is heard in unbroken succession.[104] Today Ch'i alone has as many people as the ancients had. Without enlarging its territory or increasing its population, provided that Ch'i put into effect a policy based on Humanity and practised true Kingship, it would be irresistible. Furthermore there has been no time in the whole of history like the present when the world has gone so long without a True King. The people have never suffered under such tyrannical government as obtains today, yet the starving might easily be fed and the thirsty given drink.

"Confucius said, 'Virtue travels faster than the edicts carried by the royal couriers.' Today, if a large state were to put into effect government based on Humanity, the rejoicing of the people would be that of a man saved from the gallows. If only princes employed one-half the good men that the ancients employed, the achievements would be double those of the ancients. It is only at the present time that this would be true."

(2A.1)

3.29

Kung-sun Ch'ou asked Mencius, "Suppose, Sir, that you were appointed Chief Minister of Ch'i, and suppose, too, that your teachings were put into practice, would you still remain unmoved,[105] even if this resulted in the King of Ch'i becoming no less than a Paramount Prince or even a True King?"

---

[103] See Additional Notes.   [104] This phrase is proverbial.   [105] See Additional Notes.

Mencius replied, "I would still remain unmoved. I attained that stage at the age of forty."[106]

Kung-sun Ch'ou said, "In that case, you, Sir, excel Meng P'en[107] by a wide margin."

Mencius said, "It is not a difficult state to attain. Indeed, Kao Tzu[108] attained it before I did."

Kung-sun Ch'ou said, "Is there a teaching on the subject of 'remaining unmoved'?"

Mencius replied, "Yes, there is. It was exemplified by Pei-kung Yu when he was training himself in 'fearlessness.' He neither shuddered nor blinked. He trained his mind to think of a beating in public as no different from a hair plucked from his head. What he would not condone in a roughly dressed serving-man, he would not condone in a major Feudal Lord. He thought as little of stabbing a powerful prince as of stabbing a serving-man. He would not pay reverence to a Feudal Lord. An insult addressed to him he returned in kind. It was exemplified by Meng Shih-she when he was training himself in 'fearlessness.' He said, 'I look upon victory and defeat indifferently, for to take the measure of the enemy carefully before sounding the advance, to occupy one's mind upon winning before engaging him, is the way to engender fear for one's opponents. I cannot after all ensure that I will win, but I can ensure that I have no fear.' Tseng Tzu was not unlike Meng Shih she; Tzu-hsia was not unlike Pei-kung Yu. Which of the two had the superior 'fearlessness' I do not know, but Meng Shih-she had the main essential.[109] In his day, Tseng Tzu asked Tzu-hsiang,[110] 'Are you an addict of "fearlessness"? I once heard the Master [Confucius] speak of the "greater fearlessness." He said, 'If on self-examination I find that I am not correct, I would tremble before a roughly dressed serving-man, but if on self-examination I find that I am correct, I would advance boldly upon thousands and ten thousands of men.'[111] Meng Shih-she took care of his physical vigour[112] and is not really to be compared with Tseng Tzu, who took care of the main essential."

Kung-sun Ch'ou said, "Might I then ask about your remaining unmoved, and Kao Tzu remaining unmoved?"

Mencius replied, "Kao Tzu said, 'Do not seek in the mind for that

---

[106] Confucius makes a not dissimilar claim; see *Analects*, 2.4.
[107] A knight of fashion.   [108] See 4.6.   [109] See Additional Notes.
[110] Disciple of Tseng Tzu.   [111] Cf. *Analects*, 8.7.   [112] See Additional Notes.

which cannot be put into words. Do not seek in the physical realm, for that which is not in the mind.' His latter phrase I concede but not the former. For the will gives orders to the physical vigour, and the physical vigour is that which imbues our physical frame. The will is in charge, physical vigour its subordinate. For this reason I say, 'He who has a firm grip on his will should do no harm to his physical vigour.' "

Kung-sun Ch'ou said, "You have already said, 'The will is in charge, the physical vigour is its subordinate' but, too, you say, 'He who has a firm grip on his will should do no harm to his physical vigour.' "

Mencius replied, "When the will is given primacy it sets the physical vigour in motion, but when the physical vigour is given primacy it sets the will in motion. A stumble, a lurch forward, these are the acts of the physical self which react upon the mind."[113]

Kung-sun Ch'ou said, "Might I then ask in what respect you are superior to Kao Tzu?"

Mencius replied, "I understand 'what can be put into words.'[114] I am adept in the cultivation of the 'greater physical vigour.' "

Kung-sun Ch'ou said, "Might I ask what you mean by the 'greater physical vigour?' "

Mencius said, "It is difficult to express in words. The physical vigour in this sense is the greatest, the most durable. If it is nurtured by rectitude it remains unharmed and permeates the entire universe. The physical vigour in this sense is the fit recipient for Justice and the Way. Without it, man is ill-nourished. It is begotten of the sum total of just deeds. It is not to be seized and held by incidental just deeds. If an act of ours does not meet with approval in the heart, then (the life-force) is ill-nourished. That is why I say Kao Tzu has never understood Justice. He thinks it is external to man.[115] One must render service to it; one must not regard it as an objective criterion. The mind must never let it out of its sight, but we must not try to make it grow. Let us not be like the man of Sung who, worried that his young plants were not growing, tugged at them (to help them grow). He returned home, full of fuss, saying, 'What a busy day! I have been helping my plants to grow.' His son hurried out to the fields to look, but the young plants had withered already. There are few men in the world today who are not

---

[113] That is to say, they are involuntary intuitive acts. Mencius supposes that Kao Tzu believes that the mind should follow the dictates of physical desire.

[114] A reference back to Kao Tzu's "Do not seek in the mind for that which cannot be put into words." Kao Tzu would mean such metaphysical entities as "Justice."   [115] See 4.9.

'helping the plants grow.' Some neglect their plants, thinking it useless to weed them. Some help their plants by giving them a tug. But this is not merely useless; it is actually harmful."

Kung-sun Ch'ou said, "What do you mean by 'I understand what can be put into words'?"

Mencius replied, "I understand what hides the other half of a half-truth. I understand the pitfalls that lie beneath extravagant statements. I understand where the path has been left, in depraved statements. I understand the emptiness that lies behind evasive statements. Engendered in the mind, they cause harm to government. When they result in governmental action they cause harm to public affairs. If a Sage were to rise again he would agree with all that I have said."[116]

Kung-sun Ch'ou said, "Confucius' disciples Tsai Wo and Tzu-kung were adept at exposition. Jan Niu, Min Tzu, and Yen Yuan were adept with words but known too for the virtue of their actions.[117] Confucius himself combined all their best qualities, but he did say, 'As far as putting things well into words is concerned, I am not very able.' Then, Master (with the claims you make), have you already become a Sage?"[118]

Mencius replied, "Oh! what sort of talk is this! Once Tzu-kung asked Confucius, 'Master you are a Sage, are you not?' Confucius replied, 'As far as being a Sage is concerned, that I cannot be, but I do study without becoming bored, and I teach without becoming tired.'[119] Tzu-kung said, 'To study thus is true wisdom, to teach thus is Humanity. With true wisdom and Humanity, you surely are a Sage already.' Even Confucius himself would lay no claim to being a Sage, so what sort of talk is this (of my being a Sage)?"

Kung-sun Ch'ou said, "With all respect, I once heard it said that Confucius' disciples Tzu-hsi, Tzu-yü, and Tzu-chang had 'one limb of the Sage,'[120] Jan Niu, Min Tzu, and Yen Yuan had 'all the limbs of the Sage' though in lesser proportions.[121] In what class would you place yourself?"

[116] Mencius makes a similar claim in 3.3.

[117] This occurs in *Analects*, 11,2a, in a slightly different form. Tsai Wo is the Tsai Yü, Jan Niu the Jan Keng, Min Tzu the Min Tzu-ch'ien, and Yen Yuan the Yen Hui of Waley's translation.

[118] See Additional Notes.   [119] Cf. *Analects*, 7.33.

[120] That is, they shared certain of his characteristics. The three disciples of Confucius mentioned here occur again in a derogatory story in 4.14.

[121] Neither this passage, nor the passages which follow citing Confucius and his disciples, occur in the present *Analects*. The Yu Jo mentioned here is the Master Yu of *Analects*, 1.

Mencius replied, "Let us leave this question aside for the moment."

Kung-sun Ch'ou said, "Well then what sort of men were Po Yi and Yi Yin?"

Mencius replied, "They were men who pursued different paths. Po Yi[122] was the sort of man who would neither serve a prince of whom he did not approve, nor direct a people of whom he did not approve. He took office in times of good government and resigned in times of bad. Yi Yin was the sort of man who said, 'Why should I not serve a prince of whom I do not approve, or direct a people of whom I do not approve?' He would take office in times of good government and bad. Confucius was the sort of man who felt that he might take office when it was proper to do so, refrain when it was proper to do so, complete the term of office, or cut it short, when it was proper to do so. These three were all Sages of the past. I have never been able to tread the path they trod. But if I had my wish, it would be to have studied under Confucius."

Kung-sun Ch'ou said, "Are Po Yi and Yi Yin men of a class with Confucius?"

Mencius replied, "Oh no! There has never been another Confucius since man first appeared on earth."

Kung-sun Ch'ou said, "Quite so, but they had things in common with him surely?"

Mencius replied, "Yes they had; either one of them might, being given sovereignty over a hundred square miles of territory, have all the Feudal Lords attending at their court, and thus have obtained sovereignty over the whole world, but not one of them would have sought that sovereignty by the commission of a single unjust deed, or by the slaying of a single innocent man. In this respect they had things in common with Confucius."

Kung-sun Ch'ou said, "Then might I ask in what respect they differed from him?"

Mencius replied, "Confucius' disciples Tsai Wo, Tzu-kung, and Yu-jo had each wisdom enough to recognize a Sage. But they would not have thought it seemly, to name in so many words one whom they loved so much.[123] Tsai Wo said, 'As I see it our Master is far more

---

[122] Po Yi who fled from the tyrant Chou but returned to serve King Wen (6.69) forms with Yi Yin (see 3.7) and Liu-hsia Hui (see 6.64) a trinity of model ministers (see 4.18, 6.64).

[123] That is, they recognized that Confucius was a Sage, but it would, says Mencius, have been maladroit to say so in so many words.

worthy than Yao or Shun.' Tzu-kung said, 'See him perform his rites and you will know the sort of government to expect from him; listen to the sort of music he enjoys, and you will know the sort of "virtue" he will exert. And a hundred generations hence, a hundred kings further on, no one will gainsay it. There has never been another like our Master since man first appeared on the earth.' Yu-jo said, 'It is not only among the people that this is so. The Ch'i-lin among beasts, the Phoenix among birds, Mount T'ai among mounds and hummocks, the Lakes and Rivers among runnels after rain are things of a class [i.e., they are peerless]. The Sage among the people is of the same class [i.e., peerless]. Sages stand out in their class, rise above its level, but from the first appearance of man upon the earth there has been no Sage who has stood out, or risen above them, in such rich measure as Confucius.' "

(2A.2)

3.30

Kung-sun Ch'ou said, "A gentleman does not teach his own son; why is this?"

Mencius replied, "The circumstances are such that it would never do. He who teaches must do so with proper detachment and if that does not work he may then show anger. But if a father shows anger he causes pain to his son. My teacher taught me with proper detachment from which he never departed. But for a father to be detached is painful both to father and son. When father and son cause pain to each other, the result is deplorable. In antiquity, fathers taught other men's sons. Between a father and his son there should be no stern admonitions to excel. If there are, they become remote from each other and remoteness is a bad augury. Indeed, it is the worst."[124]

(4A.19)

YO-CHENG TZU

We have already met Yo-cheng Tzu in the employ of the Prince of Lu inter-ceding on Mencius' behalf. When it was proposed in Lu to offer Yo-cheng Tzu this post, Mencius was "so delighted that he could not sleep." Among

---

[124] See Additional Notes.

Mencius' pupils, he is the only recorded success. Mencius thought at one time that Yo-cheng Tzu "inclined towards the good," but Yo-cheng Tzu seems to have fallen short of expectation, as the following two stories tell. When asked his opinion of Yo-cheng Tzu Mencius gives him a rather low grade.

3.31

Huo-sheng Pu-hai asked, "What sort of a man is Yo-cheng Tzu?"

Mencius replied, "He is good and reliable."

Huo-sheng said, "What do you mean 'good' and 'reliable'?"

Mencius replied, "By 'good,' I mean 'that which we properly may wish for'; by 'reliable' I mean 'having it within himself.'[125] When goodness and reliability are fully realized in a man, I call him 'excellent'; when so realized as to dazzle the beholder, I call him 'a great man'; but when realized in such measure as to change the life of the beholder, I call him 'a Sage.' One with the attributes of a Sage, but who is unknowable, I call 'a god.' Yo-cheng Tzu I place among the 'good and reliable' but below the next four ['excellent,' 'great,' 'sage' and 'divine']."

(7B.25)

3.32

Yo-cheng Tzu at the instigation of Tzu-ao[126] came to Ch'i. He presented himself before Mencius. Mencius said, "So, Sir, you have come to see me after all!"

Yo-cheng Tzu said, "Master, why do you speak like this?"

Mencius said, "How many days have you been here?"

Yo-cheng Tzu replied, "I came a few days back."

Mencius replied, "It is precisely because you came 'a few days back' that I speak in this way, and very properly so, do you not think?"

Yo-cheng Tzu said, "But I have not yet made any arrangements for my accommodation!"

Mencius replied, "Have you been taught that you must make arrangements for your accommodation before presenting your respects to your seniors?"

Yo-cheng Tzu said, "I am guilty of an offence."[127]

(4A.24)

[125] Being substantially what he says he is and doing what he says he will do.
[126] See 2.7.   [127] A way of saying "I am sorry."

3.33

Mencius said to Yo-cheng Tzu, "Your coming here at the instigation of Tzu-ao was purely for the purpose of filling your stomach. I would never have thought that you, Sir, having learned the Way of the ancients, would have been governed by such considerations."

(4A.25)

KAO TZU

Kao Tzu, of whom two stories are told here, does not seem to have been the most apt of pupils. He should not be confused with the Kao Tzu of 3.29 and 4.6 (their names are spelled differently) or the Kao Tzu of 3.21, a namesake, but quite a different person. Kao Tzu has been introduced to the reader already in 2.16.

3.34

Kao Tzu said, "The music of Yü the Great[128] was better than that of King Wen."

Mencius replied, "Why do you say that?"

Kao Tzu said, "Because the bell-thong knob is nearly worn through."

Mencius said, "Is that sufficient proof? Is it the fine fettle of a pair of horses that makes the ruts in the road to the city gate?"

(7B.22)

3.35

Mencius said to Kao Tzu, "There are footpaths in the hills, which, if they are suddenly put to heavy use, become roads, but which soon after such use become overgrown with grass again. Your mind, Sir, is overgrown with grass!"

(7B.21)

CH'EN TZU (CH'EN CHIN)

Ch'en Chin was with Mencius towards the close of Mencius' tenure of office in Ch'i, as we have seen from 2.10, 2.12, and 2.13. In the following, we see

[128] See Introduction to 6.43 and to 6.52.

that Ch'en Tzu is still perplexed at the idea of "a gentleman refusing office."

3.36

Ch'en Tzu said, "Under what circumstances did the True Gentleman in antiquity engage in the public service?"

Mencius replied, "Three stipulations governed his accepting office, and three his handing in his resignation.

"First. If he were received with the utmost respect, with all the requirements of protocol fully met, and if he were assured that the prince would do as he said he should, then he would accept office. But if on taking office, though there were no remission of politeness or respect, he found that the prince did not do what he said he should then he resigned.

"Second. Though he were given no assurance that the prince would do as he said he should, providing that he were received with the utmost respect, with all the requirements of protocol fully met, he would still accept office. But if on taking office there were a remission of politeness or respect, then he resigned.

"Finally, if he had had nothing to eat for days, so famished that he had not strength to leave his house, and his prince, hearing of these straits, say 'He is one of our great men, and although I cannot aspire to his principles, or follow out his instruction, it would be a disgrace upon the state if such a man were to starve. I must relieve his necessities'—under those circumstances a True Gentleman might accept office but only one sufficient to relieve his necessities."[129]

(6B.14)

WU-LU TZU

Wu-lu Tzu is the eager disciple and would-be pundit of 2.11.

3.37

A man of Jen asked Wu-lu which of the two, eating itself, or the rules we obey when eating, was the more important. He answered, "The

---

[129] Such office, for example, as that of a night watchman or a gatekeeper; see Additional Notes, 3.17, note 57.

rules we obey when eating." The man asked, "Which of the two, sex itself, or the rules which govern the enjoyment of sex, is the more important?" He answered again, "The rules which govern its enjoyment." The man continued, "Would you still insist on this, if I could only save my life by eating in disregard of the rules, but would die by insisting on them? Would you insist on the rule that a man must go personally to receive his bride if, being unable to do so, he could not then get married?" To this Wu-lu could not give an answer.

On the next day he went to Tsou and reported this to Mencius. Mencius said, "What is so difficult about answering a question like that? If you only read the measure at the top, a piece of wood an inch long can be made to appear higher than a ridge pole. Gold is heavier than feathers, as the saying is, but that is not to say that the gold for a tiny clasp would weigh more than a cart-load of feathers. If your questioner wants to deduce from the cases he adduces that eating and sex are *always* more important than the rules we obey in enjoying them, then why does he stop there? Why not go and ask him, 'If you could get food to eat only by twisting your older brother's arm and forcibly taking it from him, would you do so? Or if you could only get a bride by climbing the wall of the house next door and abducting your neighbour's virgin daughter, would you do so?' "[130]

(6B.1)

Of the rest, Ch'en Tai, P'eng Keng, T'ao Ying, and Meng of Hsien-ch'iu are known to tradition as "disciples,"[131] but nothing more is known of them, while men like Pei-kung Yi, Pai Kuei, and Kou Chien of Sung are either fellow philosophers, or statesmen who appear in the Works merely as interlocutors.

3.38

Ch'en Tai said, "Properly speaking, is it not petty to refrain from seeking audience with the princes? Suppose by doing so, you were to discover a great prince—he might become the Ideal King. Or, a lesser figure, he might become Paramount Prince? After all does it not say in the *Manuals*,[132] 'By bending one foot, you might make ten feet straight'? Surely this is a possibility."

---

[130] These, we must suppose, were unthinkable courses of action in Mencius' day.
[131] As also is Ch'ung Yü, see 2.8 and 2.14.   [132] See 1.28, Additional Notes, note 109.

H

Mencius replied, "In earlier times Duke Ching of Ch'i[133] was hunting. He summoned his huntsman by signalling to him with a plumed
flag. The huntsman would not come. The Duke was about to kill him.
But, 'the knight of stout heart ever remembers that he may end up in
the gutters; the brave knight never forgets that he may lose his own
head.' What lesson did Confucius wish to draw from this? It is this:
'do not respond to a summons improperly given.' If now, I call upon
the princes without the appropriate summons, what would be said of
me? As to your quoting, 'by bending one foot you might make ten
feet straight,' the context refers to attaining benefits. If that were my
object then I would bend ten feet to make one foot straight. In days
gone by, Chao Chien Tzu forced Wang Liang to drive his courtesan,
Hsi, at the hunt. They did not take a single bird the whole day. The
courtesan reported to her master that Wang Liang was the poorest
chariot driver in the world. Someone conveyed this to Wang Liang.
Wang Liang asked if he might try again. After much urging he was
permitted to do so. Ten birds were taken in a single morning. In reporting to her master, the courtesan described Wang Liang as 'the finest
chariot driver in the world.' Chao Chien Tzu promised her that Wang
Liang would always drive for her. On being told of this, Wang Liang
said he could not do so. He said, 'For her sake I confined myself strictly
to the rules of the chase; and she failed to take a single bird all day.
For her sake I cheated and she took ten birds in a morning. The *Book
of Songs* says[134]

> Without a fault in horsemanship
> The arrows are fired—they find their mark.

I am not used to driving for petty people.[135] I beg leave to tender my
resignation.' As a driver he scorned to be classed with such huntsmen.
For he would not be classed with such, though game were taken mountains high. If now I were to pervert my principles and go running after
them [the princes], what would be said of me? And, Sir, you are in
further error. He who 'bends' himself will never be able to straighten
out others."

(3B.1)

---

[133] Cf. 3.18.   [134] *Songs*, 261.

[135] *Hsiao-jen*, "petty people," i.e., people who are non-U. In his opening question Ch'en Tai
suggests that Mencius is *hsiao*, "petty minded," i.e., not quite behaving like a gentleman.

3.39. P'ENG KENG

P'eng Keng asked, "To be followed by a baggage-train of dozens of carriages, to have hundreds of men in attendance, and so circulate among the princes, feeding at their expense, is this not gross?"

Mencius replied, "We may not receive a single bowl of rice from another, if to do so were to contravene our principles. But if it were consonant with our principles, then we might accept an empire, just as Shun accepted the Empire from Yao. I do not think that Shun was gross, do you?"

P'eng Keng said, "No, but for a knight to accept his food from a prince when rendering him no service, this I think improper."

Mencius replied, "If, Sir, the products of labour are not put into circulation and the interchange of services ensured, so that, by the surplus of one, the needs of the other may be supplied, then the farmer will have a grain surplus and the women a surplus of cloth. But if, Sir, you put these things into circulation, then carpenters and carriage-wrights will gain their means of subsistence from you. Suppose we have one who is filial at home and pays his duty to his elders abroad. He upholds the Way of the Former Kings, awaiting a pupil to whom he can confide that Way. Yet he does not obtain a means of livelihood from you. What can be said, then, of the respect you feel for carpenters and carriage-wrights and your lack of respect for Humanity and Justice?"

P'eng Keng said, "The carpenter and carriage-wright carry on their crafts in order to make a living. Does the True Gentleman advocate the Way in order to make a living?"

Mencius replied, "How could such be his motive? But he does render a service to you and is deserving of payment and should be paid. Do you pay a man because he wishes to be paid, or do you pay for the work he does?"

P'eng Keng replied, "I pay him because he wishes to be paid."

Mencius said, "Suppose a man is repairing your house. He smashes your tiles, and makes marks on the plaster. His wish in all this is to be paid. Do you pay such a man?"

P'eng Keng said, "No."

Mencius continued, "Then you do not pay because a man wishes to be paid; you pay him for the work he does."

(3B.4)

3.40. T'AO YING

T'ao Ying asked, "If, when Shun was the Son of Heaven, his father Ku-sou[136] had committed a murder, what would Kao Yao, the Minister of Justice, have done?"

Mencius replied, "He would have placed him under arrest."

Tao Ying continued "Quite so, but would not Shun have prevented him?"

Mencius replied, "How could Shun have prevented him? He knew from whence the law was received."

T'ao Ying asked, "What then would Shun have done?"

Mencius replied, "Shun looked upon abdicating the Empire as of no more consequence than discarding a worn-out shoe. He would have secretly carried off his father and fled, and making for the coast have dwelt there. He would have lived his life cheerfully, forgetting the Empire with delight."

(7A.35)

3.41. MENG OF HSIEN-CH'IU

Meng of Hsien-ch'iu asked Mencius if the following saying were an authentic utterance of Confucius. "The knight replete with virtue is a loyal subject however much his prince may fail him, and a loyal son no matter what the father does! When Shun stood with his face to the south[137] and Yao, at the head of the Feudatory faced north and paid him homage, Ku-sou too faced north and paid (his son) homage. When Shun saw this his discomposure showed on his face.[138] Confucius said, 'At that moment, the world was in grave peril, most grave.' Is this authentic?"[139]

Mencius said, "No, it is not. The True Gentleman would not say such a thing. This saying emanates from some village pedant of eastern Ch'i. (What really happened was this.) When Yao was aging, Shun shared the throne with him. And then, as the *Yao Tien*[140] says, 'In the twenty-eighth year Fang Hsun [i.e., Yao] died; the people mourned

---

[136] See Introduction to 6.43 and to 6.52.

[137] The stance of an Emperor. For Yao, Shun, and Ku-sou, see Introduction to 6.43 and 6.52.

[138] A ritual *faux pas;*[1] see Additional Notes, 1.4, note 26.

[139] See 3.3. This passage suggests that spurious, or at least contested, *Sayings of Confucius* were in circulation already at this time. See Introduction to 6.73.

[140] In the *Book of Documents*, cf. *Documents*, p. 5.

for him for three years as though mourning their own kith and kin. Everywhere the sound of music ceased.' Confucius said, 'There are neither two suns in the sky, nor two kings over the people.' Shun had already become Son of Heaven and had lead the Feudatory in mourning for three years. In the version you quote there would have been two Sons of Heaven!"

Meng of Hsien-ch'iu said, "I now understand, thanks to your instruction that Shun never treated Yao as a subject, but may I ask why Shun never treated Ku-sou as a subject? For it says in the *Book of Songs*[141]

> Under the wide Heavens,
> All land is the king's.
> Right up to the frontier
> All are his subjects.

If Shun was Son of Heaven already, might I ask why it was that Ku-sou was never treated as a subject?"

Mencius replied, "This song is not speaking of matters such as this. It refers to toiling in the king's business, yet having insufficient to support one's parents.[142] It is as though the poet were saying, 'Nothing I do but is for the king; am I the only good worker?' That is why I say that those who interpret the *Book of Songs* should not do violence to the poet's intention, by singling out one line. They should try to think through the poet's intention; in this way they will understand the poem. And similarly with a single line. Take the line, for example, in the song 'Milky Way':[143]

Of the black-haired people that remain in Chou, not one survived.

If we take this literally, there was no one left in Chou!

"(To return to your question.) Of all the attainments of a filial son, none surpasses that of bringing honour to his parents. And of all the honouring, none surpasses that of supporting them, by virtue of being ruler of the world. To be the father of the Son of Heaven is the supreme honour. To be supported by one's son, as Son of Heaven, is the acme of 'being supported as a parent.' The *Book of Songs*[144] says,

> Forever expressing filial thoughts
> His filial thoughts become exemplars.

---

[141] *Songs*, 285.   [142] I.e., the song is a protest, not a statement of monarchical principle.
[143] *Songs*, cf. Karlgren, *Odes*, 258.   [144] *Songs*, 248.

The *Book of Documents*[145] says,

> With reverence he received Ku-sou,
> With veneration and with awe.
> Ku-sou too complied in kind.

This was 'being a loyal son no matter what the father does.' "

(5A.4)

3.42

Pei-kung Yi asked Mencius about the ranks and emoluments of the House of Chou.[146]

Mencius replied, "We cannot now know the precise details, for the Feudatory, fearing the harm that might ensue, have done away with the records;[147] however, I know the system in broad outline:

"The principle title was that of Son of Heaven. The next was that of duke. The next was that of lord. The next that of earl. The next was *Tzu* and *Nan*, both equal in rank. Altogether there were five kinds of title. A ruler constituted one rank, a minister a second rank, a great officer a third rank, a knight of the first grade a fourth rank, a knight of the middle grade a fifth rank, and a knight of the lower grade a sixth rank. Six ranks in all. The Son of Heaven had, under his direct control, a thousand miles, Dukes and lords each one hundred miles, earls seventy miles, and *Tzu* and *Nan* each fifty miles. Four grades of feudal holding were recognized: Those whose personal holdings did not exceed fifty miles and had no access to the Son of Heaven, except through a Feudal Lord. They were known as "dependant holders." Those who were ministers to the Son of Heaven, who were given land equal to that of the holding of a Feudal Lord. Those who were Great Officers and were given land equal to that of an earl. Those who were knights of excellence and were given land equal to that of a *Tzu* or *Nan*.

"In a major state where the domain was a hundred miles square the ruler's increment was ten times that of his ministers; a minister's four times that of a Great Officer; a Great Officer's twice that of a knight of the first grade; a knight of the first grade's twice that of a knight of the middle grade; a knight of the middle grade's twice that of a knight of the lower grade; a knight of the lower grade and a commoner in official

[145] *Documents*, cf. Legge, II.ii.21.   [146] I.e., under the model kings, Wen and Wu.
[147] See Additional Notes.

service had equal emoluments. Emoluments, that is, sufficient for him to have a substitute to till his fields.

In a state of the next degree, where the domain was seventy miles square, the ruler's increments were ten times that of his ministers; the minister's three times that of a Great Officer and the Great Officer's twice that of a knight of the first grade; a knight of the first grade's twice that of a knight of the middle grade; a knight of the middle grade's twice that of a knight of the lower grade; a knight of the lower grade and a commoner in official service had equal emoluments, sufficient, that is, to have a substitute to till his fields.

"In a minor state, where the domain was fifty miles square, the ruler's increments were ten times that of his ministers. The minister's twice that of the Great Officer; the Great Officer's twice that of the knight of the first grade; the knight of the first grade's twice that of the knight of the middle grade; the knight of the middle grade's twice that of the knight of the lower grade; the knight of the lower grade and the commoner in official service had equal emoluments, sufficient, that is, to have a substitute to till his fields.

"The yield retained by a cultivator, who was given one hundred *mou* to cultivate and to fertilize was as follows: a top-grade farmer, grain for nine people; lower top, grain for eight people; middle-grade farmer, grain for seven people; lower middle-grade, grain for six people; lower-grade farmer, grain for five people. A commoner in official service had his emoluments computed in accordance with this scale."

(5B.2)

3.43

Pai Kuei said, "My water conservancy measures are superior to those of Yü."[148]

Mencius replied, "There, Sir, you are wrong. Yü's measures were consistent with the way of waters. He used the Four Seas for his drainage area. You, Sir, use the adjacent states as your drainage area. Waters running beyond their courses, we call 'uncontrolled waters.' Uncontrolled waters are floods. And floods, the Humane man detests. There, Sir, lies your error."

(6B.11)

[148] See Introduction to 6.43 and to 6.52.

3.44

Pai Kuei said, "I should like to see the taxes assessed at one-twentieth of the yield. What would you think of that?"

Mencius said, "What you propose is the system of the pastoral Mi peoples. Would you like to see a kingdom of some ten thousand households with only one potter?"

Pai answered, "No, there would not be enough pots to use."

Mencius replied, "The Mi peoples do not grow the five grains with the exception of millet. They have no fortified cities, no palaces and great houses, no temples with rites and sacrifices; they have none of the gifts and entertainments required by a Feudatory. They have no ordered administrative machinery, so that a twentieth suffices for their needs. How could we, in the central states, dispense with all social obligations and with our rulers? Even with a shortage of potters a state cannot sustain itself; how much less can it dispense with its princes. If you wish to make taxes lighter than the taxation of Yao and Shun, then we in the central states will become a series of lesser and greater Mi's, but if you wish to make them heavier, then we shall be governed by greater or lesser Chiehs."[149]

(6B.10)

3.45

Mi Chi said, "Gossip credits me with being utterly unreliable."

Mencius said, "You need not worry yourself about that. A true knight despises this constant gossiping. The *Book of Songs*[150] says,

> My sad heart aches
> I am disliked by all these petty people.

This might have been said of Confucius.

> And though he did not dispel their displeasure,
> he did not abase his good name.

This might have been said of King Wen."[151]

(7B.19)

---

[149] For Yao and Shun, see Introduction to 6.43 and to 6.52. For Chieh, see 6.69.
[150] *Songs*, 75.
[151] *Songs*, 240.

3.46. KOU CHIEN OF SUNG

Mencius said to Kou Chien of Sung, "You, Sir, like to travel from court to court. Let me tell you my views on this subject. If in doing so you gain recognition, then be content, but if you fail to gain recognition, then too be content."

Kou Chien said, "How can one always 'be content'?"

Mencius replied, "Honour virtue, delight in Justice; then you may be content. For a knight in financial straits does not lose sight of Justice, and in success he does not depart from the Way. In financial straits without losing sight of Justice—that is his satisfaction. In success and not departing from the Way—thus the people never lose their sense of expectation from him. In antiquity, when a man attained his goal, his beneficence flowed down to the common people; when he failed to attain it, he cultivated his person and so became famous in his generation. So that if you meet with financial straits, ensure that you are good yourself, and if you meet with success ensure that you do good to the whole world."

(7A.9)

3.47. CHIAO OF TSAO

Chiao of Tsao asked, "Is it true that any man might become a Yao or a Shun?"

Mencius replied, "Quite true." He continued, "I understand that King Wen was ten feet in height, T'ang the Successful was nine feet, while I myself am nine feet and four inches. This is merely a matter of what one eats.[152] Now what should I do to become like Yao or Shun?"

Mencius replied, "What has your height got to do with this? To become like Yao and Shun is simply a matter of doing so. Here is a man whose physique was so poor that he could not control a duck. He was a weakling. Now he says he can lift three hundred pounds. He has become a strong man.

"If he can lift the sort of weight that Wu Huo[153] lifted, then he becomes another Wu Huo. Men should surely not get so concerned about the things they are not master of when they simply fail to do them. A younger brother walks slowly and follows after his elders. If he

---

[152] We must, of course, understand that the ancient Chinese "foot" and "inch" were shorter than our own, but even so Chiao was evidently a very tall man.

[153] See Introduction to 6.78.

hurried and stepped in front of them we would say he was not a proper younger brother. It would not be a matter of his being incapable of walking slowly, but of his failing to do so. The Way of Yao and Shun is nothing less than the way of a filial son and a younger brother.[154] Do you, Sir, clothe yourself in the garments of Yao, repeat to yourself his sayings, walk as he walked, and you will become another Yao. But clothe yourself in the clothes of Chieh, repeat to yourself his sayings, walk as he walked, and you will be another Chieh."[155]

Chiao said, "I am being received in audience by the Lord of Tsou and shall ask him for lodging, for I wish to stay here, to study further with you."

Mencius replied, "The Way is like a great road; it is surely not difficult to understand. The sickness of men is that they do not seek it. If you, Sir, return to your home and seek for it, there will be teachers enough."

(6B.2)

3.48. CHOU HSIAO

Chou Hsiao asked Mencius, "Did the gentlemen of antiquity accept office?"

Mencius replied, "They did. The *Records* say, 'If Confucius were three months out of office, he was quite distracted. As he passed from one state to another, he invariably carried with him his gift of introduction.' Kung-ming Yi[156] said, 'Among the men of antiquity, to be out of office for three months was a matter for condolence.'"

Chou Hsiao said, "A matter for condolence! Is that not taking things too seriously?"

Mencius replied, "For a knight to lose his office is comparable to a prince losing his kingdom. The *Rituals* say, 'A prince ploughs in person with the assistance of the people, so as to provide the sacrificial millet. His consort tends the silkworms and unravels the cocoons, so as to provide sacrificial garments.' If the animals be not whole, and the millet not pure, or the garments unprepared, he would not dare to offer the sacrifices. And, too, a knight, lacking the fields,[157] similarly would not sacrifice. When the victim is slain, but the vessels and the garments are not prepared, he would not dare to offer it in sacrifice.

---

[154] I.e., a mode of behaviour of which every one is capable.
[155] See Introduction to 6.69.   [156] See 1.27.
[157] For the knight's fields, see 1.32.

Neither could he offer its meat in hospitality. Is not this a matter for condolence?"

Chou Hsiao said, " 'On passing from one state to another he invariably carried a gift of introduction': what does that mean?"

Mencius said, "A knight in office is like a farmer who ploughs. Would such a farmer, on departing from the state, leave his plough behind?"

Chou Hsiao said, "The State of Tsin, after all, has offices for gentlemen, but I have never heard that it was a matter for such concern. And if it is such a matter why are gentlemen so exacting in the matter of accepting office?"

Mencius replied, "When a man is born it is hoped that he might one day set up a household. When a daughter is born it is hoped that she might one day have a home to go to. All men have this feeling for parenthood. But if the children, without waiting for the orders of their parents and the agreement of the marriage brokers, bore holes through the wall to catch a glimpse of each other, or even climb over the wall to be with each other, their parents and all good citizens will regard them with contempt. In antiquity men always desired to be in office, but loathed to do so by improper means. To take office by improper means is of the same order as 'boring holes through walls.' "

(3B.3)

Chapter Four

MENCIUS AND
HIS RIVALS

HEDONISTS AND UTILITARIANS

In its beginnings, Confucianism was a local, and unsuccessful, movement. It did not come into prominence until nearly two hundred years after the death of Mencius. In his own day Mencius complained that "the whole world has succumbed to the teaching of Yang Chu and Micius."[1] Underlying much of Mencius' teaching an awareness is betrayed of the teachings of these two powerful figures, though little occurs in the Works by way of direct reference to them.

Yang Chu's philosophy is known to us only through the cautionary references to it in the works of his rivals. The work sheltering under his name, The Garden of Pleasure,[2] is almost certainly a much later compilation. Yang Chu is represented in tradition as the advocate of unbridled Hedonism. He certainly represents that wing in the Chinese tradition which is concerned with self-awareness and self-cultivation, with the individual as opposed to society. His name is linked by Mencius with the slogan wei ngo, *"I act in my own interests." He is credited with saying that he would not pluck a hair from his body to save the world. Mencius nowhere identifies any of his antagonists specifically as a follower of Yang Chu. But the spirit of Hedonism is all-pervasive at the Courts and it may well be that, though inarticulate, the philosophy of Yang Chu in fact "flooded the world" at that time. As a philosophical principle Hedonism comes closest to direct expression in Mencius in the words of Kao Tzu. He argues that pleasure is the principle by which one determines that* jen *(Humanity) is "internal" and* yi *(Justice) "external."[3]*

---

[1] See 3.3. Possible dates for Yang Chu are c. 395-335 B.C. and for Micius c. 486-390 B.C. Micius, like Mencius and Confucius, is known to occidental readers by a latinized form of his name used by the early Jesuits. His Chinese name is Mo Ti or Mo Tzu ("Master Mo"), hence the terms Mohist, to describe his teaching, and Mohism of his teaching.

[2] See Additional Notes.   [3] See below, 4.6 ff.

The philosophy of Micius is as well documented as is that of Mencius himself. The present work, Mo Tzu,[4] however, presents a synoptic view of the developments of doctrine, from its early statements to its later developments. We are concerned with Mohism as it was known to Mencius. To Mencius, Mohism was above all the philosophy that opposed "universal love" to the Confucian "familial duty." The Mohists believed that "if all men were to love each other equally and without qualification," if they were to "love each other as they loved themselves," there would be a revolutionary basis in society for all of the political and economic solutions they proposed for the governing of the state. To the Confucians the state was essentially the projection of the family. The bonds of society were thus an extension of the grades of affection and duty that bound together the various degrees of kinship. To the Mohists this was stultifying. It perpetuated hereditary class distinctions and interests, which inhibited the rise of the egalitarian state, where the competent governed in the interests of the majority. Against the Confucian criterion of yi, "Justice," the Mohists opposed the criterion of li, "utility" or "profit." Where the Confucians asked if a thing were "right," the Mohists asked if it conduced to "the greatest benefit of the greatest number." The Mohists had no time for antiquity. The Confucians regarded antiquity as the ultimate authority. On the grounds of utility the Mohists condemned waste, and particularly the convention at the time for lavish and expensive burial rites. For Mencius, it was sufficient that such rites had the authority of antiquity.[5] Indeed the Rites comprised a code of conduct that the True Gentleman unswervingly observed. The Mohists were organized into fraternities and maintained a strict ascetic discipline within their bands. Their devotion in the defence of a prince whom they served became proverbial. They are credited with a number of inventions in military engineering.

Mencius thus, the proponent of a restoration to a former order of things, was opposed by two conflicting streams of thought—by the Mohists, who advocated innovation, a new basis for society, and a new ordering of society; and by the followers of Yang Chu, who, despairing of society, sought in the cultivation of individual integrity a solace from the banes of the society they knew. Neither Mohism nor Hedonism, for all their gains in the fourth century B.C., had a long lease of life. Other and more volatile forces were to arise before the problems of the state were to be settled. But once settled, it was the Confucians who, in the end, came into their own. In Mencius' day, however, they had made little headway.

[4] See Additional Notes.   [5] See 1.35 and 2.8.

4.1

Mencius said, "Yang Chu's teaching is summed up in the words, 'I act in my own interests.' Even if he could help the whole world by plucking a single hair from his body, he would refuse to do so. Micius' teaching is summed up on the words 'Love all equally.'[6] Even if he had to wear his body to the bone to help the world, he would have done so. Tzu-mo[7] takes up the middle position, and in doing so he is nearer the truth. But in taking up a middle position on principle without considering the special circumstances attendant in each case, he takes up a unique position.[8] What I dislike in these 'unique positions' is that they make a travesty of the Way. They make one point and overlook a hundred others."

(7A.26)

4.2

Mencius said, "Those who defect from the Mohists turn to Yang Chu. Those who defect from Yang Chu turn to us. When they do so, accept them without further ado. To try to argue with them is like recovering a stray pig and hobbling it after it is put back in its sty."

(7B.26)

4.3 MOHISTS

Yi Chih, a follower of Micius, sought to meet with Mencius through one of the disciples, Hsü Pi. Mencius said, "I really would like to see him, but I am still unwell. When my illness is better, I shall go and see him." Yi Chih accordingly did not come. On a later occasion he again sought a meeting with Mencius. Mencius said, "I can see him today. If we do not correct error the Way will remain obscure. I will put him right. I understand that Yi Chih is a Mohist. The Mohists advocate simple funerals.[9] Master Yi hopes to change the world thereby. He surely cannot believe that without a simple funeral the deceased is not honoured! For, if so, since he gave his own parents a lavish funeral he has dishonoured them!" Master Hsü told Yi Chih what Mencius

---

[6] See 6.15.   [7] See 2.15.   [8] See Additional Notes.
[9] Even in modern times the lavishness of burial rites has kept peasant families in crippling debt. See also 1.35 and 2.8.

had said. Yi Chih said, "The Confucians advocate the Way (of the ancients). In antiquity men ruled 'just as an infant is held in the arms.'[10] What does that phrase mean? To me, it means that one should love all regardless of class or rank. And that love should begin with love to our near kin." Hsü Pi reported this to Mencius. Mencius said, "Does Yi Chih really think that the feelings one has for the newly born child of a neighbour would be comparable to the love that one has for an older brother's son? What he should have deduced from the phrase that he cites is this. A baby crawling about, about to fall into a well, commits no crime.[11] Furthermore, when Heaven begets a life, it does so through a single root-stock, yet Yi Chih (supposes that life stems from) two root-stocks.[12] It may well be that in the remote past there was the custom of not burying one's own kin, but simply of casting them into a ditch, so that later, passing the ditch, upon seeing the foxes and wildcats gnawing at the bodies, and the flies and gnats biting at the flesh, sweat broke out upon the face, and the eyes were turned away. Sweat broke out indeed, not on account of what others might think but as a sign on the face of feelings felt deep in the heart. Probably they returned home, collected baskets and spades, and covered the bodies with earth. To cover them was assuredly the right thing to do. The filial son and the Humane man in covering the bodies of their deceased kinsfolk must surely be acting in accordance with the Way."[13]

Hsü Pi informed Yi Chih of what Mencius had said. Yi Chih after a moment's reflection said, "He has taught me something."

(3A.5)

4.4

While Mencius was at Shih Ch'iu in the State of Sung, he met Sung K'eng. Sung K'eng was about to leave for the State of Ch'u. Mencius said, "Where, Sir, are you going?" Sung K'eng replied, "I have heard that Ch'in and Ch'u are preparing for war. I am going to see the King of Ch'u to see if I can talk him into desisting. If he is not agreeable I shall go and see the King of Ch'in and see if I can talk him into desisting. Of the two I hope to succeed with at least one."

Mencius said, "Without going into detail, what in broad outline will your arguments be?"

[10] See Additional Notes.   [11] See Additional Notes.   [12] See Additional Notes.
[13] See Additional Notes.

Sung K'eng said, "I shall argue on the grounds of *li* (utility)."

Mencius said, "As far as your objective is concerned, it is great, but as for your arguments they will never do. If you persuade the kings of Ch'u and of Ch'in to disband the Three Armies in the pursuit of profit, the officers of the army, delighting to be disbanded, will set off in the pursuit of profit. Ministers will serve their princes for the love of profit. Thus prince and minister, father and son, brother and brother, discarding the principles of *jen* (Humanity) and *yi* (Justice), will conduct their intercourse from motives of profit. This has never happened without disaster to the state.[14] But if you persuade the kings of Ch'u and of Ch'in to disband the Three Armies from considerations of Humanity and Justice, the officers of the army, delighting to be disbanded, will look with favour upon Justice and Humanity. Ministers will serve their princes from motives of Justice and Humanity. Sons will serve their fathers from motives of Justice and Humanity; younger brothers will serve their older brothers from motives of Justice and Humanity. Thus, prince and minister, father and son, and brother and brother, having rejected the motive of profit, will conduct their relationships from considerations of Humanity and Justice. This only happens under an Ideal Prince. Why must you use that word 'profit'?"

(6B.4)

4.5

The Duke of Lu[15] was proposing to make Shen Tzu[16] general of the Lu armies. Mencius said, "Putting commoners into the field without training them first is to sacrifice them needlessly. In the days of Yao and Shun, one who needlessly sacrificed the people would never have been tolerated. Even if Lu, by so doing, in a single battle defeated Ch'i and so recovered Nan-yang it would never do." Shen Tzu was exceedingly angry and said, "I profoundly disagree with that." Mencius said, "Let me make myself clear. The domain appropriate to a Son of Heaven is a thousand miles square. With less, he would have insufficient to entertain the Feudatory. The domain appropriate to a Feudal Lord is a hundred miles square. With less he would have insufficient to fulfil the feudal obligations recorded in his Ancestral Shrine. When the Duke of

---

[14] In 1.21 Mencius makes a similar case against "utility" to the King of Liang. See also 6.54.
[15] Presumably Duke P'ing of Lu.
[16] See Additional Notes.

Chou was enfeoffed with the State of Lu, his domain was a hundred miles square. It is not true that a hundred miles was not enough so that he had to add to it. When the T'ai-kung was enfeoffed with the State of Ch'i his domain too was a hundred miles square. It is not true that a hundred miles was not enough so that he had to add to it. Yet the State of Lu today is five hundred miles square. Do you, Sir, imagine that if a True King were to arise, Lu would be increased in size or lessened? Even if to do so were merely a matter of taking land from here and adding it there, a Humane King would not do so. And how much less would he do so when it could only be done at the cost of men's lives? In serving his prince a True Gentleman obtains preferment by seeking to lead his prince, keeping his mind steadfastly upon Humanity."

(6B.8)

Kao Tzu and Human Nature

It was in his dispute with Kao Tzu that Mencius declared himself on the problem of the nature of man. We know little about Kao Tzu. Mencius said of him that he had attained that stage of cultivation called "remaining un-moved." Mencius said further that Kao Tzu had attained that stage before he, Mencius, had.[17] *From Kao Tzu's concern with the definition of terms, his distinction between the subjective and the objective, he seems, in intellectual temper, close to the Mohists; but in his preoccupation with man's nature and with distinguishing between those things that pertain to the self and those which are external, and with his denial of the principle of universal love, he is closer in spirit to the Hedonism of Yang Chu.*

Kao Tzu regarded man's nature as something with which he is endowed at birth, something neither good nor bad—a set of tastes and sensibilities, awarenesses capable of responding to inner and outer stimuli. The feelings proper to man, such as Humanity, he felt were the product of these senses. The duties proper to man, such as Justice, he felt were the product of external stimuli, to which the senses responded.

Mencius regarded man's nature as the endowment which differentiates him from the animals. It is inherently good. Humanity and Justice are its intrinsic qualities. Unimpeded man acts with Humanity and Justice. It is only under the pressure of external conditions that man acts evilly.

[17] See 3.29.

The problem of the nature of man was not raised by Confucius. Mencius' position was rejected by his successor in the Confucian trinity, Hsun Tzu. Hsun Tzu argued that man was born evil, but that with training and discipline he could become good. The Han Confucian, Wang Ch'ung, however, rejected both, opting for a position closer to Kao Tzu. He argued that man's nature was amoral, having a potential for both good and evil.

4.6

Kao Tzu said, "The nature of man is comparable to the nature of the wood of the willow tree. Such things as Justice and Humanity are comparable to cups and bowls carved in willow wood. To make man's nature Humane or Just is comparable to making cups and bowls from willow wood."

Mencius replied, "But when the wood is carved into a bowl, is its nature left unscarred? No! It becomes a bowl only at the price of suffering damage to its original nature. If that is so, then must a man suffer damage to his original nature in order to become Humane and Just? In such a view, to make men Humane and Just is to violate their nature. From what you say, one would be forced to such a conclusion."

(6A.1)

4.7

Kao Tzu said, "The nature of man is comparable to water trapped in a whirlpool. Open a channel for it on the east side and it will flow away to the east. Open a channel for it on the west side and it will flow away to the west. This is because man's nature is neither inherently good nor bad, just as it is not inherently in the nature of water to flow to the east or to the west."

Mencius replied, "It is assuredly not in the nature of water to flow to the east or to the west, but can one say that it is not in the nature of water to flow upwards or downwards? Man's nature is inherently good, just as it is the nature of water to flow downwards. As there is no water that flows upwards, so there are no men whose natures inherently are bad. Now you may strike forcefully upon water, and it will splash above your head. With a series of dams, you may force it uphill. But this is surely nothing to do with the nature of water; it happens only after the intrusion of some exterior force. A man can be made to do evil, but this is nothing to do with his nature. It happens only after the intrusion of some exterior force."

(6A.2)

4.8

Kao Tzu said, "What I mean by nature is the thing that gives life. Mencius asked, "Do you mean that in the sense that you would say that whiteness is the thing that whitens?" Kao Tzu said, "Yes, certainly!' Mencius continued, "Then it would follow that the whiteness of a white feather and the whiteness of white snow are comparable, and similarly that the whiteness of white snow and the whiteness of white jade are comparable?" Kao Tzu said, "Yes, certainly." Mencius replied, "With that line of reasoning would you not have to say that the nature of a dog and the nature of an ox are comparable, and so the nature of an ox and the nature of a man are comparable?"

(6A.3)

4.9

Kao Tzu said, "What I mean by nature is food and colour (the taste and senses). I regard Humanity as pertaining to these senses and not external to them. Justice, on the other hand, is something external; it does not pertain to the senses."

Mencius said, "How can you say that the one is inherent and the other external?" Kao Tzu said, "To a man who is my senior I pay, in Justice, the deference due to his seniority. This is not because paying such deference is an intrinsic part of *me*, I react to the stimulus of his seniority just as I see a white thing as white, since I am actuated by its whiteness, which is external to myself. It is for this reason that I say such things are external."

Mencius said, "If in speaking of the whiteness of a white horse, we say that it differs in no way from the whiteness of a white man, I suppose we must say that the 'seniority' (old age) of an old horse differs in no way from the 'seniority' of an old man. In which case, in what does Justice repose? In 'seniority' itself or in him who responds to seniority as he, in Justice, should?" Kao Tzu said, "I feel love for my younger brother, but I feel no love for the younger brother of a man of Ch'in. My brother provokes a feeling of pleasure within me, and so I say it is inherent. To a man from Ch'u who is my senior I pay the deference due to his seniority, just as I would pay deference to a senior of my own family. My doing so provokes a feeling of pleasure within my seniors. So accordingly I say that Justice is an external thing." Mencius said, "My enjoyment of a dish cooked by a man of Ch'in differs in no way from my enjoyment of a similar dish cooked by my own people. This is true of a number of similar material things. Since it is so, would you still assert that the enjoyment of food is something external?"

(6A.4)

4.10

Meng Chi-tzu asked Kung-tu Tzu, "Why is Justice said to be 'internal' in origin?" Kung-tu Tzu said, "It is the thing we do prompted by the respect we feel and so we say it is 'internal' in origin." Meng Chi-tzu said, "Suppose a man in the village is a year older than your older brother. To whom should you show the greater respect?" Kung-tu Tzu said, "To my older brother." Meng Chi-tzu said, "When pouring wine to whom would you offer the wine first?" Kung-tu Tzu said, "To the man in the village." Meng Chi-tzu said, "Then surely whether you feel respect or deference is prompted by this person or that. It comes from without not from within." Kung-tu Tzu could not answer this. He asked Mencius. Mencius said, "Ask him which he respects the more, his uncle or his younger brother. He will say 'My uncle.' Ask him which he respects the more, his younger brother when impersonating a corpse[18] or his uncle. He will say 'My younger brother.' Then ask him, 'And what of the respect due to your uncle?' He will say, 'It is the position my brother occupies that occasions this.' You, Sir, can then reply, 'My respect normally is directed to my brother, but when the occasion demands it is directed to the man in the village.' "

When Meng Chi-tzu was told this, he said, "When the occasion demands it I respect my uncle, and when the occasion demands it I respect my younger brother. This surely is determined from without,

---

[18] At a funeral. The impersonation was usually done by an adolescent boy to offer a temporary repose for the spirit of the deceased.

and not from within." Kung-tu Tzu replied, "In winter I drink hot water; in summer I drink it cold. Then is my desire to drink determined from without?"

(6A.5)

4.11

Kung-tu Tzu said, "Kao Tzu says, 'Man's nature is neither good nor bad.' Others say man's nature may tend in either direction. They say in the reigns of the good kings Wen and Wu the people were disposed to do good. In the reigns of the bad kings Yu and Li[19] the people were disposed to do evil. Still others say some men's natures are good while others are bad. These say that, under a good sovereign like Yao, a bad man like Hsiang appeared; and that, to a bad father like Ku-sou, a good son Shun was born; that, with a nephew of a senior branch as evil as Chou on the throne, such good uncles as Ch'i, Lord of Wei, and Prince Pi Kan lived.[20]

"Now, Sir, you say, 'Man's nature is good.' I suppose that these others are wrong?"

Mencius said, "It is of the essence of man's nature that he do good. That is what I mean by good. If a man does what is evil he is guilty of the sin of denying his natural endowment. Every man has a sense of pity, a sense of shame, a sense of respect, a sense of right and wrong. From his sense of pity comes *jen* (Humanity); from his sense of shame comes *yi* (Justice); from his sense of respect, *li* (the observance of rites); from his sense of right and wrong, *chih* (wisdom). *Jen, yi, li,* and *chih* do not soak in from without; we have them within ourselves. It is simply that we are not always consciously thinking about them. So I say, 'Seek them and you have them. Disregard them and you lose them.' Men differ, some by twice, some by five times, and some by an incalculable amount, in their inability to exploit this endowment. The *Book of Songs*[21] says,

> Heaven gave birth to all mankind
> Gave them life and gave them laws.
> In their holding to them
> They lean towards the virtue of excellence.

[19] Kings of Chou in the eighth century B.C., under whom western Chou declined; cf. 6.10 and 6.43, and see Introduction to 6.69.

[20] See Additional Notes, 3.28, note 103.   [21] *Songs,* 142.

Confucius said, 'This poet really understood the Way,' Thus, to possess life is to possess laws. These are to be laid hold upon by the people, and thus they will love the virtue of excellence."

(6A.6)

4.12

Mencius said, "When the harvest is good, the younger people are for the most part amenable, but when the harvest is lean, they are obstreperous. Their reacting differently under these differing circumstances is not due to the nature with which Heaven has endowed them but to those who create these overwhelming conditions. Sow the barley and cover it with soil. Providing that the ground is uniform and the barley is sown at one time, it will spring to life, and in due time all the barley will ripen. However, differing circumstances do arise; some ground is rich, some is poor; some well watered, some not; not all is equally well-tended. Even so, things of a kind resemble each other. And can we doubt that human beings are any different? The Sages and we ourselves are things of a kind. Lung Tzu[22] said, 'The sandal-maker may not know beforehand the size of his customer's feet, but we can be sure that he will not make the sandals the size of baskets.' Sandals resemble each other; men's feet are things of a kind. All men relish flavourings in their food. But it took an Yi Ya[23] first to discover those flavourings. Suppose Yi Ya's nature differed in kind from those of other men, just as the nature of horses and hounds differs from that of a man. How could it have happened that, whatever flavourings humans like, all derive from Yi Ya? As far as flavourings are concerned, the world is indebted to Yi Ya, but this could only happen because all men's palates are similar.

"This, too, is true of the ear. For music, the world is indebted to K'uang the Music Master.[24] But this could only happen because all men's ears are similar. This, too, is true of the eyes. No one would deny that Tzu-tu[25] was handsome, unless he was blind.

"Therefore, the human mouth enjoys its flavourings, the ear its music, the eye its beauty. These things are all alike. And is this not true of the things of the heart? What are those things that all hearts have in common? I say, 'the underlying principle, the essential Justice.'

[22] See 1.32, note 120.   [23] Fabled cook of Duke Huan of Ch'i; see Introduction to 6.78.
[24] See Introduction to 6.78.   [25] See Introduction to 6.78.

"The Sages (differ from us only) in being the first to discover those things which all hearts have in common. The underlying principle and the essential Justice evoke joy in our hearts just as rich meat delights our palate."

(6A.7)

4.13

Mencius said, "All this talk of 'man's nature'[26] is just so much 'ifs and therefores' and each 'therefore' is argued on the basis of self-interest. What I so dislike about these clever people is the way that they delve away at their arguments. If only they would dig away as Yü did when he drained off the Flood,[27] then I would not dislike these clever people so. When Yü drained off the Flood, he drained off the unserviceable. If these clever people would do the same, then their cleverness would be great indeed! If they sought the reasons for the height of the Heavens or the distance of the stars, they could sit down and calculate the solstices of a thousand years to come!"

(4B.26)

THE AGRONOMISTS

Though Mencius names Yang Chu and Mo Tzu as his most formidable rivals, theirs were far from being the only philosophies with which he had to contend. During his visit to the principality of T'eng he ran into the Agronomists. These were the advocates of a return to the simple life, where every man became his own prime producer. They identified themselves with the cult-hero Shen Nung, 'the god of Agriculture,' and sought to elevate the cultivation of the soil to the noblest of human pursuits. This was another of the 'restoration' philosophies, proposing a return to the primeval order of things when kings 'sowed the grain for the food they ate.' Mencius regarded this as a misinterpretation of history. In explaining this, Mencius gives us a fine description of the Chinese version of the Flood legend.

4.14

Hsü Hsing, an advocate of the teachings of the god of Agriculture, came to T'eng from Ch'u. Presenting himself at the palace gate, he

[26] I.e., by the Hedonists.   [27] See 3.3. and 4.14.

announced himself to Duke Wen, saying, "I, a man from distant parts, have heard that you, My Lord, practise Humane government. I would like to have a plot of land here and to become your subject." Duke Wen gave him a place to live. Hsü Hsing's followers numbered some twenty or thirty men. All wore shirts of coarse haircloth. They made rope sandals and wove grass mats for a living.

Ch'en Hsiang and his young brother Ch'en Hsin, both disciples of Ch'en Liang, arrived in T'eng from Sung carrying their ploughs upon their backs. They too said, "We have heard that you, My Lord, are putting into practice the policies of the Sages, and we would like to become the subjects of a Sage."

When Ch'en Hsiang met Hsü he was overjoyed. He renounced all that he had hitherto learned from Ch'en Liang and studied with Hsü Hsing. Ch'en Hsiang met Mencius and told him that Hsü Hsing had said of Duke Wen, "He is indeed a Worthy Prince, but even so he has not yet heard of the Way, for a Worthy Prince should both plough and eat with his people, preparing his own meals while conducting the government. But so far, T'eng still has his granaries, arsenals, and storehouses, and thus oppresses the people in order to provide for himself. Whence does his worthiness derive?" Mencius replied, "Hsü Hsing insists on planting his own grain before he eats, does he not?" Ch'en Hsiang replied that he did. Mencius said, "Hsü Hsing insists on weaving his own cloth before he clothes himself, does he not?" Ch'en Hsiang replied that he did not; he wore coarse haircloth. Mencius asked, "Does he wear a cap?" Ch'en Hsiang replied that he did. "What sort of cap?" asked Mencius. "A cap of coarse cloth," answered Ch'en Hsiang. "Did he weave the cloth himself?" asked Mencius. "No," replied Ch'en Hsiang, "he gets it in exchange for his grain." "But why," pursued Mencius, "does Hsü Hsing not do his own weaving?" Ch'en Hsiang replied, "It would be to the detriment of his sowing." Mencius asked, "Does Hsü Hsing cook with cooking pots and plough with an iron ploughshare?" Ch'en Hsiang answered, "Yes." "Did he make them himself?" asked Mencius. "No," replied Ch'en Hsiang, "he gets them in exchange for his grain." Mencius replied, "Procuring utensils and tools by bartering grain would surely not be 'oppressing' the potter and the caster, and the potter and the caster by bartering his wares for grain would surely not be 'oppressing' the cultivator. But why does Hsü Hsing not become his own potter and caster, so that he can get all that he needs from his own establishment? Why does he behave in this confused fashion, bartering with the artisans? What can be said of Hsü Hsing's 'not involving himself in complications'?" Ch'eng Hsiang said, "You cannot both conduct your own farming and engage in the myriad activities of the artisans." Mencius replied, "If that is so, can you both conduct your own farming and engage in the business of government? There are pursuits proper to great men and pursuits proper to lesser men. Further, to make for yourself, in a single lifetime, all the things that the myriad craftsmen make (if you insist that all you use should be made by yourself) would have everyone completely worn out. Therefore it is said, 'Some labour with their hands, and some labour with their minds. Those who labour with their minds govern others. Those who labour with their hands are governed by others. Those who are governed provide food for others. Those who govern are provided with food by others.' This is universally regarded as just.

"In the days of Yao, when the earth was still not levelled off, and the flood waters flowed without restraint, inundating the world, when the trees and grass grew thick and bird and beast roamed everywhere, before the edible grains were grown, and bird and beast pressed upon man, when the earth was criss-crossed with animal tracks, then Yao grieved. He raised up Shun and commissioned him to regulate the earth. Shun sent Yi with a burning torch to set fires in the hills and fens, and to burn them off. The birds and beasts fled for safety. Yü diverted the Nine Rivers, cleared courses for the Ch'i and T'a, directing them towards the sea. He drew off the Ju and Han, banked up the Huai and Szu, directing them into the Yang-tse. Then only could the peoples of the central states grow food to eat.

"Yü pursued his task for eight years and during that time passed his own gate three times without going in. Though he wished to do his own ploughing, could he have done so? The Lord of Millet[28] taught the people to plant and reap, and to cultivate the five edible grains. When the grains ripened the people enjoyed a sufficiency. But there is a truth about man. Though he is well fed, warmly clothed, and safely housed, if he be not taught, he is not far removed from the birds and beasts. A Sage would be concerned at this. Shun appointed Hsieh as his Minister for the People, to teach them the duties of man to man,

[28] Legendary ancestor of the Chou House; see 6.99 and Introduction to 6.52.

of the love that should exist between father and son, of the just dealing that should exist between prince and subject, of the distinctions that should be observed between man and woman, of the precedence proper among old and young, of good faith between friends. Yao said, 'Encourage them, lead them forward, correct them, keep them straight, support and protect them, make them content. Then bestir them to virtue.' The concern of the Sage for the people is of this kind.

"Had such Sages time to do their own ploughing? Yao's sole concern was that he might not get the services of Shun. Shun's sole concern was that he might not get the services of Yü and of Kao Yao.[29] It is only a common farmer whose sole concern would be that he failed to get his hundred acres ploughed! By *hui* (kindness) we mean the sharing with others of our riches. By *chung* (fidelity) we mean teaching others to do good, but by *jen* (Humanity) we mean gaining a man (*jen*) to benefit the whole world. Thus, to give over the world to a man is easy, but to obtain a man that will benefit the world is most hard.

"Confucius said, 'How great Yao was as a sovereign! Heaven only is really great, and Yao matched up to it. Vast was his greatness; the people could not put a name to it. And what a prince Shun was! Majestic indeed! He governed the world, but its government meant nothing to him.'[30] In their governing the world, can it be said that Yao and Shun did not put their whole hearts into it? Certain it is that they were not preoccupied with ploughing. I have learned that we might improve[31] the barbarians with our own culture, but never that our culture might be improved by that of the barbarians! Ch'en Liang was born in Ch'u. He liked the Way of the Duke of Chou and of Confucius. He came north to study it in the central states. None of our northern scholars could better him. He was what one calls a most distinguished scholar. You, Sir [i.e., Ch'en Hsiang], and your brother studied with him for a score or more years. He died, and now you turn your back on him.[32] When, in earlier days, Confucius died, after the three years of mourning the disciples put their affairs in order, to return home. They entered Tzu-kung's presence and bowed. As they looked at each other they wailed to the point where they lost their voices. Then they returned

---

[29] See 3.40.

[30] In the sense that he was not *engagé*. He could surrender the government without a question if Heaven ordained it. For Confucius' remark, compare *Analects*, 8.18 and 19.

[31] Literally "change," but here, as often, "change for the better, improve."

[32] By attaching themselves to Hsü Hsing. As Confucians, they had turned from the true path.

to their homes. Tzu-kung himself came back, built for himself a house on the site, and lived there alone for three years. Then he finally returned home.

"On another occasion Tzu-hsia,[33] Tzu-chang, and Tzu-yü, feeling that Yu-jo resembled the Sage, sought to serve him as they had served Confucius. They tried to urge Tseng Tzu to join them. But Tseng Tzu said, 'This is not proper. What has been washed in the great rivers, and bleached by the autumn sun, is glistening white. It cannot be improved.'[34] Now, gentlemen, how differently from Tseng Tzu you have behaved. You left your Master and studied with this southern barbarian with his shrike-like voice. His teaching is not that of the Former Kings. I have heard of birds leaving the dark canyon for the high trees, but never of their leaving the high trees for a dark canyon. In the *Lu Sung*[35] it says,

> When the Ti and the Jung were smitten
> When Ching and Hsü were suppressed.

The Duke of Chou was at that moment about to smite them, yet you, Sir, propose to study with them! This is not a change for the better!"

Ch'en Hsiang said, "Under Hsü Hsing's teaching, there would be no fluctuation in market prices or fraudulent dealing in the state. Even a small child sent to market would not be swindled. If cloth and silk lengths were standardized, the price of cloth could be standardized too. If the weights of hemp and silk in hanks were standardized, the price of yarn, could be standardized too. If the grain measures were standardized, the price of grain could be standardized too. If the quality of shoes were standardized, the price of shoes could be standardized too."

Mencius said, "Inequalities are of the very nature of things. Some are twice, some five times, some ten, a hundred, a thousand, or even ten thousand times the worth of others. If, Sir, you want to heap all together and make them the same, the whole world will be thrown into confusion. If shoes of good and poor quality were similarly priced, who would make the good shoes? If we followed Hsü Hsing's teaching, men would be led on to swindle each other. Who then could bring order to the state?"

(3A.4)

---

[33] See the Additional Notes.   [34] I.e., it is "gilding the lily."
[35] In *Book of Songs*, see *Songs*, 251.

4.15

*In Ch'i itself the principles of Hsü Hsing had found a sympathizer in the
person of Ch'en Chung Tzu, the scion of an ancient local family. Mencius
conceded his altruism but thought the philosophy he embraced turned men into
earthworms. The Agronomists, however, were protesting at the inequalities
of a social and economic system in which the disparities between the wealth
of the classes were so drastic. Ch'en Chung Tzu, not surprisingly, was thought
a traitor to his class. The Ambassador for Ch'i was asked at the Court of Chao,
"Is Chung Tzu of Wu-ling still alive? He neither serves the prince nor assists
the family and shuns the company of his peers. He sets an example of utter
fecklessness. I am surprised that he hasn't been executed!"*

K'uang Chang[36] said, "Ch'en Chung Tzu surely is a man of the utmost
integrity. He went to live in Wu-ling and for some days was without
food, so weak that he could neither see nor hear. By his well there was a
plum tree, its fruit half eaten by maggots. He crawled forward to the
tree to get the plums. He had to eat mouthfuls before he began to see
and hear again."

Mencius said, "Of all the scholars of Ch'i, Ch'en Chung Tzu to me
stands out as the thumb among the fingers, but even so, in what does his
integrity consist? It is only an earthworm that could carry out fully
the principles he holds. Earthworms eat mould and tunnel below to the
Yellow Springs for drink! But the house Ch'en now lives in—was it
built by a saint like Po Yi or by a scoundrel like the brigand Chih?[37]
Such things we never know." "But," said K'uang Chang, "he himself
makes rope sandals, his wife making the rope. And these he barters for
food." Mencius replied, "Ch'en Chung Tzu is a member of one of
Ch'i's noble families. His older brother, T'ai, has estates at Ko, with a
revenue of ten thousand *chung*. But Ch'en Chung Tzu thinks these are
ill-gotten gains and refuses to touch them. He shunned his brother, left
his mother, and went to live in Wu-ling, Returning home on a visit,
when his brother had received a gift of a goose, he frowned and said,
'What are you going to do with that cackling thing?'[38] Later his
mother killed the goose and offered it to him to eat. His older brother

[36] The friend of Mencius; see 1.15.
[37] See Introduction to 6.78.
[38] The "gift," we must suppose, he thought was a bribe, or some illicit exaction from a tenant.
At all events Ch'en Chung Tzu could not bring himself to call the goose by its proper name.

at that moment came in from outside and exclaimed, 'This is the meat of that "cackling thing"!' Whereupon Ch'en Chung Tzu ran outside and vomited. He refused to eat what his mother had offered him, but will eat what his wife gives him. He refused to live on his brother's estate, but will live in a place like Wu-ling! Can he, in these circumstances, fulfil the obligations of the station in life to which he was born? People like Ch'en Chung Tzu have to become earthworms to carry out fully the principles they hold."

(3B.10)

4.16

Mencius said, "Even if Ch'en Chung Tzu were offered the State of Ch'i, suppose that it offended his notion of Justice, he would not accept it and so everyone trusts him. But his acts of Justice are merely scruples about accepting a dish of rice or a bowl of soup. In these scruples he is without a peer. But his notions of Justice do not preclude his abandoning the duties of kinsman to kinsman, of prince to subject, of superior to inferior. Surely we cannot trust a man in major matters merely because he has shown scruples over minor ones!"

(7A.34)

THE ACADEMY

We know that King Hsüan of Ch'i, under whom Mencius served as a minister, founded the Chi-hsia Academy.[39] *To this Academy, King Hsüan invited the scholars of his day, rewarding those who pleased him with high-ranking sinecures and large houses. We know the names of several prominent members of the Academy, some of whom subsequently became famous. But the Academy is not mentioned in the* Works, *and Mencius appears to have met with but one of its members. The* Works, *however, are full of hidden reproaches of "idle scholars engaged in pointless discussions,"*[40] *of the "chill shades" under whose baneful influence King Hsüan treated so lightly the teachings of Mencius.*[41] *We know that the King offered Mencius himself a house and a pension, after his resignation from office, and of Mencius' scornful rejection of the offer.*[42]

---

[39] Or perhaps revived it. Some accounts attribute the foundation to Hsüan's predecessor, King Wei, in 357 B.C.

[40] See 3.3.   [41] See 1.19.   [42] See 2.13.

Shun-yü K'un was a member of the Academy. He is said to have written a philosophical work but it has been lost. He was given high rank without duties and a large house by King Hsüan. In his encounter with Mencius he treats mockingly the Confucian emphasis upon li (ritual), jen (Humanity), and hsien (worthies), and Mencius' own retreat from office. He gives no hint of his own philosophical position.

4.17

Shun-yü K'un said, "It is prescribed in the *Rites*, is it not, that 'in giving and receiving, a man and a woman should not touch hands'?"

Mencius said, "That is so."

Shun-yü said, "Suppose my sister-in-law is drowning, may I give her my hand?"

Mencius replied, "Only a wild animal would refuse to do so. Men and women do not allow the hands to touch as a matter of good manners, but overriding conditions govern the rescue of a sister-in-law from drowning."

Shun-yü K'un said, "The whole world is drowning, yet you do not offer a hand. Why is this?"

Mencius replied, "When the world is drowning I offer it my Way, but if my sister were drowning I would offer her my hand. Do you, Sir, propose to offer the world your hand?"

(4A.18)

4.18

Shun-yü K'un said, "He who places his 'fame and deeds' at the public disposal acts in the interests of others. He who refuses to do so acts in his own interests. You, Sir, once ranked among the Three Ministers, but before the efficacy of your 'fame and deeds' could be felt, you resigned from office. Is this really the way a Humane man behaves?"

Mencius replied, "Po Yi, though a worthy, remained in a lowly station because he would not serve a perverse prince. Yi Yin presented himself five times before the worthy King T'ang and five times before the tyrant Chieh. Liu-hsia Hui[43] neither thought it a disgrace to serve a degenerate prince nor to accept a minor post. All these pursued different

---

[43] See 6.64.

courses, although their objective was the same. And what was the objective they had in common? It was *jen* (Humanity). True Gentlemen seek to be Humane—no more, no less. Why should they pursue identical courses?" Shun-yü K'un said, "In the days of Duke Mu of Lu, the government was in the hands of Kung Yi-tzu. Tzu-liu and Tzu-szu[44] were his ministers. Yet that was a time of the severest encroachment upon the territory of Lu.[45] From this it appears that 'worthy men' are of no particular advantage to a state." Mencius replied, "Yu did not avail himself of the services of Po-li Hsi and so he lost his state. Duke Mu of Ch'in did so and became Paramount Prince. In this case failure to use a worthy man resulted in the loss of the state. In the case you cite, though Lu was encroached upon, it was not lost." Shun-yü K'un said, "When Wang P'ao was living on the banks of the river Ch'i, the people of Ho-hsi became adept at the staccato style of singing. When Mien Ch'ü was living in Kao-t'ang the people of western Ch'i became adept at the andante style of singing. The manner in which the wives of Hua Chou and Chi Liang wailed at their husbands' funerals changed the mourning pattern of the entire state. The gifts we innately possess manifest themselves beyond ourselves. I have never yet met a man with an aptitude which did not result in effective action. Therefore, I say, there are no 'worthies' today, for if there were I would certainly know about them." Mencius replied, "Confucius was Minister of Justice in Lu. His prince failed to avail himself of Confucius' services. At the sacrifices the portion of roast meat that should properly have been proffered to Confucius was never sent. Without even doffing his cap, Confucius took his leave. Those who did not know him thought he left because of the roast meat, but those who knew him realized that it was because of a breach of ritual. As far as Confucius was concerned, he left office on a matter of punctilio, not wishing to leave without cause. The common run of men certainly do not know about the motives that actuate a True Gentleman."

(6B.6)

---

[44] See Introduction to 6.73.
[45] In a series of attacks by Ch'i in 412, 411, and again in 408 B.C. Each time Lu had to cede territory to Ch'i.

ꕷꕷ

COMMENT ON
THE TIMES

The world of the fourth century B.C., as Mencius knew it, was a very different place from the world of his ideals—the Utopia of antiquity. In so far as he comments at all upon his own times, it is to deplore them. In the world of real politics, in contrast to the world of idealized history, the rich got richer and the poor got poorer. At the courts, resourceful generals and agile politicians, rather than men of virtue, secured office. The advocates of war, the architects of power blocs, and the negotiators of land grabs found their policies more persuasive than those of the gentle claims of Justice and Humanity. Such men, if Mencius had had his way, he would have put among the first to be punished.

POLITICIANS

5.1

Ching Ch'un said to Mencius, "What great men are Kung-sun Yen and Chang Yi![1] When they are aroused, the princes tremble, but when they are at ease, the whole world is quiet."

Mencius replied, "When did they become great men? Have you, Sir, never learned the *Rites*? On becoming a man, at the capping ceremony, the father instructs his son. Upon marriage, the mother instructs her daughter. When she leaves home, the mother accompanies her daughter to the gate, admonishing her, saying, 'You are going to your new home. Be respectful, be careful, do not disobey your husband.' Compliance is the criterion in the proper course for women.[2] But he who properly might be called a great man is one who dwells in the

---

[1] See Additional Notes.   [2] See Additional Notes.

broad mansion of the world, takes his place in its seat of rectitude, pursues the Great Way of the world, who, gaining his ambition, shares it with the common people, but who, failing to gain his ambition, pursues his principles in solitude. He is one whom riches and honours cannot taint, poverty and lowly station cannot shift, majesty and power cannot bend. Such a one I call a great man."

(3B.2)

5.2

Mencius said, "There are those who claim to be excellent tacticians and strategists—this is a great offence. If a prince loves Humanity, then he has no enemies to oppose him. When the punitive expedition turned south, the northern Ti peoples resented it; when it turned eastwards, the western Yi peoples resented it. They said, 'Why are we put last?'[3] When King Wu attacked Yin, he had three hundred chariots and three thousand warriors. He said, 'Do not be afraid; I shall give you peace; I have no quarrel with the people.' The people bowed low, like a deer shedding its antlers. The word *cheng* (punitive expedition) is a synonym of *cheng* (correction). When all men wish to correct themselves, what need is there for warfare?"

(7B.4)

5.3

Mencius said, "Those who serve princes today promise to enlarge his landholdings and enrich his treasuries and arsenals. They are called 'good ministers' but in antiquity they would have been called 'plunderers of the people.' If a prince's face be not set toward the Way, if his inclination is not towards Humanity, and his ministers seek to make him richer, they are 'enriching a Chieh.'[4] Some promise to negotiate advantageous treaties for their Prince so that he will be successful in war. These, too, are called 'good ministers' but in antiquity they would have been called 'plunderers of the people.' If a prince's face be not set towards the Way, if his inclination is not towards Humanity, and his ministers seek to make him more powerful in battle, they are 'supporting a Chieh.'

[3] Cf. 1.16, note 68.   [4] See Introduction to 6.69.

K

"No prince today, pursuing the path they presently follow, without a complete change of present practice, could rule the world for a single day, even supposing he were offered it."

(6B.9)

5.4

Mencius said, "Shame plays an important part in man. But the cunning devisers of tricks and devices have no use for shame. If one differs from other men[5] in having no sense of shame, in what will one be like other men?"[6]

(7A.7)

5.5

Mencius said, "When Ch'iu[7] was steward of the Chi family, upon whom Ch'iu's virtue exercised not the slightest effect, he even imposed, on their behalf, a double exaction of grain. On another occasion Confucius said, 'Ch'iu is no follower of mine. My little ones, if you were to beat the drums and set upon him, I would not say you nay.' From this we see that any who contributed to the enrichment of a ruler but who failed to practise Humane government would have been rejected by Confucius. And how much more so would they be rejected who urge, on their prince's behalf, counsels of war. To settle territorial disputes by war, when the bodies of the slain choke the countryside, to settle disputes over cities by war, when the bodies of the slain choke the walls—this is what may be called 'governing property and living off human flesh.'[8] Death is too good for such crimes. Therefore, I say, 'The highest punishment should be meted out to the propagators of war, the next highest punishment to those who advocate blocs among the princes, and the next highest to those who would sequester grass lands to be brought under cultivation for the princes."

(4A.15)

---

[5] *Pu jo jen*, "not like other men," is used in 6.33 for a freak. One might therefore translate: "To have no sense of shame is to be a freak, not only in this but in other things too."

[6] This curiously veiled reference is thought to be to the coterie at Court who had the prince's ear, to the discomfiture of Mencius. He says, no doubt with justice, that they were quite unscrupulous.

[7] Ch'iu is Jan Ch'iu. For this story compare *Analects*, 11.16.

[8] Cf. 1.23 and 3.3.

5.6

Mencius said, "The setting up of border posts in antiquity was to prevent violence. Today they are set up for the purpose of engaging in violence."

(7B.8)

THE WEALTHY

5.7

Mencius said, "When giving advice to the great,[9] one should treat them with contempt, paying no attention to the awesomeness that attends them. Their vast halls several fathoms high, with their flying rafters protruding several feet—these, even if I had my choice, I would not have. The great areas of food set before them, their attendant girls in the hundreds, even if I had my choice, I would not have. The rounds of music, the drinking of wine, the spurring and galloping of the chase with a thousand carriages in attendance—these, even if I had my choice, I would not have.

"Nothing that such people have would I wish to have. All that I have is in accordance with the regulations of antiquity. Why should I be impressed by them?"

(7B.34)

5.8

Mencius said, "To hold the reins of state is not difficult. The difficulty lies in not offending the great families. That which the great families desire, the state desires. That which the state desires, the whole world desires. Therefore in abundant measure must one's virtuous teaching inundate the entire continent."

(4A.6)

5.9

Mencius said, "The treasures of a Feudal Lord are three: his lands, his peoples, and his governance. But calamity will fall on his person if he regards pearls and jades as the treasures of state."[10]

(7B.28)

[9] I.e., rich and socially prominent. Mencius also uses *great* in other connections; see, for example, 5.1.
[10] There are a number of stories of fabled jades and famous pearls, the "treasures of state" over which princes fought battles.

5.10

Bestow upon a man the "families of Han and Wei" [i.e., great wealth]
and if he can still look upon himself with indifference he surpasses the
commonalty by a wide margin.

(7A.11)

THE PRETENTIOUS

5.11

In Ch'i there was a wife and a concubine living together. When their
goodman went out he ate and drank well. On his return home, when
asked by his wife with whom he had been eating and drinking, he
invariably said that it was with some rich or well-connected person.
The wife, observing to the concubine that, even so, no one of any consequence ever visited the house, said that she was going to follow him
and see for herself. She got up early next morning and followed him,
but nowhere in the city did anyone stop and speak to him. At last he
reached the Outer East Wall where some people were sacrificing to the
dead among the graves. He begged scraps from them. Getting little,
he moved on to further groups. It was in this way that he ate and drank
so well. The wife went home and said to the concubine, "It was to our
goodman that we looked with expectation for the rest of our lives.
And this is what happens." And so they stood weeping together in the
courtyard and reviling him. All unaware of this, the goodman came
swaggering in from outside, and began to boast to his wife and concubine.

From the True Gentleman's viewpoint, there are few wives and
concubines who have no cause to weep and to be ashamed at the ways
in which their menfolk seek for riches and honours, for profit and
advancement.

(4B.33)

5.12

Mencius said, "The man of deference does not look down upon others.
The frugal man does not take from others. A ruler who looks down upon
and takes from others fears only that they will disobey him. How can

such a ruler become frugal and deferential? Certainly not by a mere tone of voice or an ingratiating smile."

(4A.17)

THE WICKED

5.13

Mencius said, "Can one possibly speak to those who are Inhumane? They feel falsely secure when danger is imminent, regard as profitable the things that make for calamity, take delight in those things which bring destruction. If one could only speak to them, would such things as lost kingdoms and ruined estates be? Once a child was singing,

> When the waters of the Tsang-lang run clear
> I wash my cap-strings.
> Then when the waters are dirtied
> I wash my feet.

"Confucius said, 'Do you hear, my little ones, what he is singing? When clear he washes his cap-strings, when dirtied he washes his feet. He has taught himself a lesson.' For a man first brings contempt upon himself before others despise him. A feudal estate sows the seeds of its own destruction before others finally destroy it. A kingdom first occasions an attack upon itself before others finally attack it. This is what the *T'ai Chia*[11] means when it says,

> When catastrophe is of Heaven's making
> We may still escape,
> When catastrophe is of our own making
> We will not survive.

(4A.9)

5.14

Mencius said, "One can have no converse with those who do violence to themselves, or have dealings with those who abandon themselves. To do violence to oneself is to speak contrary to Propriety and Justice. To

---

[11] In the *Book of Documents*; see Legge, IV.v.ii.3.

abandon oneself is to say, 'I cannot take my place with men of Humanity and Justice!' Humanity is for man a house of security. Justice is for man a path of straightness. To let the house of security go untenanted, to let the path of straightness go untrodden, is a pity indeed."

(4A.11)

Chapter Six

THE TEACHINGS
OF MENCIUS

HUMANITY AND JUSTICE

The words jen *and* yi, *which I have translated "Humanity" and "Justice,"*[1] *are the key tenets of Mencius' system. Humanity (*jen*) is the attribute of being a man (*jen*)*[2] *as a man at his best instinctively feels both he and others should be. It is the sympathy he has "naturally" for a fellow human being in trouble. It is a quality with which a man is born, but which he must "guard in the thoughts" and cultivate. Confucius used the word* jen *for a very nearly unattainable human perfection—a quality almost transcendental—which he would only attribute to the Divine Sages of antiquity. But to Mencius, "all men can be a Yao or a Shun" and the gentleman "who is a gentleman indeed" not only may, but does, assiduously cultivate* jen. *Mencius nowhere defines* jen *more closely than this, but rather speaks of the consequence of being* jen. *For the man who is* jen, *wisdom rather than folly, honour rather than disgrace, felicity rather than catastrophe, results. For the prince who has this quality, the goals of True Kingship are realized—the prosperity of his state, the perpetuating of his line, and ultimately the allegiance of the whole world.* Jen *engenders* te, *"power"— a prestige and a moral persuasiveness which is the very opposite of* pa, *"physical force." Men everywhere, according to Mencius, find* jen *irresistible, for* jen *renders* pa *completely ineffective.* Yi, *"Justice," is the doing of what is right in seeing that others get their rights. "Rights" are not codified and referable to a system of law, but derive from custom: such things, for example, as the time-honoured "right" ·of the people to gather kindling in the forests, the "right" to the duties of a filial son by his father, the "right" of the people to a level of existence sufficient to maintain their aged in comfort. But it is also*

[1] See Additional Notes.   [2] See Additional Notes.

"right" to give and receive the niceties of courtesy, to behave and deport oneself according to the Rites.

In short, a man is jen *when he is what he should be, and* yi *when he does what he should do. Just what he should be and do in the Mencian view, we gather not from abstract definitions, but from the examples he gives.*

6.1

Mencius said, "It is a feeling common to all mankind that they cannot bear to see others suffer. The Former Kings had such feelings, and it was this that dictated their policies. One could govern the entire world with policies dictated by such feelings, as easily as though one turned it in the palm of the hand.

"I say that all men have such feelings because, on seeing a child about to fall into a well, everyone has a feeling of horror and distress. They do not have this feeling out of sympathy for the parents, or to be thought well of by friends and neighbours, or from a sense of dislike at not being thought a feeling person. Not to feel distress would be contrary to all human feeling. Just as not to feel shame and disgrace and not to defer to others and not to have a sense of right and wrong are contrary to all human feeling. This feeling of distress (at the suffering of others) is the first sign of Humanity. This feeling of shame and disgrace is the first sign of Justice. This feeling of deference to others is the first sign of propriety. This sense of right and wrong is the first sign of wisdom. Men have these four innate feelings just as they have four limbs. To possess these four things, and to protest that one is incapable of fulfilling them, is to deprive oneself. To protest that the ruler is incapable of doing so is to deprive him. Since all have these four capacities within themselves, they should know how to develop and to fulfil them. They are like a fire about to burst into flame, or a spring about to gush forth from the ground. If, in fact, a ruler can fully realize them, he has all that is needed to protect the entire world. But if he does not realize them fully, he lacks what is needed to serve even his own parents."

(2A.6)

6.2

Mencius said, "All men have things they cannot tolerate, and if what makes this so can be fully developed in the things they can tolerate, the result is Humanity. All men have things they will not do, and if what makes this so can be fully developed in the things they will do, then Justice results. If a man can fully exploit the thing in his mind which makes him not wish to harm others, then Humanity will result in overwhelming measure. If a man can fully exploit the thing in his mind which makes him reluctant to break through or jump over (other people's) walls, Justice will ensue in overwhelming measure. If a man can fully exploit the reluctance he feels in the use of the salutation *ju* and *erh*[3] wherever he goes he will act justly. When a knight says something which he should not have said, and by doing so gains his end, or when by failing to say something he should have said similarly gains his end, this is only in principle the same as 'breaking through other people's walls.' "

(7B.31)

6.3

Mencius said, "Of all seeds, the five grains are the best. But if they do not come to fruit, then the *t'i* and *pai* are better.[4] With Humanity it is the same. It is a question of its coming to fruit—nothing more."

(6A.19)

6.4

Mencius said, "It is by what he guards in his thoughts that the True Gentleman differs from other men. He guards Humanity and propriety in his thoughts. The man of Humanity loves others. The man of propriety respects others. He who loves others is in turn loved by others. He who respects others is in turn respected by others. Suppose someone treats us badly. The True Gentleman will look for the reason within himself, feeling that he must have failed in Humanity or propriety, and will ask himself how such a thing could in fact have happened to him. If after examination he finds that he has acted Humanely and with

[3] Pronouns of a direct and less direct form of address. The first is informal and intimate, but would be *gauche* if used to a superior. The latter indicates deference and would be comic if used, for example, to a child.

[4] Said to be wild, as opposed to cultivated, grain plants, with a very low yield. The "five grains" are the edible crops of the farmer: rice, millet of two kinds, wheat, and pulse.

propriety, and the bad treatment continues, he will look within him-self again, feeling that he must have failed to do his best. But if on examin-ation he finds that he has done his best, and the bad treatment con-tinues, he will say, 'This person, after all, is an utter reprobate; I will have done with him. If he behaves like this, how does he differ from an animal? Why should I be put out by an animal?'

"Therefore the True Gentleman spends a lifetime of careful thought, but not a day in worrying. There are things to which he does give careful thought. 'Shun,' he says, 'was a man. I too am a man. But Shun became an examplar to the whole world, an example that has been passed down to us who come after, while I, as it were, am still a mere villager.' This is a matter about which he might take careful thought—taking careful thought only that he might be like Shun. As to those things about which the True Gentleman worries—they do not exist. What is contrary to Humanity he would not be. What is contrary to propriety he would not do. As to 'spending the day worrying,' the True Gentleman simply does not worry."

(4B.28)

6.5

Mencius said, "Is the arrow-maker any less Humane than the armourer because his main concern is that his arrows should do the utmost damage, while the armourer's concern is that the least damage might be done? Is the shaman more Humane than the coffin-maker (because the shaman is interested in the patient's recovery, while the coffin-maker is inter-ested in his death)? And, too, in the matter of the choice of the doctrine one follows[5] one cannot be too careful.

"Confucius said, 'It is Humanity that adorns a village. What can be said of the wisdom of him who chooses to live where Humanity is not?'[6] Humanity is the patent of honour bestowed by Heaven, the house of security where man should dwell. Since none can prevent us being Humane, not to be Humane is folly. Not to be Humane, not to be wise, is to lack a sense of propriety and to lack a sense of Justice. Such a person is the bondservant of others. To be a servant, and to be ashamed of one's servitude, is like the bow-maker being ashamed of his bows, and the arrow-maker of his arrows. Rather than be ashamed of such servitude

[5] See Additional Notes.   [6] *Analects*, 4.1.

it were better to be Humane. To be Humane is like engaging in archery. The archer adjusts his person before shooting. Having shot and failed to hit the bull's eye, he does not rail against those who have shot better. He seeks the remedy in himself."

(2A.7)

6.6

Mencius said, "If one is Humane then glory results, but if one is not Humane then disgrace results. For a man to fear disgrace, and yet to continue contrary to Humanity, is like fearing the damp and continuing to live in a low-lying place. Rather than fear disgrace, it were better to ennoble virtue, and to accord honour to the knights who exemplify it.[7] When worthy men are in positions of authority, the competent carry out their duties. At such times as the state is in repose, its policies and laws can be made clear to all. Even a major state will stand in fear of such a state. In the *Book of Songs*[8] it says:

> Before the days of cloud and rain came
> I took the mulberry roots
> And wove them into a window and door,
> You people down below!
> Who dares insult me now?

Confucius said, 'How well the author of this song knew the Way! Who dares to impugn the man who governs his House and State well?' But today, at such times as the state is in repose, its officers abandon themselves to pleasure and indolent ease. They are merely seeking catastrophe for themselves. Catastrophe or happiness are invariably self-sought. The *Book of Songs*[9] says:

> Think always of being the fit recipient of the
>   Charge.
> Seek for yourself its many blessings.

and the *T'ai Chia* says:[10]

---

[7] It was King Hui of Liang who "feared disgrace" and sought for "honour"; see 1.20.
[8] *Songs*, 231; see Additional Notes.
[9] *Songs*, 241.
[10] In the *Book of Documents;* see Legge, IV.v.ii.3.

When catastrophe is of Heaven's making
We may still escape.
When catastrophe is of our own making
We will not survive.

The *Songs* and the *Book of Documents* are here referring to this."

(2A.4)

6.7

Mencius said, "A Paramount Prince[11] was one who, pretending to Humanity, resorted to force. Such a one had need of the rule of a major state. A True King is one who, practising Humanity, resorts only to virtue. Such a one has no need of a major state. T'ang the Successful had a state of only seventy miles square, and King Wen a state of only a hundred miles square. They were True Kings. Allegiance which is gained by the use of force is not an allegiance of the heart—it is the allegiance which comes from imposing upon weakness. Allegiance which is gained by the exercise of virtue is true allegiance. It is the response of joy felt deeply in the heart. Such was the allegiance that Confucius gained from his seventy followers. The *Book of Songs*[12] says:

From the West, from the East,
From the North and from the South,
There was no thought of not rendering allegiance.

The *Songs* here refer to the allegiance of the heart."

(2A.3)

6.8

Mencius said, "When a minister is not up to remonstrating with his prince, then it is not enough to find fault with his government. It is only a great man who can rectify error in the prince's mind. If the prince is a man of Humanity, then nothing in his state but will be Humane. If the prince is a man of Justice, then nothing in his state but will be Just. If the prince is a man of rectitude, then nothing in his state but will be upright. Once the prince is corrected, the good government of the kingdom is assured."

(4A.21)

[11] See Introduction to 6.70.   [12] *Songs*, 247.

6.9

If the prince is a man of Humanity then nothing in his state but will be Humane.

If the prince is a man of Justice, then nothing in his state but will be Just.

(4B.5)

6.10

Mencius said, "The Three Dynasties[13] gained the Empire by Humanity and lost it by Inhumanity. States rise and fall, and are held and are lost for the same reason. If the Son of Heaven is Inhumane he will lose his Empire. If the Feudatory are Inhumane they will surrender their altars.[14] If ministers and Great Officers are Inhumane they will forfeit their family shrines. If knights and commoners are Inhumane they will not keep their four limbs intact. If a man abhors death and destruction, yet delights in the Inhumane, it is as though he were revolted by drunkenness, yet allowed himself to be urged to drink more wine."

(4A.3)

6.11

Mencius said, "Humanity extinguishes Inhumanity just as water extinguishes fire. Men of Humanity today are like a cup of water used to extinguish a wagon-load of burning kindling, which, when it fails to extinguish such a fire, is said to show that water is ineffectual against fire. But the Inhumane are in a more serious plight than they (the Humane). The Inhumane are, after all, headed in the end for destruction."

(6A.18)

FAMILIAL DUTY[15]

To the man of Justice and Humanity, "the duty from which all others spring"[16]

[13] I.e., of Hsia, Shang, and Chou. The House of Chou, though *de jure* still rulers, had "lost" their Mandate in the eighth century under King Yu and King Li (see 4.11 and 6.43).

[14] That is, the altars of the soil and crops, the proprietorship of which was the patent of feudal tenure.

[15] Other references to familial duty are 3.5, 3.11, 3.12, 3.41, 6.52, etc.   [16] 6.13.

is his duty towards his parents. Hsiao, "filial piety," the son owes to his father, and t'i "the duty of the younger brother," the brother owes to his older brother. Familial duty derives from the ancient religion where the ever present ancestors stored up the virtus *of the line, and to whom worship was offered, and whose help was invoked for the fortunes of the family. This was later extended to "serving the parents while they are still living." And hence was developed the Confucian teaching of filial duty. In later Confucianism* hsiao *becomes almost a metaphysical principle, but in Mencius' time it still lies within the realm of precept.*

The Mohists developed this idea even further. The duty we owe to parents, they argued, we owe in equal measure to all mankind. Thus, incongruously perhaps, Confucians and Mohists saw an antithesis between "familial duty" and "universal love," though both argued that the one led eventually to the other.[17]

6.12

Mencius said, "Humanity attains its finest flower in the service of parents. Justice attains its finest flower in obedience to older brothers. Wisdom its finest flower in the realization of these two things and consistently adhering to them. Ritual attains its finest flower in the formulation of these two things into a disciplined pattern. Joy has its finest flower in the pleasure that is derived from these two things. In pleasure they grow, and growing they are irrepressible. And being irrepressible all unknowingly the feet take up the measure and the hands begin the dance."[18]

(4A.27)

6.13

Mencius said, "Of all my duties, which is the greatest? My duty to my own parents! Of all that is held in trust by me which is the greatest? The preservation of my body! I have heard of those who, having kept their bodies inviolate, could serve their parents, but not of those who, failing to do so, still served their parents. Whichever duty I fail to perform, it must not be my duty to my parents, for that is the duty from which all others spring. Whichever trust I fail to fulfil, it must not be that of keeping my body inviolate, for that is the trust from which all others arise.

[17] See 6.34: "The Humane include all within their affections."   [18] See 1.4, note 26.

"When Tseng Tzu[19] was providing for his father, Tseng Hsi, he invariably served wine and meat. On removing the dishes at the end of a meal he would ask his father to whom the remainder should be given. If asked if there was any more, he always answered yes. When Master Tseng in his turn was being provided for by his son Tseng Yüan, Tseng Yüan too served wine and meat, but on removing the dishes at the end of the meal he did not ask his father to whom the remainder should be given, and, if asked if there was any more, he always said no. This was because he intended to serve anything left over again the next day. Tseng Yüan's duty to his aged father was what might be called 'ministering to the mouth and body' (the outer shell of observance), while that of Tseng Tzu to his father was what might be called 'ministering to the heart' (an observance of sincerity).[20]

"It is familial duty as exemplified by Tseng Tzu that has my approval."

(4A.20)

6.14

The Way lies close at hand, yet men seek for it afar. Duty is not hard, yet men seek it in the most difficult things. If each man individually were to treat his own kin as properly they should be treated, and respected his elders with the respect that is due to them, the whole world would be at peace.

(4A.12)

6.15

Mencius said, "A True Gentleman loves all living creatures, but does not treat all with Humanity. He treats all human beings with Humanity, but does not treat them all with familial affection.

"He who feels the love of family towards his own kin will feel Humanity for all men. He who feels Humanity for all men will be kind to all living creatures."[21]

(7A.45)

---

[19] See Introduction to 6.73.

[20] Or, as we should say, the "letter of the law" in contrast to the "spirit of the law."

[21] In the Mencian system, *ai*, "love" is contained within *jen*, "Humanity," and *jen* is contained within *ch'in*, "family love." *Ch'in* and *jen* take priority over *ai*. In the Mician system *ai* is supreme, and *chien ai*, "universal love," takes priority over *jen* and *ch'in*.

6.16

Mencius said, "Three things delight the True Prince, but being sovereign of the universe is not one of them. His first delight is that his parents are still living and that his brothers give no occasion for anxiety. His second delight is that he can look at Heaven unabashed and face his fellow men without a blush. His third delight is to gain the allegiance of the world's most talented men, and to instruct and train them. These are his three delights, but being sovereign of the universe is not one of them."

(7A.20)

6.17

Mencius said, "The support of parents during their lifetime does not by itself meet the requirements of the supreme duty; these are only met in full when parents have been properly interred."

(4B.13)

6.18

Mencius said, "There are three contraventions of the rules of filial piety,[22] and of these the greatest is to have no progeny. It was for this reason that Shun married, even at the cost of failing to inform his parents. The True Gentleman would regard the reasons which prompted Shun to marry as cancelling out his obligation to inform his parents first."[23]

(4A.26)

MAN'S NATURE AND HIS FATE

Man's nature, hsing *(about which several theories were held in Mencius' day),*[24] *was to Mencius innately good, and this was attested by the universality of a sense of kinship and of right and wrong. It is in this that man differs from other living creatures. But the* hsing *can "be hacked away at" and atrophy and disappear if not "nurtured" aright. Nurturing the* hsing *consists in "guarding the mind" (ts'un hsin), for the mind is the repository of "Humanity" and "Justice." It is the* hsing *and* hsin *that determine what we are. It is our*

---

[22] See Additional Notes.   [23] See 3.11.
[24] See 4.6 ff., where Mencius argues the matter with Kao Tzu.

ming, "*fate*," *that governs our fortunes and determines our lease on life.
Ming was originally a patent to a fief-holder, given by the Son of Heaven,
as heaven's deputy, to a feudatory. In extended usage it is our "lot in life"—
the fate ordained by Heaven. While a man can "guard his mind" and determine his conduct. he cannot determine his fate, which is in Heaven's hands.*

*Though all men are innately good, the realization of that good comes with
self-cultivation and self-knowledge.*

6.19

The difference between a man and an animal is slight.[25] The common
man disregards it altogether, but the True Gentleman guards the distinction most carefully. Shun understood all living things, but saw clearly
the relationships that exist uniquely among human beings. These
relationships proceed from Humanity and Justice, It is not because of
these relationships that we proceed towards Humanity and Justice.

(4B.19)

6.20

Mencius said, "Bull Mountain was once beautifully wooded. But,
because it was close to a large city, its trees all fell to the axe. What of its
beauty then? However, as the days passed things grew, and with the
rains and the dews it was not without greenery. Then came the cattle
and goats to graze. That is why, today, it has that scoured-like appearance. On seeing it now, people imagine that nothing ever grew there.
But this is surely not the true nature of a mountain? And so, too, with
human beings. Can it be that any man's mind naturally lacks Humanity
and Justice? If he loses his sense of the good, then he loses it as the mountain lost its trees. It has been hacked away at—day after day—what of
its beauty then?

"However, as the days pass he grows, and, as with all men, in the still
air of the early hours his sense of right and wrong is at work. If it is
barely perceptible, it is because his actions during the day have disturbed
or destroyed it. Being disturbed and turned upside down the 'night
airs' can barely sustain it. If this happens he is not far removed from the
animals. Seeing a man so close to an animal, people cannot imagine
that once his nature was different—but this is surely not the true nature

---

[25] See Additional Notes, 3.3, note 11.

L

of the man? Indeed, if nurtured aright, anything will grow, but if not nurtured aright anything will wither away. Confucius said, 'Hold fast to it, and you preserve it; let it go and you destroy it; it may come and go at any time no one knows its whereabouts.' Confucius was speaking of nothing less than the mind."

(6A.8)

6.21

Mencius said, "I am fond of fish, but, too, I am fond of bear's paws. If I cannot have both, then I prefer bear's paws. I care about life, but, too, I care about Justice. If I cannot have both, then I choose Justice. I care about life, but then there are things I care about more than life. For that reason I will not seek life improperly. I do not like death, but then there are things I dislike more than death. For that reason there are some contingencies from which I will not escape.

"If men are taught to desire life above all else, then they will seize it by all means in their power. If they are taught to hate death above all else, then they will avoid all contingencies by which they might meet it. There are times when one might save one's life, but only by means that are wrong. There are times when death can be avoided, but only by means that are improper. Having desires above life itself and having dislikes greater than death itself is a type of mind that all men possess— it is not only confined to the worthy. What distinguishes the worthy is that he ensures that he does not lose it.

"Even though it be a matter of life or death to him, a traveller will refuse a basket of rice or a dish of soup if offered in an insulting manner. But food that has been trampled upon, not even a beggar will think fit to eat. And yet a man will accept emoluments of ten thousand *chung* regardless of the claims of propriety and Justice. And what does he gain by that? Elegant palaces and houses, wives and concubines to wait on him, and the allegiance of the poor among his acquaintance! I was previously speaking of matters affecting life and death, where even there under certain conditions one will not accept relief, but this is a matter of palaces and houses, of wives and concubines, and of time-serving friends. Should we not stop such things? This is what I mean by 'losing the mind with which we originally were endowed.' "

(6A.10)

6.22

Mencius said, "To the hungry all food is sweet; to the thirsty all water is sweet. Such cannot judge when food and drink is as it should be. Their hunger and thirst blunt their palate. And it is not surely only the mouth and belly that are affected by hunger and thirst; they affect the minds of men. If, though he suffers from hunger and thirst, a man can remain unaffected in his mind, it need occasion him no regret that, in this, he is not like other men."[26]

(7A.27)

6.23

Mencius said, "In the nurturing of the mind, there is no better method than that of cutting down the number of desires. A man who has few desires, though he may have things in his mind which he should not have, will have but few of them. A man who has many desires, though he may have things in his mind which he should have, will have but few of them."

(7B.35)

6.24

Mencius said, "It is the man who has stretched his mind to the full who fully understands man's true nature. And understanding his true nature, he understands Heaven. To guard one's mind and to nourish one's true nature is to serve Heaven. Do not be in two minds about premature death or a ripe old age. Cultivate yourself and await the outcome. In this way you will attain to your allotted span."

(7A.1)

6.25

Mencius said, "It is of their essential nature for the mouth to be concerned with taste, for the eye with colour, for the ear with sound, for the nose with smell, and for the four limbs to seek rest and repose. But in these functions, there is, too, the element of Heaven's purposes. The True Gentleman does not call this element 'essential nature.'

[26] That he is, so to say, a freak; see 5.4.

"Humanity is concerned with father and son, Justice with prince and subject, the Rites with host and guest, wisdom with worthy men, and being a Sage with the Way of Heaven. These are Heaven's purposes, but, too, there is in them an element of the 'essential nature.' The True Gentleman does not call this element 'Heaven's purposes.' "27

(7B.24)

6.26

Mencius said, "Nothing, but is preordained. We should accept obediently our rightful lot. Therefore he who understands Heaven's ordinances does not walk below high walls, but when he dies in the full discharge of his principles he has fulfilled the lot that Heaven has ordained for him. He who dies, however, in a felon's chains cannot be said to have fulfilled the lot that Heaven ordained for him."

(7A.2)

6.27

Mencius said, " 'Seek and we find; let go and we lose.' Seeking is only of value in finding, when what is sought lies with us to seek. But there is a principle in seeking. When what we are to find is already preordained then seeking itself is of no value. What is sought is beyond our control."

(7A.3)

6.28

Mencius said, "The functions of the body are the endowment of Heaven. But it is only a Sage who can properly manipulate them."

(7A.38)

6.29

Mencius said, "A man cares about all parts of his body without discrimination, and so he nurtures all parts equally. There is not a square inch of skin that he does not care about, and so he tends all of his skin equally. His decision as to what is most effective for himself comes

27 See Additional Notes.

from within himself. The human body has parts which are large and parts which are small. He does not treat one to the detriment of the rest. But he who gives preferential treatment to the lesser parts of the body becomes a lesser man. He who gives preferential treatment to the great parts becomes a greater man.

"Suppose a wood-lot owner neglected the timber trees and looked after the undergrowth; he would be a very poor wood-lot operator. A doctor who treated one finger and neglected the back and shoulders would be a very befuddled physician. Men despise one who lives only to eat and drink, because he develops the lesser functions of his body and neglects the greater. If he wishes not to neglect the greater, should he not regard his mouth and belly as a 'single square inch of skin?'"

(6A.14)

6.30

Determination is like digging a well; if water is not struck after digging for nine fathoms, one might as well abandon the well.[28]

(7A.29)

6.31

Mencius said, "If a man love others, and his love is not reciprocated let him think about his own feelings for Humanity. If a man govern others, and they fail to respond, let him think about his own wisdom. If a man extend courtesies to others, and is not in turn treated with courtesy, let him think about his own sense of reverence. If a man pursue a course, and his way is impeded, let him seek the remedy in himself. With these things correct within himself, the whole world will turn to him. The *Book of Songs*[29] says,

> Think always of being the fit recipient of the Charge
> Seek for yourself its many blessings."

(4A.4)

6.32

Mencius said, "Anyone who really wishes to grow a small tree like the *t'ung* or *szu* tree learns how to tend it. But in the matter of one's own

[28] I.e., there is no virtue in setting one's sights upon the unattainable (cf. 6.27).   [29] *Songs*, 241.

person, there are those who do not learn how to tend it, not so much because they have a greater love for a tree than for themselves, but because of a heedlessness that is very deep-seated."

(6A.13)

6.33

Mencius said, "Suppose a man has a little finger which is crooked, and which he cannot straighten out. He feels no pain; neither does it affect his work. He will, even so, go as far as Ch'u or Ch'in if there were someone there who could set it straight again. Why? Because it makes him different from other men.[30] If a man's little finger makes him different from others, he knows enough to feel embarrassed about it. If a man's mind makes him different from other men and he does not know enough to feel embarrassed about it, then that is what I call 'being unaware of things of like kind.' "

(6A.12)

6.34

Mencius said, "The wise take all knowledge for their province, but are most concerned about important things. The Humane include all within their affections, but are most concerned with affection for the worthy. Yao and Shun in their wisdom did not know everything— they were concerned with things of the first priority. The Humanity of Yao and Shun was not impartially displayed to all men—they were concerned most with affection for the worthy. Those who are meticulous about the light mourning worn for distant relatives, but neglect the deep mourning for close relatives, who gulp and guzzle at meals yet ask questions about the propriety of biting meat with the teeth—these are examples of not being concerned with the important things."

(7A.46)

6.35

Mencius said, "A Humane word does not affect men so profoundly as a Humane reputation. Good government does not affect them so profoundly as gaining their allegiance by good teaching. Good government the people respect, but good teaching the people love. By good

[30] I.e., a freak; see 5.4.

government one may elicit the people's wealth, but by good teaching
one elicits their hearts."

(7A.14)

6.36

Mencius said, "Most people do things without knowing what they do,
and go on doing them without any thought as to what they are doing·
They do this all their lives without ever understanding the Way."

(7A.5)

6.37

A man cannot be shameless. Shamelessness is the shame of having no
sense of shame.

(7A.6)

6.38

Mencius said, "All things are complete within ourselves. There is no
joy that exceeds that of the discovery, upon self-examination, that we
have acted with integrity. And we are never closer to achieving Humanity than when we seek to act, constrained by the principle of reci-
procity."

(7A.4)

6.39

Mencius said, "Humanity is the mind of man. Justice, the path he
follows. If by closing the way he fails to follow it, then he loses his
mind and has no way of retrieving it. How sad this is! If a fowl or a
dog stray we know how to find them again, but if the mind strays we
have no such recourse. The whole purport of learning is nothing more
than this: to regain the mind that has strayed."

(6A.11)

6.40

Mencius said, "The True Gentleman pursues knowledge profoundly
according to the Way, wishing to appropriate it for himself. Having

appropriated it, he abides with it in perfect assurance. Abiding with it in assurance, he stores it deeply, and storing it deeply he draws from it whichever way he moves, as though he were encountering a spring. For this reason the True Gentleman wishes to appropriate knowledge for himself."[31]

(4B.14)

6.41

Mencius said, "Those men who have the wisdom of virtue, and many-sided knowledge, will often be found to have discovered it in personal distress. Like the orphaned servant or the concubine's son, they take careful thought as though in imminent danger, and anticipate trouble with profound care. That is why they succeed."[32]

(7A.18)

6.42

Mencius said, "The abilities men have which are not acquired by study are part of their endowment of good. The knowledge men have which is not acquired by deep thought is part of their endowment of good. Every baby in his mother's arms knows about love for his parents. When they grow up, they know about the respect they must pay to their elder brothers. The love for parents is Humanity. The respect for elders is Justice. It is nothing more than this, and it is so all over the world."

(7A.15)

WHAT HISTORY TEACHES

To Mencius, just as the square and compasses is to the craftsman, so is history to the True Gentleman. It provides him with his standards. Mencius derived his knowledge of history from the Book of Documents, *from the* Book of Songs, *and from other literary sources.*[33] *But, though he thought that written history had its value,*[34] *it was not to be taken always at its face value. To*

---

[31] This does not, I confess, make very much sense. There is reason to suppose that the text is corrupt.

[32] On the uses of adversity, see also 6.61.

[33] See Additional Notes, 1.28, note 109.   [34] Cf. 6.48.

Mencius, the history of the world was the progress in cycles from primordial perfection to modern-day chaos, and any documentary sources that appeared to contradict this, he promptly rejected.[35] *Mencius develops this descent from the Divine Sages to the Model Kings, and from the Model Kings to Confucius in a number of passages.*[36] *The path downwards is, however, arrested by exemplary figures and hastened by cautionary ones. Looked at another way, history to Mencius was a series of catastrophes, each holding out, however, promise of recovery, and so he is saved from complete pessimism. Heaven, as it were, steps in about every five hundred years*[37] *with a Sage King, or one like Confucius, "who would have been King"*[38] *to "save the world." Mencius, then, has no deterministic view of history. He believed that primordial perfection was always recoverable if only men would seek for it. They do not do so through heedlessness of history's lessons.*

For Mencius the past was peopled with figures some of whom we now know to be mythical or legendary, though some are unquestionably historical. The important thing, however, in reading Mencius is to understand history as its author envisioned it. In this view, the world began with a Deluge and it was made habitable through the labours of the three heroes, Yao, Shun, and Yü. These ruled "all under Heaven" in turn. Of them, Yao and Shun appointed their successors, but with Yü the principle of hereditary tenure was established. Thereafter the world was governed by dynastic houses; that of the Hsia founded by Yü; that of the Shang or Yin founded by T'ang the Successful (c. 16th cent. B.C. to 11th cent. B.C.); and that of the Chou (c. 11th cent. B.C.), founded, upon the revolt of King Wen by his son, King Wu. The "Three Emperors" and the "Three Dynasties" each had their ministers, and these ministers, together with their sovereigns, are the Worthies—men in whom Humanity and Justice, familial duty, wisdom, and integrity were exemplified at their highest. Their governmental policies are the "Way of the Former Kings," a return to which is Mencius' political programme. By contrast, the Three Emperors had each some venal relative, and the dynasties of the Hsia, Shang, and Chou had each an evil descendant by which the dynasty was threatened or lost.[39] *These provide Mencius with his cautionary figures— a reminder that virtue, however powerful, can spend its course. But not entirely. Even during these "evil times" there are men such as Po Yi (in the*

---

[35] Cf. 6.46. [36] Cf. 2.14, 3.3. [37] See 6.49.

[38] Cf. 3.8, where it is said that, but for someone to present him, Confucius would have been Son of Heaven.

[39] In the case of the Chou the dynasty was still, of course, nominally intact, but its "virtue" had run out under King Yü and King Li in the eighth century (see 4.11 and 6.43).

*Shang Dynasty) and Liu-hsia Hui (at the collapse of western Chou) who are
not corrupted. Yi Yin, Po Yi and Liu-hsia Hui form a sort of Trinity of pure
men in a corrupt age.*

*Thus the past, to Mencius, was peopled with the uncompromisingly good
in whom was revealed the Way, and the utterly bad—fit only for the "punishment of Heaven" and history's cautions against turning from the Way. But
History, too, held out its expectations. And in Mencius' time these expectations were overdue. It was perhaps this that led Mencius to suppose that he
might be, after all, "the man whom Heaven has chosen."*[40]

6.43 THE SQUARE AND COMPASSES

Mencius said, "The perfect square and the perfect circle come only from
the set square and compasses. The perfect exemplars of man's relation
to man come from the Sages. Both he who, as a prince, wishes to follow
fully the way of princes, and he who, as a subject, wishes to follow fully
the way of subjects, should take Yao and Shun as his model. He who
does not serve his prince as Shun served Yao does not show reverence
for his prince. He who does not govern his people as Yao governed the
people deprives his people. Confucius said, 'Two courses only lie
before us, that of Humanity and that of Inhumanity.'

"He who oppresses his people overmuch will be slain and his state
will perish. He who oppresses his people, though he does not do so
overmuch, will still find his person in danger and his kingdom im-
perilled. Oppressive rulers earn such titles as 'The Dark' or 'The Cruel.'[41]
They may be good fathers to their sons and kindly to their grandsons,
but for a hundred generations to come such epithets remain with them
unchanged. The *Book of Songs*[42] says,

> Yin's warning beacons were not far off
> During the reign of the last sovereign of Hsia.

This song warns of these things."

(4A.2)

6.44

Mencius said, "With eyes as sharp as those of Li Lou[43] or with hands as

---

[40] Cf. and 6.49 with 2.14.

[41] *Yu,* "Dark," and *Li,* "Cruel," were the posthumous names of two Chou kings at the close of
western Chou. They are mentioned in 4.11.   [42] *Songs,* 242.   [43] See Introduction to 6.78.

skilled as those of Kung-shu[44] one could still not draw a perfect circle without the aid of compasses, or a perfect square without the aid of a set square. With an ear as keen as that of K'uang the Music Master[45] one could still not strike the five notes accurately without the aid of the pitch-pipes. Even with the principles of a Yao or a Shun one could still not govern the world in peace without Humane government. There are princes with Humane hearts, or with a reputation for Humanity, but whose peoples gain no benefit therefrom, and whose example will not bear emulation by generations to come. This is because they do not put into practice the Way of the Former Kings.

"Therefore I say, 'Competence alone is insufficient for the conduct of government; laws by themselves will not get put into effect.' The *Book of Songs*[46] says,

> Neither offending nor forgetting,
> In everything following the ancients' code.

It has never happened that one who followed the example of the Former Kings has erred.

"The Sages passed on to us the compass, the square, the level, and the line, having laboured to the point of blindness in contriving them so that we can make things square or round, level or straight. The usefulness of these things is incommensurable. They passed on to us the pitch-pipes, having laboured to the point of deafness in contriving them, so that we can strike accurately the five notes. The usefulness of the pitch-pipes is incommensurable. They passed on to us the principles of government based on fellow-feeling, having laboured their minds to the point of exhaustion in contriving them, so that Humanity might overshadow the world. It is truly said, 'To attain a great height, start from a hill top; to attain great depth, begin in the hollow of a marsh.' Can he be said to be truly wise, who, to attain the best in government, does not start with the Way of the Former Kings?

"It is for this reason that only men of Humanity ought properly to occupy high position. To lack Humanity and to be highly placed is to spread abroad evil among the populace. When the prince has no principles by which to measure, his subordinates have no standards to maintain. If the Court does not remain true to principles, the workmen

---

[44] I.e., Kung-shu P'an, the dexterous mechanic of Lu (seventh century); see Introduction to 6.78.
[45] See Introduction to 6.78.   [46] *Songs*, 172.

will not keep true to standards. If the ruler contravenes Justice, lesser men will contravene the penal code. It will then be a matter of sheer luck that the state survives. Truly it is said, 'It is not the imperfection of defensive walls, or the paucity of arms, that constitutes disaster for the state. It is neither a failure to increase the acreage of arable land, nor an inadequate accumulation of goods and wealth, that constitutes the losses of a state. It is a ruler who lacks propriety, and subordinates who lack learning, and, when plunderers of the people prosper, it is these things that bring about the overthrow, in short order, of the state. The *Book of Songs*[47] says,

> Since Heaven is about to trample under foot,
> You should not be so talkative.

The word 'talkative' here means 'to chatter.' He who serves his prince without Justice, who enters and retires from office without the observance of protocol, he is an example of a mere chatterer. Truly it is said, 'To urge a difficult course upon a prince is to show respect for him; to set the good before him and to bar the way to evil is to show reverence for him.' But he who says, 'Our prince has not the ability,' he it is who deprives his prince.'"[48]

(4A.1)

6.45

Mencius said, "The carpenter and the carriage-wright can give a man a set square or compass, but they cannot make him skilful."

(7B.5)

6.46 ON HISTORY BOOKS AND THE INFLUENCE OF HISTORY

Mencius said, "Rather than believe all that we read in the *Book of Documents*, it were better that there were no *Book of Documents*. From the chapter 'Wu Ch'eng,'[49] for example, I have abstracted two or three exemplary passages, but no more. Though the man of Humanity is never opposed, the 'Wu Ch'eng' describes the most Humane [King

---

[47] *Songs*, 301 (see Karlgren, *Odes*, 254).   [48] Cf. 2.1 and 2.16.
[49] See Legge, V.iii.9.

Wu] attacking the most Inhumane [Chieh the Tyrant] and says that 'the blood flowed till the pestles were afloat in the mortars.' How *could* that be?"

(7B.3)

6.47

Mencius said, "The *Spring and Autumn Annals* have no examples of 'just wars,' though they do contain examples of some wars better justified than others. The word *cheng*, 'a punitive expedition' [which occurs in the *Annals*], properly speaking, refers to one in authority attacking one under his jurisdiction. States of equal rank cannot properly *cheng* each other."

(7B.2)

6.48

Mencius said, "When the manifestations of True Kingship were seen no more, the *Songs* were composed. When songs were composed no more, then spring and autumn annals were compiled. The *Ch'eng* of the State of Tsin. the *T'ao Wu* of the State of Ch'u, and the *Ch'un Ch'iu* of the State of Lu are works of this kind. They are concerned with the affairs of Huan of Ch'i and Wen of Tsin,[50] and they are written in the annalistic style. Confucius said, 'Their just purport, though I say so myself, I deduced.' "[51]

(4B.21)

6.49

Mencius said, "A little more than five hundred years passed from the times of Yao and Shun until the times of T'ang the Successful. Men like Yü the Great and Kao Yao knew Yao and Shun at first hand, but T'ang knew them only by hearsay. A little more than five hundred years elapsed from the times of T'ang until King Wen. Men like Yi Yin and Lai Chu knew T'ang at first hand, but King Wen knew him only by hearsay. A little more than five hundred years elapsed from King Wen

[50] See Introduction to 6.70.   [51] See Additional Notes.

to Confucius. Men like T'ai-kung Wang and San Yi-sheng knew King Wen at first hand, but Confucius knew him only by hearsay. A little over a hundred years have elapsed from the time of Confucius until the present. Today we are not so far removed from the times of the Sage, and, more seriously, are close by the place where he lived. But there is no Sage! Is there not to be one?"

(7B.38)

6.50

The fructifying influence of a True Gentleman ends after the lapse of five generations. That of a lesser man ends, too, after five generations. I could never have been a pupil of Confucius in person; even so, though I say so myself, I have gleaned his teachings from others.

(4B.22)

6.51

A Sage is the teacher of a hundred generations—such men, for example, as Po Yi[52] and Liu-hsia Hui[53]. And so, when the story of Po Yi is told, the dull man becomes reasonable, and the weak man strengthens his resolve. When the story of Liu-hsia Hui is told, the mean man becomes open-hearted, and the boorish man becomes generous.

Inspiring they were a hundred generations ago; a hundred generations later, no man hearing of them but is similarly aroused. Could this be so of one who was not a Sage? And how much more inspiring it must have been to those who knew them intimately.

(7B.15)

The "Confucius of the Analects," as Mr Waley has pointed out[54] saw in the founders and expanders of the Chou Dynasty the culmination and climax of the glories of the classical age. Confucius' hero was the Duke of Chou. For Confucius the preceding dynasties of Hsia and Shang are shadowy eras, and the Divine Sages he barely mentions. By Mencius' time, less than two centuries after Confucius, the picture of antiquity had changed considerably. For one thing it stretched back further in time. The Divine Sages—for Confucius, demi-gods—are completely "historicized" and secularized. "Any man might become a Yao or a Shun."[55] Antiquity, too, is much more heavily populated. The "Emperors" now have ministers, and many new names appear. They

---

[52] See 3.29.   [53] See 6.64.   [54] *Analects*, Introduction, p. 13.   [55] See 3.47 and cf. 2.5.

provide the Confucian calendar of saints and sinners with a number of new exemplars. Much "research," too, has been undertaken into the society of antiquity. Mencius speaks confidently of its fiscal system and its laws,[56] whereas in Confucius' time the Master doubted whether even Shang culture could really be reconstructed on the evidence supplied by Sung, in which it was then popularly supposed to have been preserved.[57]

Two hundred years after Mencius, historical studies had developed further. The father of Chinese history, Szu-ma Ch'ien, speaks of Five Emperors and Three Dynasties. These form the foundations of Chinese "traditional history." From such sources much of the traditional dating has been evolved.

Today Chinese history begins on the firm ground of evidence with the Shang Dynasty, about which, thanks to the momentous excavations at Anyang and elsewhere, far more is known than classical historians dreamed possible. Prior to Shang, modern scholars speak of the Late and Early Neolithic, basing their periodization upon stratification rather than upon the rationalizations of legend of traditional history.

But in the Mencian view, it is the times of Yao and Shun that represents antiquity at its zenith, and Mencius characterizes his teaching as "the Way of Yao and Shun."[58]

This is how the period of the Sages looked to Mencius:

THE SAGE KINGS

Kings	Worthy Ministers	Cautionary Figures
Yao	Shun	
(two daughters, 3.17)	(to whom Yao offered the throne)	Yao's nine sons (3.17)
		Tan Chu, a son (3.8)
Shun	Yü	Ku-sou (Shun's father)
(married Yao's	(to whom Yao offered the	Hsiang (Shun's brother,
two daughters, 3.11)	throne)	3.8, 3.9)
	Hsieh, Minister of the	The "sons of Shun"
	People (4.14)	Kung-kung
	Kao Yao, Minister of	Huan T'ou
	Justice (3.40)	The Prince of San Miao
Yü the Great	Yi (Premier, and Yü's	K'un (Yü's father, 5.3)
Ch'i (his son and	nominee for the Throne, 3.8)	
successor, 3.8)		

[56] See, e.g., 3.44.   [57] See *Analects*, 3.9.

[58] See 1.27, 2.1, 3.7, 3.20, etc. In 4.14 earlier Confucianism is referred to as "the Way of the Duke of Chou and of Confucius." Though important for Confucius, the Duke of Chou is for Mencius a lesser figure. The Way, for him, is pre-eminently "the Way of Yao and Shun."

And this is how the Three Dynasties looked to Mencius:

THE THREE DYNASTIES

	Good Kings	Bad Kings	Exemplary Figures
HSIA	Yü the Great Ch'i (his son)	Chieh the Tyrant	

SHANG
(c. 16th-11th
cent.)
	T'ang the Successful
	T'ai-ting ⎰
	   Wai Ping (succeeds
	   ⎱ T'ang)
	   Chung Jen
	T'ai Chia (3.34, 3.38)
	"Six or seven Worthy
	    Kings"
	
	Wu Ting
			Yi Yin (T'ang's tutor,
			later his premier)
			
			Lai Chu (6.49)

		Chou the Tyrant	Lord of Wei (step- brother), Pi Kan and Lord of Chi (uncles to Chou) Po Yi Chiao Chi (minister who defected to the Chou House, 6.61, 3.28) T'ai-kung Wang (3.28)
WESTERN CHOU (c. 11th cent. to c. 8th cent.)	King Wu		Duke of Chou (enfeoffed with Lu) T'ai-Kung Wang (en- feoffed with Ch'i)
		Yu the Dark Li the Cruel (6.43, 4.11)	

Before their accession, the House of Chou, as it appears in *Mencius*, looked like this:

Legendary Ancestors

The Lord of Millet (Hou Chi)
Liu the Duke (1.14)
> *Posthumously dignified as "kings"*
"King" T'ai (Ku-kung T'an-fu)

(Wang Chi)

"King" Wen (Lord of the West)

King Wu (first Son of Heaven)   Duke of Chou (brother and minister)

6.52

Mencius said, "Shun alone was the sort of person who could regard the spectacle of the entire world turning with delight in allegiance to him as a mere tuft of grass.[59] But, even so, he could not bring himself to think of himself as a man, because he had not the approval of his parents, or to think of himself as a son, because he could not comply with his parents' wishes. It was because Shun observed the principles of duty to parents in their entirety that his father, Ku-sou, was, in the end, contented, and, with Ku-sou contented, the whole world was led to change. With Ku-sou contented, everywhere the duties of father and son were firmly established. This is an example of filial duty at its finest."

(4A.28)

6.53

Mencius said, "When Shun was living far in the hills, among the woods and rocks, the wild deer and the boar were his travelling companions. There was very little to distinguish him from the mountain country folk, until he heard a good word or beheld a good deed. Then he was like the great rivers bursting their banks; like a great flood, nothing could stop him."

(7A.16)

6.54

Mencius said, "He who, rising at cock-crow, exerts every effort to be

[59] A thing of no account.

M

good is a disciple of Shun. He who, rising at cock-crow, exerts every effort in the pursuit of gain is a disciple of the brigand Ch'ih.[60] If you wish to know what separates Shun from the brigand Ch'ih, it is no other than this: it is the margin that lies between making profits and being good."

(7A.25)

6.55

Mencius said, "When Shun was living on wild herbs[61] he behaved as though he would continue to do so all his life. But when he became Son of Heaven and was dressed in rich robes, played the lute and had the two daughters [of his predecessor Yao, to attend him], he behaved as though he had always had these things."

(7B.6)

6.56

Mencius said, "Shun was born in Chu-feng, but moved to Fu-hsia, and died in Ming-t'iao. He was a member of the eastern Yi tribe. King Wen was born in Chou, by Mount Ch'i, and died in Pi-ying. He was a member of the western Yi tribe. Shun and King Wen were separated in space by more than a thousand miles, and in time by more than a thousand years, but the aspirations they realized in the central states were as complementary as the two parts of a contract-tally.[62] The Sages from first to last observed identical principles."

(4B.1)

6.57

In Yao and Shun it was inherent; in T'ang and Wu it was self-cultivated; but in the Paramount Princes it was merely borrowed. But since it was borrowed for so long and never returned, how were men to know that it[63] was not theirs?

(7A.30)

---

[60] See Introduction to 6.78.
[62] See Additional Notes.
[61] I.e., in dire poverty.
[63] See Additional Notes.

6.58

Mencius said, "In Yao and Shun it was inherent; T'ang and Wu returned to it.

"When every movement, every gesture, is governed by the precise Rite, this is the acme of virtue in all its richness. The wailing at the lament for the dead must not be for the benefit of the living. The pursuit of the path of virtue without deviation must not be for the sake of the emoluments. A man must tell the truth, but not merely as a matter of conventional rectitude. A True Gentleman carries out the law, waiting upon the Will of Heaven."[64]

. (7B.33)

6.59

Mencius said, "Yü the Great disliked good wine, but liked good talk. T'ang the Successful held fast to the middle way, employing worthy men no matter where they came from. King Wen regarded his people as one attends a wounded man. He looked expectantly towards the Way, though he was not to see it realized.[65] King Wu was neither negligent of those who were near, nor forgetful of those far off. The Duke of Chou longed to unite in his person the virtues of these three kings, so that there might be seen in his life the four duties they exemplified. When he did not match up to them, he looked up, pondering the matter. He continued throughout the night. If favoured with an answer to his problem, he remained seated awaiting the sunrise."

(4B.20)

6.60

Mencius said, "Tzu-lu[66] was pleased when anyone told him of his faults. Yü the Great bowed on hearing something well said. The great Shun went further still. On observing excellence in others, he emulated it; forsaking his own way, he followed the good in others. He took

---

[64] I.e., the virtue of the rite lies in the attitude of the performer and not in its performance; cf. 6.13.

[65] It was his son, King Wu, who was to see the Way realized when the Chou House became Sons of Heaven.

[66] A disciple of Confucius.

pleasure in taking his example from what he thought to be good in others. From his early life when he ploughed and sowed, made pots and fished, until the time when he became Emperor, there was nothing that he had not learned from others. Therefore there is, for the Princely Man, nothing greater than to become good in concert with his fellows."

(2A.8)

6.61

Mencius said, "Shun rose to high office from the irrigated fields, Fu Yüeh was summoned from among his planks and mud-pounding,[67] Chiao Chi from among his salt and fish,[68] Kuan Yi-wu from the hands of the law officer,[69] Sun-shu Ao from his retreat on the coast,[70] and Po-li Hsi from the market place.[71] Thus it is that, when Heaven is about to confer high office on a man, it first exercises his mind with suffering and flexes his muscles with toil. It inures his body to hunger and his person to poverty. It frustrates him in his undertakings so that his mind is stimulated, his nature toughened to endure, and he develops capabilities he lacked.

"All men err, but can afterwards change their ways. They are straitened in mind, buffeted in spirit, but later may rise up again. It is evident in their looks, revealed in their words, and later results in understanding.

"And so it is with the state. If there are no model families and wise counsellors within the state, and no hostile states and troubles abroad, then the state will perish.

"So we learn that what is begotten in sadness and sorrow draws to its end in peace and happiness."

(6B.15)

6.62

Duke Ching of Ch'i[72] said, "He who can neither give orders nor take orders is a man to be set aside as of no account." Tears came into his eyes as he gave his daughter in marriage to the Prince of Wu.[73] Today

---

[67] He was a builder.   [68] He began life as a fisherman and became Minister of Chou, see 3.28.
[69] I.e., Kuan Chung; see Introduction to 6.70.
[70] He became Premier of the Duke Chuang of Ch'u, one of the Paramount Princes; see introduction to 6.70.
[71] Po-li Hsi was in the service of Duke Mu of Ch'in and is one of Mencius' exemplary statesmen; see 3.14 and 4.18.   [72] See Additional Notes, 1.2, note 17.
[73] The people of Wu were thought barbarous by their more northerly neighbours, and this marriage was contracted under duress.

the minor states model themselves on the major states and scorn to take orders from them. This is like a pupil scorning to take orders from his tutor. Rather than scorn such orders, it were better that they modelled themselves on King Wen. Any major state which modelled itself on him for five years, or a minor state for seven years, inevitably would command the allegiance of the whole world. The *Book of Songs*[74] says:

> The descendants of the House of Shang
> Are numbered in the hundreds of thousands,
> But God most High has already ordained
> That they pay allegiance to Chou.

> They pay allegiance to Chou.
> Heaven's charge is not held in perpetuity.
> The knights of Shang are most adept,
> Pouring the libations in the capital of Chou.

Confucius said, 'Humanity can never be an attribute of all men, but if the prince loves Humanity, no one in the world will oppose him.' Today there are those who hope that no one in the world will oppose them, but lacking Humanity they are like a man who seizes something hot without first wetting his hands. The *Book of Songs* says:[75]

> Who can hold a heated thing
> Without first wetting his hands?

(4A.8)

6.63

The common people await a King Wen before they bestir themselves. but the knight of distinction bestirs himself without a King Wen.

(7A.10)

The Exemplary Ministers

YI YIN, PO YI, LIU-HSIA HUI, AND THE T'AI-KUNG

6.64

Mencius said, "Po Yi kept his eyes and ears from evil sights and sounds, He would neither serve a prince nor give orders to a people of whom he

---

[74] *Songs*, 241.   [75] *Songs*, 302 (see Karlgren, *Odes*, 257).

did not approve. Under good government he took office; under bad government he resigned. He could not bear to live in the vicinity of a perverse court or of a perverse people, though he took the view that to be among villagers was like sitting in Court dress upon a pile of mud and ashes.[76] Under the regime of the tyrant Chou he went to live on the shores of the North Sea, waiting for the day when the world would be clean again. Thus it is that today, on hearing the story of Po-yi, the dull man becomes reasonable, and the weak man strengthens his resolve.

"Yi Yin, on the other hand, said, 'Why should I not serve a prince or give orders to a people of whom I do not approve?' He took office under governments good or bad. He said, 'In creating the people Heaven ordained that those who have knowledge should teach those who have not knowledge yet, that those who understand should teach those who do not understand yet. I am one of Heaven's creatures who have such understanding, and I am going to teach those who have not, in accordance with this principle.' He took upon himself the heavy responsibility of mankind, feeling that if the beneficence of Yao or Shun did not reach to the lowest man or women, it was as though he personally had pushed them into a ditch.

"Liu-hsia Hui[77] thought it no disgrace to serve a corrupt prince, neither did he decline a minor post. On taking office he did not try to hide his worthiness, but invariably carried out his office according to his principles. If dismissed he showed no resentment. In poverty he did not pity himself. Living among villagers he was at ease, behaving as though he was loath to leave them. His principle was, 'You are you, and I am I. You may stand by my side stark naked but you can never defile me.' Thus it is that today, on hearing the story of Liu-hsia Hui, the boorish man becomes open-hearted, and the mean man generous.

"When Confucius was leaving the State of Ch'i, he set off while the rice was still being rinsed.[78] When he was leaving the State of Lu he said, 'I shall be leaving by and by.[79] This is the proper way to leave

---

[76] For a courtier, life among peasants was distasteful, yet despite this he would not attend a corrupt court; cf. 6.67.

[77] Liu-hsia Hui (seventh century) was a statesman of Lu, proverbial for probity (*Analects* 18.2; cf. 15.13 and 18.8). With Po Yi and Yi Yin he forms a trinity of just men in a corrupt age (see 4.18 and 6.67).

[78] "While the rice was still being rinsed" means that he left without waiting for it to be cooked The meal was ordered but, such was his haste, he left before it was ready to serve.

[79] He dallied, as if loath to go.

the state in which one's parents were born. Confucius was the sort of person who, when the occasion called for a quick departure or for a delayed one, when the occasion called for entering office or retiring from office, did so."

Mencius said, "Po Yi was the pure one among the Sages, Yi Yin was the official *par excellence* among the Sages, Liu-hsia Hui was the reconciler *par excellence* among the Sages, but Confucius alone was the one among the Sages with a sense of the appropriateness of the occasion. In Confucius we have what we would call the quintessence of harmony. The quintessence of harmony is when the bronze and the jade instruments are in perfect accord. The bronze instruments begin the theme, and the jade instruments complete it. And so it is the duty of wisdom to begin the theme, and the duty of sageliness to complete it. Wisdom is like the virtuosity of a musician, and sageliness the strength he reveals in performance. It is like an archer, aiming at targets beyond the hundred paces. The arrow finding its mark is a matter of his strength, but its striking the bull's-eye is not so much a matter of his strength, but of his skill."

(5B.1)

6.65

Mencius said, "To avoid the tyrant Chou,[80] Po Yi[81] had gone to live on the North Sea coast, but hearing of the rise of King Wen he bestirred himself saying, 'I surely should return! For I have heard that the Lord of the West [i.e., King Wen] delights in taking care of the aged.' To avoid the tyrant Chou the T'ai-kung had gone to live on the coast of the Eastern Sea,[82] but hearing of the rise of King Wen he bestirred himself saying, 'I should surely return! For I have heard that the Lord of the West delights in taking care of the aged.' These two men were among the most distinguished of the elderly men of their day, yet they returned (to the capital). It was a matter of the world's fathers turning in allegiance (to King Wen), and, since the fathers paid him allegiance, to whom could the sons pay allegiance (but to King Wen)? If any of the princes were to put into effect the policies of King Wen, within a period of seven years they would inevitably become rulers of the world."

(4A.14)

---

[80] See 6.69.   [81] See 3.29.   [82] For this he was awarded the fief of Ch'i; see 4.5.

6.66

Po Yi was living on the shores of the North Sea avoiding the Tyrant Chou. Hearing of the rise of King Wen, he said elatedly, "Now surely is the time to go back! I have heard that the Lord of the West is adept at the proper care of the aged." The T'ai-kung was living on the shores of the Eastern Sea for the same reason, and his reaction was the same as that of Po Yi. If today there were a prince who was adept at the proper care of the aged, then men of Humanity everywhere would feel that they personally must go to him.

Let the five-acre homesteads plant mulberry trees along the walls, and let their womenfolk rear silkworms on them, and then the aged might have silk to wear. Five laying hens and two brood sows (if no impost of labour is made during the breeding seasons) would ensure that the elderly did not go without meat. On the hundred-acre farms let the peasants till them (and not be called away for corvée duty), and then whole households need not starve. When it is said that the "Lord of the West was adept at caring for the aged" it refers to the control he exercised over the villages and fields, teaching the villagers to plant mulberry trees, training their wives, enabling them to care for their elderly. One cannot keep warm at fifty without silk, or feel replete at seventy without meat. When they are neither warm nor well fed, they freeze or starve to death. Among the common people in King Wen's time, there were no aged people who starved or froze to death.

(7A.22)

6.67

Mencius said, "Po Yi would not serve under a prince of whom he did not approve, or make friends contrary to his principle of making friends. He would neither take his place in an evil man's Court, nor even speak with such a man. To do so, for him, would have been like squatting in dust and ashes in his Court robes and cap. This feeling which he had of hatred for evil was such that, if he were standing with a villager whose cap was not properly adjusted, he would look straight through him, bidding him begone, as though he were besmirched by his presence. Thus it was that though summoned with fair words by a Feudal Lord, he would decline the summons. He declined it because he felt it would defile him to accept.

"Liu-hsia Hui thought it no disgrace to serve a corrupt prince; neither did he think it bemeaning to serve in a minor post. On taking office he did not try to hide his worthiness, but invariably carried out his office according to his principles. If dismissed he showed no resentment; in poverty he did not pity himself. And so it was that he said, 'You are you, and I am I. You may stand at my side stark naked, but you can never defile me.' Therefore, he associated with others with perfect ease, but never lost his integrity in the process. On wishing to hand in his resignation, if pressed to stay, he would stay. He did so because he felt it would defile him to go."

Mencius said, "Po Yi was perhaps over-scrupulous, Liu-hsia Hui a little contemptuous of his fellow men. Over-scrupulousness and contempt are not things a gentleman should emulate."

(2A.9)

6.68

Mencius said, "Liu-hsia Hui would not be turned from his purposes for the three most senior offices of state."[83]

(7A.28)

The Evil Kings

Chieh, the last of the Hsia line, and Chou, the last of the Shang line, whose names are often coupled together, are ominous figures in Confucian thought. They are the prototypes of the king whose virtue has run out, and from whose house Heaven is to withdraw its Mandate to govern. Growing legend furnishes ever-increasing depth and detail to the enormities of Chieh and Chou.[84] They are to provide, in the "mirror for princes,"[85] a warning for evilly disposed monarchs. A Chieh or a Chou may legitimately be slain and supplanted.[86] The Mandate of Heaven tempers the principle of hereditary succession in Chinese history, since kingship, though hereditary, is always subject to Heaven's approval, and the rise of a Chieh or a Chou[87] gives sanction to revolt and lends legitimacy to a change of line.

[83] Cf. *Analects*, 18.2.   [84] See Waley, *The Way and its Power*, p. 126.

[85] Later, a favourite epithet for "history."

[86] See 1.1. and 3.8. In 6.43 and 4.11 there is a suggestion that the House of Chou, too, had its Chieh and Chou in King Li and King Yü.

[87] Chieh and Chou, like Maverick and Quisling, give their language a new word; see 3.44, 3.47 and 5.3.

6.69

Mencius said, "When Chieh and Chou lost the Empire, they lost the people. And by 'losing the people' I mean 'losing their sympathy'. There is a way to gain the Empire. It is to gain the people, and having gained them one gains the Empire. There is a way to gain the people. Gain their sympathy, and then you gain them. There is a way to gain their sympathy. Share with them the accumulation of the things you wish for, and do not impose upon them the things you yourself dislike.

"The people turn in allegiance to Humanity, as surely as water flows downwards or as a wild animal takes cover in the wilderness. Just as the otter drives fish into the deep pools, and the hawk chases small birds into the dense covert, so did the tyrants Chieh and Chou drive the people into the arms of T'ang and King Wu. If today, there were among the princes one who loved Humanity, the present Feudatory would, as it were, be his 'drivers.' However little such a prince may wish to become the Ideal King, he would have no choice. Those today who aspire to become the Ideal King are rather like the prescribing of a three-year-old herb for an ailment already seven years gone. If the herb is not in stock, the patient may not live long enough to get it. If such princes have not determined upon Humanity, they may continue for the rest of their lives in sorrow and shame, and be overtaken by death (before their Humanity matures).[88] The *Book of Songs*[89] says,

> What can be the good of it?
> You will, all of you, be overwhelmed.

This has reference to these things."

(4A.10)

The Paramount Princes

The Chou Dynasty, under which Mencius lived, and which had begun so propitiously with the model King Wen and King Wu, had in his day reached its nadir. Since the eighth century the royal house had been a cipher. Real power reposed with the Feudal Princes whose city-states were virtually autonomous. In a loose confederacy some centuries before, a powerful prince among them had been chosen as Paramount Prince and under the system of the Paramountcy some states such as Ch'i and Tsin had been very rich and powerful.

[88] Just as a prescription that takes three years to prepare is useless for a patient in a critical condition, so, too, the times are too critical to await a prince who needs years before his "Humanity" matures.   [89] *Songs*, 302 (see Karlgren, *Odes*, 257).

It was the memory of this, their more recent history, that excited the princes of Mencius' day. They sought for ministers like Tzu-ch'an of Cheng[90] *and Kuan Chung and Yen Ying of Ch'i,*[91] *whose names were already proverbial in the popular mind, to regain for them the Paramountcy. And not only the princes. Even Mencius' followers wondered if their master's political programme was likely to produce "results such as those once obtained by Kuan Chung."*[92] *But the Paramountcy and its ministers were, to Mencius, reprehensible. It was the "way of Force" and diametrically opposed to the "Way of the Former Kings."*[93] *It was illegitimate. It was sovereignty "merely borrowed"*[94] *and not Heaven-ordained. The Paramount Princes was a subject about which it was best not to speak (1.5). Under the Paramountcy the people may have "seemed happy" (in the popular mind it was a time of prosperity), but they did not "turn to the good."*[95] *With the popular heroes of the more immediate past, Mencius contrasts men like Liu-hsia Hui, the statesman who would not be defiled, and Po-li Hsi, the "most wise," and expresses great indignation when he himself is compared to Kuan Chung, to whose behaviour Mencius says "he would not stoop."*[96] *This is recent history as it concerns Mencius:*

	Princes and Ministers		Good men in evil times
7th cent.	Duke Wen of Tsin*		
	Duke Huan of Ch'i*	Kuan Chung (Premier)	
	Duke Mu of Ch'in*		Po-li Hsi (Premier)
			Liu-hsia Hui of Lu
6th cent.	Duke P'ing of Tsin (r. 556-531)	Hai T'ang (Premier)	
		Tzu Ch'an of Cheng (d. 522)	
	Duke Ching of Ch'i (r. 547-490)	Yen Tzu (Premier) (d. 505)	
	Duke Ling of Wei (r. 534-493)		
5th cent.		Meng Hsien Tzu† (d. 554)	
		Chi Huan Tzu† (d. 492)	Confucius
		Chi K'ang Tzu† (d. 461)	(551-479) and his circle
	Duke Hsiao (Ch'u) of Wei (r. 492-481)	Yang Hu (dictator of Lu, (fl.505)	
	Kou-chien, King of Yüeh (r. 496-465)		
	Duke Mu of Lu (415-383)		Tzu-szu (483-402) and his circle

* Paramount Princes.   † Oligarchs in Lu.

[90] See 6.72.   [91] See 1.2.   [92] See 3.28, also 3.29 and 3.38.   [93] See 6.7.
[94] See 6.57.   [95] See 6.71.   [96] See 2.1 and cf. 3.28.

6.70

Mencius said, "The five Paramount Princes offended against the Three Founding Kings. The Feudatory today offend against the Paramount Princes. The nobles today offend against the Feudatory.

"When the Son of Heaven visited a Feudal Lord it was called *hsün-shou*. A Feudal Lord's visit to the Court was called *shu-chih*. In spring, the sowings came under review so that the shortages (of seed) might be made good, and in the autumn the harvest was inspected so that help might be sent where the yield was deficient.[97] Upon entering a state, when the ground was being brought under cultivation and the fields were well kept, when the aged were looked after and the worthy honoured, and if men of distinction filled its offices, then the Emperor would offer congratulations and mark this with a gift of land. But if, upon entering a state, the land was let run wild, the aged neglected, worthy men passed by, if extortioners held office, then the Emperor would issue a reprimand. One failure to attend at Court meant a loss of title, two failures a loss of territory, three failures and a Feudal Lord was removed from his tenure by the Six Armies.[98] Thus it was that the Emperor passed sentence, but did not engage in the attack himself. The Feudal Lords engaged in the attack,[99] but did not themselves pass sentence.

"The Paramount Princes, however, forced one Feudal Lord to attack another. That is why I say the Paramount Princes offended against the Three Kings.[100]

"Duke Huan of Ch'i was the most powerful of the five Paramount Princes. At the meeting of the Princes at K'uei-ch'iu,[101] the sacrificial animal was bound and the documents attached to it, but the blood-smearing ceremony was not carried out.[102] The first article of the covenant read, 'We will put the unfilial to death, but will not allow an heir-apparent to be displaced. We will not recognize a concubine as a rightful wife.' The second article read, 'We will honour worthy men and cultivate the talented, so that recognition will be given to the man of

---

[97] Cf. 1.2.   [98] The Imperial forces.

[99] It was their feudal duty to provide chariots and men for such attacks.

[100] By arrogating to themselves the Kings' prerogatives.

[101] In 650 B.C.; see *Tso Chuan*, Duke Hsi, 9.

[102] Solemn agreements were ratified by burying copies of the documents with a sacrificial animal, the blood of which was smeared on the mouths of representatives of each of the contracting parties.

virtue.' The third article read, 'We will treat the elderly with respect, and the young and tender with kindness. We will not be negligent of visitors or travellers.' The fourth article read, 'Knights will not be given office hereditarily, nor will we allow plurality in office. In filling offices we will seek the right man. No prince has authority to put a noble to death.' The fifth article read, 'There will be no sharp practice in the matter of land boundaries or restrictions on the sale of grain; there will be no feudal tenure given without prior notification!' The covenant then continued, 'All we who thus covenant together, having made this solemn covenant, declare that we return to our states in amity.'

"Now the Feudatory today contravene every article of this agreement. And so I say the Feudal Lords offend against the five Paramount Princes. He who perpetuates his prince's crimes commits the lesser offence, but he who takes the initiative in his prince's crimes commits the greater offence. The nobles today take the initiative in their prince's crimes. Therefore I say, 'The nobles today offend against the Feudal Lords.'"

(6B.7)

6.71

Mencius said, "Under the Paramount Princes the people seemed happy, but under a True King they seem unmoved. Though he slay them they bear him no resentment. Though he benefit them, he takes no credit for doing so. Daily the people turn to the good, though they do not know what makes them do so. Wherever the True Gentleman visits, a change ensues; whatever he cherishes becomes spirit-fraught; all high and low and Heaven and earth are in harmonious flow. How can it be said that such a man 'helps things but slightly?'"[103]

(7A.13)

6.72

After Tzu-ch'an[104] had obeyed the call to take charge of the government of Cheng, he continued to offer a ride in his carriage to those

[103] See Additional Notes.

[104] The noted Premier of Cheng, who died in 522 B.C. He occurs also in *Analects*, 14.10 and 5.15. Confucian circles regard him as an equivocal figure. But the *Tso Chuan* makes clear that he was a statesman of stature.

wishing to ford the Tsin and Wei. Mencius said, "It was kindly of him, but it showed a misconception of the duties of a prime minister. Each year, in the eleventh month the foot-bridges and in the twelfth month the bridges for carriages should be repaired. Then the people would not be put to the inconvenience of wading across rivers (in winter). Let the ruler do all that he should, and then, when he travels abroad, he may properly expect men to step out of his path. What time would he then have to ferry any and every man across rivers? For in the practice of government the days are too short to please everyone."

(4B.2)

Confucius and His Circle

Mencius said that if he had had his wish, it would have been to have studied under Confucius.[105] *But "the fructifying influence of a True Gentleman ends after the lapse of five generations" and, continues Mencius, "I have gleaned his teachings from others.*[106] *Mencius lived well over a hundred years after the death of Confucius.*[107] *In the intervening five generations the teachings of the Master had undergone considerable development in the hands of his followers. So, too, had notions about the person of Confucius himself. His legend had begun to grow. Stories were circulating about Confucius that obviously bear the marks of hagiology or of spiteful gossip. Already to Mencius, Confucius was a Sage, a word that in Confucius' lifetime was reserved for remote deities of the past. And further, he was the Sage "far more worthy than Yao or Shun," the Sage that "stood out and rose above" the rest. "There has never been another like our Master since man first appeared on the earth."*[108] *Confucius was already well on the way to apotheosis.*

And, too, legend is beginning to provide Confucius with a career of worldly success of which no hint is given in the early Analects.[109] *For Mencius he has become the Minister of Justice in Lu*[110] *and has held office under two princes in the State of Wei.*[111] *And in the realm of the "might have been" Mencius says that, but for a technical hitch, Confucius would have been Son of Heaven.*[112] *Thus Confucius became for posterity "the king they never crowned."*

After Confucius' death at least two of his disciples set up "schools" of their

[105] 3.29.   [106] 6.50.   [107] 6.49.   [108] 3.29.   [109] See Waley, *Analects*, Introduction, p. 13.
[110] 4.18.   [111] 3.19.   [112] 3.8.

own. Of these Tseng Tzu figures most prominently in Mencius. *Tseng Tzu (c. 505-436 B.C.) was Confucius' most important disciple. Two stories of his filial piety, for which he and his school later became proverbial, are preserved in* Mencius.[113] *There is a hint of subsequent rivalry between the schools of the disciples of Confucius,[114] and Mencius depicts Tseng Tzu in the better light, thus suggesting that Mencius' own teachers were in the Tseng Tzu tradition.[115] This is certainly true in the case of Kung-ming Yi and Kung-ming kao, both pupils of Tseng Tzu. Mencius several times quotes from a collection of their sayings.[116]*

Of the latter-day Confucians, Mencius is our only source for a cycle of stories about Tzu-szu (c. 483-402 B.C.), the grandson of Confucius. Mencius makes him a sort of model tutor to princes, and he exemplifies Mencius' ideal of the minister-teacher of 2.1. He is the man whom princes "would not take the liberty of summoning" and whom a prince, "if he has a matter to discuss, will call and see." Duke Hui of P'i acknowledges Tzu-szu as his "teacher,"[117] and Duke Mu of Lu (c. 415-383 B.C.) treats him with great deference,[118] even offending in his eagerness to obtain Tzu-szu's favours. For this side of Duke Mu's character Mencius *is our only source.*

How did Mencius know all this? Certainly in part from the oral tradition passed from master to pupil. This is the "I have heard it said" of, for example, 1.29 and 2.3. Not that all that was said was received uncritically. In 3.41 and 3.6, sayings are repeated to Mencius by his pupils with the question "Is this true?" On these occasions Mencius points out that the sources—a village pedant or gossip-mongers—are untrustworthy, for, if what is alleged about Confucius in such sayings were true, "would he still be Confucius?" But, too, Mencius has written sources. He quotes a Record.[119] *He quotes recognizably from the work we now know as the* Analects.[120] *But a new* Analects *could be compiled from* Mencius *from material there which does not occur in the present* Analects.[121]

In at least one particular, a misreading of Mencius *has added to legend, the legend that Confucius composed the state annals of Lu. Mencius says he "worked on," that is, studied them, and "deduced their just import."*

---

[113] See 6.13 and 3.27.

[114] I.e., between that of Tzu-hsia and Tseng Tzu; see 3.29 and 4.14.

[115] The contrast between the "knight of the way" and the "knight of fashion" (see 3.29), which Mencius develops, has a foreshadowing in a remark of Tseng Tzu's. See *Analects*, 8.7.

[116] See 1.27.   [117] 3.13.   [118] See 2.15, 3.17, and 3.18.

[119] See 3.48.   [120] See, for example, 1.28, 3.20, 3.29, 4.14, 5.5, 6.5, 6.99.

[121] From such passages as 1.23, 3.3, 3.6, 3.8, 3.10, 3.18, 3.19, 3.20, 3.21, 3.28, 3.29, 3.38, 3.48, 4.11, 4.18, 5.13, 6.6, 6.7, 6.20, 6.43, 6.48, 6.62, 6.64, 6.73, 6.74, 6.75.

6.73

Hsü–tzu said, "Confucius frequently spoke about water with admiration. He said, 'Water! Ah Water! What can we learn from water?'" Mencius said, "The fountain rumbles forth ceasing neither day nor night, filling first its basin, and then flowing on until it is lost in the seas! The fountain is like those whose roots are deeply set—it was this lesson that Confucius drew from it. Where there is no spring, where, in the seventh and eighth months in the season of rain, the dikes fill up, they dry out again almost before one's eyes. So it is with the True Gentleman. He would be ashamed of a reputation that exceeded his deserts."

(4B.18)

6.74

Mencius said, "On climbing the eastern hill, the City of Lu looked small to Confucius. When he climbed Mount T'ai the whole world looked small to him. So it is that he who has looked upon the sea finds it difficult to think of any other waters. He who has travelled to the gate of a Sage finds it difficult to think of anyone else's sayings. There is an art in looking at water. One must look at the ripples of the waves. If the sun or the moon is shining, their form and light are reflected in them. Water is the sort of thing that does not flow on until every indentation is filled. The gentlemen whose mind is set upon the Way perfects one pattern before proceeding to the next."

(7A.24)

6.75

When Confucius was leaving the State of Lu he said, "I shall be leaving shortly." This is the way that one should leave the state in which one's parents were born. When he left Ch'i he set off while the rice was still being rinsed. This is the way to leave a state other than one's own.[122]

(7B.17)

6.76

Mencius said, "The reason that the True Gentleman [i.e., Confucius]

[122] A doublet; see 6.64.

was in dire straits in Ch'en and Ts'ai was because he was out of touch
with the ruling classes there."[123]

(7B.18)

6.77

When Tseng Tzu was living at Wu-ch'eng, it was raided by some
bandits from Yüeh. Some said, "Bandits are coming; should we not
leave?" Whereupon Tseng Tzu fled. He left instructions with his
servant, saying, "Let no man lodge in my house for fear that he break
or damage my plants. When the bandits withdraw have the walls
repaired, for I shall be coming back." The bandits withdrew, and Tseng
Tzu returned to his house. His followers said, "We have treated you,
Master, with such loyalty and respect, yet when the bandits came you
were the first to flee and you did so in full sight of the common people.
Only after the bandits had withdrawn did you return. Surely that was
not proper?"

Shen-you Hsing said (to the followers), "This is something you do not
understand. Formerly when Shen-you was involved in the troubles
of Fu Ch'u some seventy men followed their Master. None was involved in the troubles. When Tzu-szu lived in Wei, bandits raided it
from Ch'i, and some said, 'Bandits are coming; should we not leave?'
Tzu-szu said, 'If I go, who will stay with the Ruler to guard the state?' "

Mencius said, "Tseng Tzu and Tzu-szu pursued identical paths.
Tseng Tzu was a teacher, a father or elder brother as it were. Tzu-szu
was a state servant, albeit a minor one. Had their circumstances been
reversed they would have acted no differently."

(4B.31)

Paragons and Proverbial Figures

*Mencius and his circle, in admitting Yao, Shun, and Yü from among the cult-
heroes of the day to their list of historical sovereigns of antiquity, are disregarding others. There was Shen Nung, the "god of Agriculture," for example,
who is preferred as the exemplar of antiquity by the Agronomists. This pre-
ference may reflect the local nature of myth-cycles but it does not do so entirely.
Yi the Archer and Li Lou of the sharp eyes occur in Mencius as names that*

---

[123] Cf. *Analects*, 11.2.

had become bywords for dexterity with the bow and for sharp sight respectively. In Mencius such heroes are merely proverbial figures. Their incorporation into the "historical" hierarchy of antiquity belongs to a later tradition.

Figures from the more recent past, too, had become proverbial. Of these Yi Ya, the fabled cook of Duke Huan of Ch'i, Kung-shu P'an the inventive mechanic of Lu (seventh century), and K'uang, the Music Master of Tsin with the perfect sense of pitch, are examples. And, too, such paragons as Tzu-tu the "Apollo" of Cheng. Wu Huo the weight-lifter, and Hsi-tzu the celebrated beauty all had names that were bywords. Certain of them in later years became the "patron saints" of artisans' guilds. Kung-shu P'an, the "god" of carpenters, has had an even more dignified elevation recently in China as the patron of technology.

The brigand Ch'ih, for Mencius and, presumably, popularly, was a name to couple with those of the evil kings, Chieh and Chou. He achieves a double notoriety with the Taoists. He becomes the man who scorns man-made, and therefore artificial, moral standards, and thus, like Robin Hood, was something of a hero.

6.78

P'eng Meng learned his bowmanship from Yi the Archer. After he had learned all that he could from him, he killed Yi because, he felt, only Yi was his superior. Mencius said, "Yi after all was partly to blame for that himself. Though Kung-ming Yi said that properly speaking no blame attached to Yi, he meant that the blame if any was slight, but he could hardly be thought to be blameless.

"The State of Cheng sent Tzu-cho Ju-tzu to make a surprise raid on Wei. Wei sent Yu-kung Chih-szu in pursuit of him. Tzu-cho Ju-tzu said, 'I feel so ill today that I cannot hold my bow. I shall be killed.' He asked his chariot-driver, 'Who is it that is pursuing us?' His driver answered, 'It is Yu-kung Chih-szu.' He said, 'Then I shall not be killed.' His driver said, 'Yu-kung Chih-szu is the best bowman in Wei, yet, Sir, you say you will not be killed. Why do you say that?' He replied, 'Yu-kung Chih-szu learned his bowmanship from Yin-kung Chih-t'a, and he in turn learned it from me. Yin-kung Chih-t'a is an upright man, and those he befriends will, too, be upright.' Yu-kung Chih-szu caught up with him. He said, 'Why, Sir, are you not holding your bow?' Tzu-cho Ju-tzu said, 'Because I am too ill today.' Yu-kung Chih-szu said, 'I, Sir, learned my bowmanship from Yin-kung Chih-t'a, and he in turn learned it from you. I cannot bear to use the skills which you have taught me to harm you. Nevertheless, this is the king's business. I dare not disregard my orders.' He drew his arrows, knocked them against the carriage-wheel breaking off their heads, fired four, and then returned."

(4B.24)

6.79

Mencius said, "When Yi the Archer was teaching his pupils bowmanship, he kept his eye firmly on the target, and he taught his pupils to concentrate on doing so too. When the master craftsman is teaching his apprentices, he uses the set square and compasses, and insists on his apprentices doing so too."

(6A.20)

6.80

Mencius said, "If Hsi-tzu had been covered with uncleanliness, people would have passed her by pinching their noses. But even an unprepossessing man might sacrifice to God on High if he prepares himself, fasts, and bathes."

(4B.25)

THE WAY

What history teaches, of course, is the Way of the Former Kings, and this "Way" is the sumum bonum *of Mencius' teaching. The word tao, "Way," is an important word in Chinese philosophy, developing from the fairly concrete "way"[124] in which the worthies of antiquity behaved and ruled (their "method," as it were) to the extreme abstraction of the Taoists of "way" as the principle which actuates the physical universe.*

6.81

Mencius said, "The omens of Heaven are no match for the advantages

[124] *Tao* in day-to-day usage was simply a "road or path."

of the earth. The advantages of the earth are no match for the common consent.[125]

"There was a village, the inner walls of which were three miles, and its outer walls seven miles. It was surrounded and attacked, but did not yield. To surround and attack it, there must have been obtained the 'omens of Heaven.' But such omens having been obtained, its failing to yield was due to 'the advantages of the earth' (a matter of a defendable site). Yet in the end it did yield and was abandoned. It was not that the walls were not high enough, or its moat deep enough, or that weapons and armour were neither sharp nor tough, or that food supplies were not ample. It was a question of 'the advantages of the earth' being no match for the common consent. Therefore it is said, 'The people are defended not by boundaries afforded by walls and mounds, the kingdom is secured not by frontiers afforded by mountains and rivers, the world pays reverence not because of the sharpness of weapons.' He who possesses the Way has many to help him. He who loses the Way has few to come to his assistance, so few indeed that in the final resort even his own kin will revolt against him. But he who has many to help him, in the final resort may find the whole world with him. He who has the whole world with him has the man whose own kin has revolted against him at his mercy. Therefore a princely man would rather not go to war, but if he does so he will be sure to win."

(2B.1)

6.82

Mencius said, "If a man does not pursue the Way, it will not be pursued by his wife and children. If he leads others from the Way, the Way cannot be pursued by his wife and children."

(7B.9)

6.83

Mencius said, "When the Way prevails, those of small virtue become the servants of those of great virtue, those of small abilities become the servants of those of great abilities. When the Way does not prevail,

---

[125] See Additional Notes.

the smaller are dominated by the greater, the weak by the strong. In either case, this is the way of Heaven, but he who obeys Heaven is preserved, and he who disobeys Heaven perishes."

(4A.7)

ON THE ECONOMY

The link between ethics and economics is, for Mencius, a close one. A "constant mind" without a "constant livelihood" is impossible (1.32, 1.5). And a constant livelihood for his people is the ruler's concern (6.70, 1.2). Indeed, it is the purpose of government "to produce the necessities of life in sufficient quantity" (7.6).

Mencius' economic policies are essentially the reinstatement of the fiscal policies and the systems of land and office tenure, which he believed were current in the days of King Wen, some seven hundred years earlier. These, he alleges, were the tithing system (see 1.32 and cf. 3.44 and 1.38), a single impost (6.85) with no further taxes such as the tax on merchandise (1.14), levies on transients (1.14). and the like; the well-field system by which land was divided into nine squares, the central or "Lord's field" being worked in exchange for the usufruct of the remaining eight (1.14 1.32); adequate employment for worthy knights, with hereditary tenure (1.32, 1.7, 1.11); the institution of public schools (1.32); free access to state lands and "sharing" the products of forest and marsh (1.3, 3.3, 1.14); and finally the recognition of, and state support for, the aged and indigent (1.5, 1.36, 1.14, 2.4, 6.66) and public relief in times of famine (1.2, 2).

The banes of the economy in his day, as Mencius sees them, are the inequities in the distribution of wealth—luxury and riches on the one hand (1.24, 1.14, 5.9, 1.4) and poverty and starvation on the other (1.36, 1.14, 1.5, 2.4, etc.). And this poverty is greatly exacerbated by the impressing of the people in the agricultural seasons (1.5, 1.20, 1.22), by the enclosures of marsh, forest, and arable land for hunting (1.14, 1.31, 3.3, 1.5), by excessive exactions to pay for Court luxury (1.24, 1.2, 1.14, 5.9, 1.4), by the improvident use of natural resources (1.22), and by tax-farming, which Mencius condemns (6.84).

Mencius was not the only critic of the economic condition of the day. The Agronomists protested at the "complications" and inequalities of the division of labour and of specialized production (4.14). Mencius justifies the division (3.39) and particularly the claims of the worthy knight upon the public purse

(3.25). *Mencius, too, defends the free price market against attempts at price control* (4.14). *The Mohists protested against waste, particularly in extravagant funerals. Mencius defends such practices based on the precedents of antiquity* (1.35, 2.8, *and* 4.3).[126]

6.84

Mencius said, "A ruler should accord honour to worthy men, and should employ the able. With the wise and competent in office, the knights of the whole world would approve, and desire to be present at his Court. In his markets, a charge should be made for space, but the merchandise should go untaxed, or (to encourage traders) orderly procedures govern the market place without charging for space. Then the merchants of the whole world would approve, and desire to establish their warehouses in his markets. At the frontiers, travellers should be inspected but not taxed, and then throughout the world those who journey will avail themselves of his highways. Cultivators should give their lawful service but pay no other dues, and then farmers throughout the world will approve, and wish to farm in his territory. The merchants should not be allowed to farm the poll and village tax; then the people of the whole world would wish to be his subjects.

"If this five-point policy were actually to be put into practice, then the peoples of neighbouring states would look upon the ruler as their own parents, and since, from the birth of man until today, no one has succeeded in mobilizing the children to attack their parents, such a ruler would be unopposed everywhere throughout the world. He who is unopposed throughout the world is the sent one of Heaven. It has never happened that the sent one of Heaven has fallen short of the Princely Ideal."

(2A.5)

6.85

Mencius said, "There are imposts upon cloth, imposts upon grain, and imposts upon a man's labour. The True Prince avails himself of one

---

[126] Another economic justification for lavish funerals is offered in the *Kuan-tzu* where such expenditure is approved on the grounds that spending strengthens the economy. See Lien-sheng Yang, "Economic Justification for Spending," in *Studies in Chinese Institutional History* (Cambridge, 1961), p. 65.

only of these imposts, remitting the other two. If he imposes two, people go hungry, but if he imposes all three families are broken up."

(7B.27)

6.86

Mencius said, "Tend the fields of grain and flax well, tax their yield lightly, and the people will be prosperous. Let food be consumed in accordance with the seasons and materials be utilized as the *Rites* prescribe, and produce will be more than enough for your needs. Water and fire are essential for the people's survival, yet such is the sufficiency of these things that no man knocking on a door in the evening and asking for water or for a light is ever refused. When a Sage governs the world, he ensures that foodstuffs are as plentiful as water and fire, and, when these conditions obtain, are the people likely to be Inhumane?"

(7A.23)

6.87

Mencius said, "Govern the people so as to ensure their comfort, and though they work hard they will not be disaffected. Order the death penalty only to ensure that life is preserved, and even in death they will not bear resentment against their executioner."

(7A.12)

THE GENTLEMAN'S LIVELIHOOD

One of Mencius' more personal concerns was the way in which a gentleman secures his means of livelihood. Ideally, of course, he should be in the prince's employ, and Mencius has much to say of the duty of princes to "employ worthy men." In practice, a gentleman was presented with a dilemma when the only employment open to him was in the service of a venal prince, or with a prince who failed to show him sufficient respect.[127] This posed problems for Mencius and his followers. Should they seek office? Or accept gifts from princes?[128] In extremity, a gentleman might take office but "only in a most junior position."[129] Otherwise, with the fortitude of a knight of the way, he must remain content in obscurity and poverty.

[127] See 6.88 and 6.91.
[128] See 6.90, 2.11, 2.13, 2.16, 2.17, 3.18, 3.19, 3.23, 3.38, 3.48.   [129] See 6.89.

Ideally, too, noble rank was bestowed on noble men. But in Mencius' day the "embroidered robes of rank" were no guarantee of nobility of spirit. Mencius derives comfort from the distinction he makes between the ranks and honours bestowed by kings, and the nobility which Heaven itself confers.

6.88

Mencius said, "The Worthy Kings of antiquity delighted in excellence and took no cognizance of influence. The Worthy Knights of antiquity did likewise. They delighted in their Way regardless of a man's influence. Thus it was that if princes did not show them the greatest respect, and afford them all the courtesies of protocol, the princes did not get to see them very often, and, not seeing them often, the chances of obtaining their services were slight."

(7A.8)

6.89

Mencius said, "One should not take office on account of poverty, though there may be times when one takes office in poverty. One should not take a wife on account of the support she may bring, though there are times when she does bring support. He who takes office on account of poverty should decline to accept an honoured position and take a lowly one, should decline high emoluments and accept low ones. What could be more just than that? Some such position, for example, as that of a gatekeeper or a night watchman. Confucius once was a mere granary clerk. He said, 'I care only that my reckonings are accurate.' He was a field overseer. He said, 'I care only that the sheep and cattle are fat and healthy.' When in a modest situation,[130] to speak of higher things is an offence. But to stand in a prince's own Court, and for one's principles not to prevail—that is a matter of which to be ashamed."

(5B.5)

6.90

Mencius said, "When one might properly either accept or not accept, to accept does damage to one's reputation for probity. When one might

---

[130] Cf. *Analects*, 9.6, where Confucius speaks of "the humble circumstances of his youth."

properly offer or not offer, to offer does damage to one's reputation for kindness. When one might properly offer one's life or not offer it, to offer it does damage to one's reputation for fearlessness.[131]

(4B.23)

6.91

Mencius said, "To support a Knight, yet not to love him, is to treat him like a pig. To love him, yet not to treat him with respect, is to treat him like a dog or horse. Deference and respect precede the offering of gifts. But one cannot falsely procure a gentleman with the deference and respect which lack the substance."

(7A.37)

6.92

Mencius said, "There are men who serve princes to seek their favour. There are ministers who ensure the security of the state's altars[132] for the pleasure they find in doing so. There are, among the common people, those whom Heaven favours, whose abilities can be used in governing the world, and who succeed in using them. There are great men by whom all things are rectified because they rectify themselves."

(7A.19)

6.93

Mencius said, "Extensive lands and many people are things a prince desires, but his delight does not lie in these things. To stand in the centre of the universe, to govern the peoples of the Four Seas, these the prince delights in, but his true being does not lie in these things. To his true being, great success adds nothing, and poverty subtracts nothing. These are the lot ordained for him. His true being lies in Humanity, Justice, propriety, and wisdom. These are rooted in his mind; they grow and give signs of life. Bright-eyed, they appear on the face, are betrayed in the set of the shoulders, manifest in every movement of the arms and legs. His every limb bears wordless testimony."

(7A.21)

---

[131] It suggests foolhardiness, not real courage (cf. 1.6).   [132] See 6.10.

6.94

Mencius said, "The people are its [i.e., the state's] most valued possession, the altars of the soil and crops its next, and the prince its least. Therefore, he who has the confidence of the people may become Son of Heaven. He who has the confidence of the Son of Heaven may become a Feudal Lord. He who has the confidence of a Feudal Lord may become a noble. When a Feudal Lord endangers the altars of the soil and crops, he is replaced. When, after the victims have been prepared and the food-offerings cleansed and the sacrifices carried out at the appropriate seasons, drought or floods ensue, then the altars are replaced."

(7B.14)

6.95

Mencius said, "All men seek to be ennobled, but each man individually has nobility within himself. He does not think about it; that is all. The ennoblements bestowed by men are not nobility at its best. Those who are on the honours list of the Chao Meng can be taken off again.[133] The *Book of Songs*[134] says,

> Having filled us with his wine,
> He has filled us with his *virtue*.

This means they were filled with Humanity and Justice, and so did not hanker after the taste of rich flesh and fine grain. Today a man whose good name reaches far, a man widely praised, has no need for the embroidered robes (of noble rank)."

(6A.17)

6.96

Mencius said, "There are patents of nobility bestowed by Heaven, and those bestowed by man. Such things as Humanity and Justice, loyalty and trustworthiness, and a tireless delight in the good—these are Heaven's patents of nobility. 'Duke,' 'minister,' 'noble'—these are noble ranks bestowed by man. In antiquity, men cultivated Heaven's titles, and the titles of man followed in due course. Today, men culti-

[133] The Chao family of Tsin, Legge suggests, were the "king-making Warwicks" of ancient China.   [134] *Songs*, 202.

vate Heaven's titles as a means of gaining man's titles, and, once they obtain them, Heaven's titles are abandoned. This is the height of self-delusion. It ends only in the loss of all title."

(6A.16)

MISCELLANEOUS

6.97

Mencius said, "Simple words of far-reaching import are good words. To hold to one's pledged word, yet to interpret it generously—this is the good way. When a gentleman speaks, his eyes do not drop below the sash,[135] but the Way is contained in his words.

"What a gentleman cherishes is the cultivation of his person, and, in doing so, the world is given peace.

"Men criticize those who neglect their own fields and tell others how to put theirs in order. They seek much in others but demand little of themselves."

(7B.32)

6.98

Mencius said, "From now on, I understand just how serious it is for a man to kill his own kin. If a father or an older brother is killed by an outsider, a man will avenge them by killing the outsider's father or brother. So that for a man to kill his own kin is not far removed from killing himself."[136]

(7B.7)

6.99

Yü and Chi[137] happened upon quiet times. Three times they passed the gates of their own homes but did not go in. Confucius thought them

[135] Ritual required that a minister addressing a king not allow his eyes to stray "above the collar or below the sash." Thus, though modest in his demeanour, the gentleman is still uncompromising in speech.

[136] He should avenge his kin by killing their slayer, namely himself.

[137] The Lord of Millet; cf. 4.14.

worthy for this. Yen Tzu[138] happened upon troubled times. He lived in a mean street, on a handful of rice and a gourdful of water a day. Others could not have endured such distress, but his happiness remained unchanged.[139] Confucius thought him worthy too.

Mencius said, "Yü, Chi, and Yen Hui [i.e., Yen Tzu] pursued identical paths. Yü thought that if one man drowned it was as though he himself were drowned. Chi thought that if one man starved it was as though he himself starved. And so it was that they took matters with such seriousness. Had the circumstances of Yü, Chi, and Yen Tzu been reversed, they would have acted no differently.

"Now if two people living with you under the same roof are fighting you should prevent them, though your hair be undressed and your cap pulled hurriedly on. But if they are fighting elsewhere in the neighbourhood, it would be wrong, with your hair in disarray, to prevent them, but, even so, if it were behind closed doors you might do so."[140]

(4B.29)

6.100

Mencius said, "One who, being in a junior position, has not the confidence of his superiors will never govern the people. There is a way to gain the confidence of one's superiors. He who is not trusted by his friends will not gain the confidence of his superiors. And there is a way to gain the trust of one's friends. He who fails to give satisfaction in his duty to his kinsfolk will not be trusted by his friends. There is a way to give satisfaction to one's kinsfolk. He who, upon examining himself, discovers a lack of integrity will not give satisfaction to his kinsfolk. There is a way to ensure personal integrity. He who is unclear as to the nature of the good will not achieve personal integrity. Therefore, integrity is the Way of Heaven, and to be concerned about integrity is the way of man. No man of integrity fails to move others. But a man lacking integrity will never move others."

(4A.13)

---

[138] Cf. *Analects*, 14.6.

[139] Cf. *Analects*, 7.9.

[140] There are several instances given in *Mencius* where punctilio may be dispensed with in extreme circumstances, but, as will be seen here, the claims of "propriety" are still very strong. The last paragraph seems to be a "chapter" on its own. It has nothing to do with the preceding.

6.101

He who seeks the allegiance of others by simply wanting their allegiance will never get it. But he who seeks to provide for others may seek the allegiance of the entire world. There has never been a True King who failed to obtain that allegiance which comes from the heart.

(4B.16)

ⓈⓈⓈⓈⓈⓈⓈⓈⓈⓈⓈⓈⓈⓈⓈⓈⓈⓈⓈⓈⓈⓈⓈⓈⓈⓈⓈⓈⓈⓈⓈⓈⓈⓈⓈⓈⓈ

Chapter Seven

MAXIMS

7.1

Mencius said, "After profound study and the most minute discussion, one may, in recapitulation, expound a matter with brevity."[1]

(4B.15)

7.2

Humanity (*jen*) is man (*jen*). Put together, the words spell out "the Way."

(7B.16)

7.3

There are instances of those who, lacking Humanity, have gained a state, but there are no instances of one who, lacking Humanity, gained the whole world.

(7B.13)

7.4

Mencius said, "Those who can steer a middle course should bring up others to do so. Those who are talented should bring up others to be talented. Then men will take pleasure in having competent fathers and older brothers. But if those who steer a middle course should neglect those who do not, and those who are talented should neglect those who are not, then the distance separating the competent and the incompetent will be measured in a few inches."

(4B.7)

---

[1] Of which the maxims which follow are, I suppose, examples.

7.5

Ritual observations which contravene the *Rites* are not true rites. Acts of justice which contravene true Justice are not acts of justice.

(4B.6)

7.6

Mencius said, "If no confidence is placed in Humane and worthy men, the state will lack substance. Without the Rites and Justice, the orders of society will be confused. Without government, the necessities of life will not be produced in sufficient quantity."

(7B.12)

7.7

Mencius said, "The worthy man, by being enlightened, enlightens others. Today men, being bewildered, attempt to enlighten others."[2]

(7B.20)

7.8

Mencius said, "No words are really unlucky words. What is really 'unlucky' is to keep worthy men in obscurity."

(4B.17)

7.9

Mencius said, "Praise is sometimes given thoughtlessly, while those who seek perfection are sometimes blamed."

(4A.22)

7.10

Mencius said, "Men talk loosely because their words are unlikely to be put to the test. Everyone wants to be a teacher; that is one of life's problems."

(4A.23)

---

[2] The text here makes play on the words "light" and "darkness" in a metaphorical sense. We have in English the word "enlighten" but not "endarken."

7.11

Mencius said, "We should speak of the shortcomings of others only when their shortcomings are likely to have disastrous consequences."

(4B.9)

7.12

The great man is one who never loses his child-like touch.[3]

(4B.12)

7.13

Mencius said, "The great man seeks no assurance that his words will be believed or that his course of action will get results. He is concerned only that in his words and actions Justice resides."

(4B.11)

7.14

Mencius said, "People commonly speak of 'the Empire, the state, and the family.' The Empire lies rooted in the state, the state lies rooted in the family, and the family lies rooted in the individual."

(4A.5)

7.15

Mencius said, "A man who has encompassed himself with profits, a lean year may not harm, but a man who has encompassed himself with virtue, a corrupt age cannot confound."

(7B.10)

7.16

Mencius said, "When knights, innocent of crime, are put to death, then the nobles may as well leave the state. When the innocent masses are butchered, then the knights may as well leave the state."

(4B.4)

---

[3] See Additional Notes.

7.17

Mencius said, "There must be things that a man will not do, before he decides about those things that he will do."

(4B.8)

7.18

Mencius said, "When the Way prevails everywhere, use it to pursue your personal cultivation. When the Way does not prevail, use your personal cultivation to pursue the Way. I have never heard of using the Way in the pursuit of other men."

(7A.42)

7.19

Mencius said, "He who gives up when he should not give up will always give up. He who treats shabbily those he should treat well will always behave shabbily. He who takes office over-eagerly may have to resign in haste."

(7A.44)

7.20

Mencius said, "A man who hankers after fame may cede a large kingdom, but if his purposes be not pure 'gifts of food' will be written all over his face."[4]

(7B.11)

7.21

Mencius said, "Confucius would never go to excess."

(4B.10)

7.22

Mencius said, "Among the vital parts of the body, the pupil of the eye has no equal. The pupil does not conceal the evil within. If all is right in the breast, then the pupil sparkles with it. But if all is not right, then

[4] See Additional Notes.

o

the pupil is dulled by it. When hearing a man speak, watch the pupils of his eyes, for there what can be concealed?"

(4A.16)

7.23
Mencius said, "If a True Gentleman has not integrity, by what will he be governed?"

(6B.12)

7.24
Mencius said, "Do not do what you should not do; do not wish for what you should not wish—there is nothing more to it than that."

(7A.17)

NOTES AND FINDING LIST

ADDITIONAL NOTES

CHAPTER I

1.2, note 17. Duke Ching of Ch'i is mentioned in the *Analects of Confucius* as consulting Confucius about government (*Analects*, XII.11), but having been unable to avail himself of the Master's services (*Analects*, XVIII.3). There seems to have existed a whole cycle of stories and sayings in Ch'i attributed to Duke Ching and his Minister Yen Tzu (d. 500 B.C.); see Mencius' comments in 3.28. We shall meet them again in 1.27 and in a doublet in 3.18, 3.38, and 6.62. In the *Analects* Yen Tzu is said to have been a man of unvarying politeness (*Analects*, V.16).

1.2, note 20. This is very free paraphrase. The text takes the form of what is clearly a citation from an earlier work with an exegetical comment upon it, which does not translate well.

1.4, note 26. Ritual (see 1.5, note 37) prescribed a series of postures and facial expressions appropriate for formal occasions. Thus princes adopted "an awe-inspiring, majestic mien." Ministers ushered into the presence of a prince walked "gingerly as though stepping on thin ice." The phrase "changed his expression" means that the King dropped his conventional pose and allowed the exasperation he no doubt felt to show on his face. After a similar lapse on another occasion (see 1.7) King Hsüan is said to have "set his face again," that is, he resumed the ritual pose he previously had held. A good description of set poses is given in *Analects*, X.16, with which see, too, Waley, *Analects*, p. 54 ff.

1.4, note 27. In evoking the plight of the peasants, description tends to fall into conventional phrases. Thus "brothers, wives, and children are separated" occurs again in 1.20. The weak and the aged "rolling into the gutters" (dead and unburied) occurs in 1.32, 1.36 and 2.4; the "able-bodied, scattering and wandering to the four quarters," in 1.36 and 2.4. This suggests perhaps a common origin, reference to which, then familiar, now escapes us. At all events it represents the extreme of governmental mismanagement when, under the threat of famine, the family breaks down and its members are driven to neglect their familial duties to both the living and the dead.

1.4, note 28. The people's reaction at the sight of the royal hunt is given in words identical with those describing their reaction on hearing the King's music. This repetition has no doubt a rhetorical force in archaic Chinese, but in English translation tends to become tedious. Where long passages are reiterated, I have tried to relieve the translation by omitting them.

1.5, note 30. Ch'i was, in fact, quite large and very wealthy, "one part in nine of the universe" as is pointed out later in the passage, and so large that it need fear no state (1.16). This is here a form of self-deprecation that good manners required.

1.5, note 37. The word *li*, which I have translated variously as "rites, propriety, courtesy, protocol, or good manners," as occasion demands, strictly denotes a rite, a form of procedure proper to the solemn ceremonies of sacrifice, of the burial of the dead, of the attainment of puberty, and of marriage (1.28, 5.1). But it also includes the rules that decorum and seemliness suggest in social intercourse, or what we should call etiquette—such things, for example, as refraining from actually touching a woman's hand when handing her something (4.17), avoiding "gulping and guzzling at meals" or "biting meat with the teeth" (6.34 and cf. 3.37). It governs the conduct of host and guest (6.25), the sort of things about which Miss Emily Post writes. *Li* is also concerned with the more formal aspects of ceremonial at Court and in diplomatic interchange, which we in recent years have come to call "protocol." For example, at Court "gentlemen may not leave their place to speak to one another" or "break ranks to bow" (2.7). *Li* is the code of *noblesse oblige*. A deposed prince has a claim on the hospitality of a fellow prince (3.17). *Li* is concerned with good manners and politeness. A child does not use the informal "yes?" when called by his father (2.1). In Han times, at least three compendiums of *Rites* were in circulation, and in Mencius' time the rites were already codified in some form for he quotes from Ritual Manuals (2.1, 3.48). Gentlemen were expected to have studied them (5.1, 3.32). In sum, *li* is the mark of the True Gentleman (6.4) who, "when every movement, every gesture is governed by the precise rite," achieves the "acme of virtue in all its richness" (6.58). *Li*, for Mencius, formulates Justice (with which *li* is often coupled [see 1.5, 1.35, 3.18, 5.14, 6.5, 6.21, and 7.6] and Wisdom into a "disciplined pattern," which for the good ritualist gives aesthetic as well as moral pleasure, for it proves irresistible. On seeing it, "all unknowingly the feet take up the measure and the hands begin the dance" (6.12).

1.5, note 38. This passage, which occurs as a doublet in 1.22, is referred to again in 6.66 where it is explained that "one cannot keep warm at fifty without silk, or feel replete at seventy without meat." This particular programme of rural development is credited by Mencius in 6.66 to King Wen.

1.6, note 41. *Yung*, "valour, bravery," is used in two senses. Here it is a term used for a sort of toughness cultivated by some knights of the period shown in doing brave but foolhardy deeds, such as wrestling with tigers (see 2.11), or feats of strength and endurance, such as lifting collossal weights (see 3.47). Such knights went through a rather tough regimen when training (see 3.29). These pursuits Mencius thought offensive to his notions of the decorum proper to a gentleman, to say nothing of the impiety towards parents that risking one's life involves (3.5). The "brave knight" of the Confucian ideal has moral courage. On a point of punctilio he insists, even though "the brave knight never knows when he will lose his head" (3.38). To risk his life otherwise is "to damage his reputation for courage" (6.90). For a comparison of the "tough knight" and the "True Knight" see Additional Notes to 3.29, note 105.

1.11, note 52. By "men of talents" Mencius has here in mind the peripatetic knights who travelled from court to court, seeking to persuade princes to put their theories of government into practice. The implication here is that the Court of Ch'i was at this time peculiarly susceptible to the *dernier cri*, and was given to receiving such men too freely.

1.11, note 53. That kings should be "the mother and father of the people" is an ancient idea in China. The state itself is conceived as an extension of the family. This notion is present in the modern word for "nation," *Kuo-chia* (*Kuo*, "city"; *chia*, "family"). Familial duty is central in the code of the Confucian gentleman, and the relation of king to subject and of minister to sovereign is often thought of as an extension of this.

1.14, note 57. The *Ming T'ang*, or Hall of Emanations, was a structure built upon a mound and surrounded by a moat. It was part of the ancient paraphernalia of kingship. In the *Ming T'ang* the rites of kings were performed, and in the moat the kings of antiquity performed a ceremonial fishing and hunting rite.

1.14, note 59. The "nine and one" system is one in which land is divided into squares, each square being so subdivided that it gives nine equal squares. The people cultivated the central square for their overlord and enjoyed the usufruct of the remaining eight for themselves (see 1.32). Because the Chinese character for "well" 井 looks like a square divided into nine the system is also called the "well-field" system.

1.15, note 66. Whatever Heaven may have ordained, the King thinks as a matter of practical politics that the annexation of Yen would provoke the other major powers to a coalition against Ch'i, much as, some twenty years previously, Ch'i together with Sung, Ch'in, and Chao had made a concerted attack on Wei (342 B.C.). In this atmosphere of *Realpolitik* it is not surprising that the idealism of Mencius had little appeal.

1.18, note 75. K'uai, King of Yen (r. c. 320-316) had allowed himself to be talked into proffering his kingdom to his minister Chih in emulation of the Sage King, Yao (see 3.10). Chih, forgetting the equally pertinent precedent of antiquity, which required that he in turn should decline the kingdom, had promptly accepted. The royal family then formed a party to contest this. It was in the confusion that resulted that Ch'i decided to intervene.

1.20, note 78. King Hui at this time was nearing the end of a reign of half a century, during which he had been almost continually at war as often on the offensive as on the defensive. Here he is summing up his losses. To attempt to be too precise about which battles he is referring to runs into difficulties. Many of his troubles came from his enmity with Han and Chao. He besieged the capital of Chao and took it in the year 353 B.C. Ch'i, coming to the relief of Chao, defeated Wei at the battle of Kuei-ling in that same year. Ten years later Wei attacked Ch'i and in this battle (343 B.C.) the King lost his eldest son. In the year following a concerted attack by Ch'i, Ch'in, and Chao upon Wei, with the Ch'in armies commanded by the redoubtable Lord of Shang, resulted in King Hui suing for peace by ceding territory to Ch'in. King Hui's enmity with Ch'u was more recent. It was in 323 B.C. that, after the defeat at Hsiang-liang, he lost eight cities to Ch'u.

1.27, note 100. Kung-ming Yi was a contemporary and pupil of Tseng Tzu (505-436 B.C.), Confucius' most important disciple. Mencius quotes his sayings elsewhere (3.48, 6.78, and 1.23, note 87), so that we may suppose Kung-ming Yi's sayings to have been collected and "passed on," just as were those of other early disciples of the Master, but we know of them only in citation.

1.28, note 107. In *Analects*, II.5, this saying is attributed to Confucius, just as a passage in 1.23 is attributed to Mencius and in 3.3 is attributed to Kung-ming Yi. We are never quite sure in early Confucian literature whether sayings are original to the speaker or quotation from the common stock of the "teachings of the School," so that attribution is sometimes difficult. A good Confucian, I suppose, would think this no problem at all since the Master himself disclaimed that he ever "made anything up," confining himself to "transmitting what was taught" (see *Analects* 7.1).

1.28, note 109. *Chih*, "will or purpose," but also used for "annals or records" (rather like our use of *testament* and *Testament*), when cited in this way refers to a collection (or collections) of documents of the past, much as *shu*, "documents," is used for the *Book of Documents*, and *shih*, "songs," for the *Book of Songs*. The *chih* have not survived. I translate *chih* here as *Manuals* since such collections were used, as were the *Book of Documents* and the *Book of Songs*, as guides to precedent and conduct. The word *chuan*, "to hand down, tradition," I have translated *Records*, and the word *li*, "rites," when used for a code of rites, I have translated *Rites* on the analogy of the above.

1.28, note 110. This was a telling thrust. Mencius would have been hard put to it to produce any documentary evidence that "three years mourning" was observed "in all three dynasties of antiquity." But for him it was sufficient that he had "heard of it" from the Confucian school; *ex hypothesi* it "happened in antiquity."

1.28, note 111. His "power" is his *te*, his virtue, whose magico-moral force is felt everywhere. This saying is proverbial (see *Analects*, 12.19) and, like most proverbs, has been used with scant regard for its origin. I have heard it used despairingly in the sense of "bowing to the inevitable."

1.31, note 114. As well it might. In the struggle for aggrandizement and power, the major states were enlarging themselves by fortifying their own or captured cities, and by building defensive walls on their expanding frontiers to protect their states. The Great Wall of China, begun some one hundred and fifty years later, followed in part the state frontiers along which walls were built by Chao in 369 B.C. and Wei in 359 B.C. The State of Ch'i in 351 B.C. began building frontier walls to protect itself from attacks by Ch'u. In "fortifying cities" far from their state capitals, the states were extending their sovereignty, often at the expense of another state. The history of Hsüeh is perhaps not untypical. It was given in fief by the kings of Ch'i to important ministers. Its revenues were increased by some Lu lands in 340 B.C. When Ch'u attacked Ch'i in 333 B.C. the Ch'u armies laid seige to Hsüeh. Mencius passed through it in c. 323 B.C. and accepted from its then incumbent a gift "to cover the cost of an escort." (He was presumably on Ch'i state business.) The rumour that it was to be fortified was not ill-founded. The King of Ch'i did so in the following year (322 B.C.) and enfeoffed a member of the Ch'i royal house there, raising the title of the fief to that of *Nan* (Baron). But the rumour was bad news for T'eng. It meant further military preparations for expansion and for war with Ch'u, under whose shadow the Principality of T'eng clung so precariously to its independence.

1.32, note 119. A commoner, who seized power in the state of Lu in 505 B.C. (see Waley's notes to *Analects*, XVI.2 and XVII.1). He is the Yang Huo of 3.23. A strict translation makes him sound sententious: "He who seeks to be rich will not be benevolent, he who wishes to be benevolent will not be rich" (Legge), whereas I take his remark to be the sort of down-to-earth talk affected by a newly-rich and not too scrupulous man.

1.32, note 124. Despite its being a Shang system. A not dissimilar programme to the one described here was suggested to the King of Ch'i (see 1.14). There, too, the well-field system and hereditary tenure are proposed, and are said to be systems used by King Wen, the father of the first king of the Chou House, King Wu.

1.32, note 125. We now know from our study of Early Chou bronze inscriptions that the words for "schools" which Mencius uses here derive from the archery grounds used in the training of young noblemen in the arts of war and the hunt. But their meanings had shifted considerably by his time. It was this according of contemporary meanings to words in ancient texts, originally meaning something quite different, that gave the Confucians scriptural authority and the sanction of antiquity for notions that were, in fact, quite recent. We would be wrong, however, to imagine that this was done in anything but good faith. Indeed in the very incident described here we see that this was so. Duke Wen, himself, as a youth had not "given himself to study, but preferred hunting and the military arts" (see 1.28). He had, in fact, gone through the training that a young nobleman in King Wen's day would have had in the "schools." Had Mencius understood his sources historically, he would hardly have been advocating "schools" to the prince as they actually existed in King Wen's day.

1.32, note 127. The House of Chou already had its *ming*, "Mandate," to feudal tenure as an "old state," but at its elevation to be "Sons of Heaven" a new Mandate had been issued. So too, suggests Mencius, the Duke might well receive a "new mandate."

1.32, note 128. From *kuei*, the jade symbol of office. This allotment is explained as providing for the means of sacrifice. It is connected, I suppose, with the ancestral rites of hereditary office-holders (cf. 3.48).

1.35, note 133. It might occur to the reader to suppose that what Mencius spent on his mother's funeral was no concern of a courtesan, but her thrust was more telling than appears, for lavish funerals were under attack by the Mohists (see 4.3) and even Mencius' own followers were disturbed by the scale of this funeral (see 2.8).

1.37, note 139. There is reason to suppose that this was the pleasure quarter of the capital. Young cadets, in a more modern era, have also discovered in such quarters congenial facilities for language study.

CHAPTER II

2.1, note 3. In suggesting that he might meet Mencius in the informality of a bed-chamber, where the punctilio of Court procedure could not be observed, the King was proposing what seemed to Mencius not only an occasion of *lèse-majesté*, but of lack of decorum towards himself. The politenesses that princes owe to gentleman is a frequent theme of Mencius.

2.1, note 6. *Nuoh* is explained as a reply lacking in formality. The son, according to the *Book of Rites* (*Li Chi* 1a. 3.14), should say *wei* and not *nuoh*. *Wei* is the sort of reply that would be expected from a servant.

2.10, note 26. In the traditional explanation of this passage *yih* is thought to be a unit of weight (twenty ounces) and *chien-chin* a metal of some kind (gold is one suggestion) of "double" value. Thus Legge reads: "a present of 2,400 *taels* of fine silver," which would be a very handsome gift indeed. Modern numismatic research has shown that *yih* was the name of a mint town in Ch'i at this period. If *chien-chin*, therefore, is the denomination "a two-unit coin," we should have a more plausible explanation of this passage. Thus: 100, 75, or 50 two-unit coins of Yih—which is precisely the way we should expect travelling expenses, or the cost of an escort, to be reimbursed. The value, then, of the piece of uncut jade in 1.13 (10.000 *yih*), though still a large sum, is more plausible than Legge's "240.000 *taels* of gold" (cf. Wang Yü-chüan, *Early Chinese Coinage* [New York, 1951], especially p. 187 ff.).

2.13, note 36. It is not clear to me that the final passage beginning with "Traders in the markets . . ." has any connection with the preceding discussion. The Han paraphrist Chao Ch'i, however, thinks that the King's suggestion to Mencius would put Mencius in the position of a market-supervisor taking his "cut" from all transactions made in the market, if he were in a position to place his own pupils in the public service. This strikes me, at least, as forced.

CHAPTER III

Chapter III, Introduction, note 2. The eminent Ch'ing scholar, Chiao Hsün (1763-1820), lists fifteen who accompanied Mencius as followers, and four who studied with him as pupils but observes that the list varies depending on who is regarded as a "disciple" (*Meng-tzu Cheng-yi*, sub. 2b. 10). These lists of course are based on actual mention in the *Works*. We have no way of knowing of any others.

3.3, note 7. This phrase in Mencius has given rise to the belief that Confucius wrote the *Annals*. All States in his day kept such annals. From a remark in the *Analects* it is clear that Confucius regarded the very wording of each entry as a portentous thing. They had to do with the "affairs of the Son of Heaven." Since the *Annals* were a sort of report to the Ancestors, a kind of heavenly book-keeping, their wording had ritual significance. A later school developed an esoteric form of interpretation of the *Annals*. The use of certain words was thought by them to convey to those in the secret "praise or blame."

3.3, note 8. Mencius evidently had access to a collection of the dicta of the Master, either other than the *Analects* as we know them, or one that was more complete. This saying does not occur in the present *Analects*.

3.3, note 9. To Mencius the monarchial structure of society and the supremacy of the family within that structure were of the essence of the ideal order of the Sages. Without these institutions men reverted to the state of "wild animals," a situation he likens to the primeval condition of the plains when human beings were driven into pits and caves.

3.3, note 11. (cf. 1.23). Properly speaking, of course, it is human beings that should engage the attention of rulers, and animals who should be regarded as a source of food. It is suggested here that the roles have been reversed. It is animals, in the horses and dogs and the game to be hunted, that occupy the attention of rulers, while their subjects are "eaten," that is, regarded as mere providers of food. Once again, the image of man becoming a wild animal is conjured up as a sign of the decline of the times (cf. 3.29, note 114). Animals are for Mencius a figure of Inhumanity (6.19, 4.14). The difference between man and an animal is slight but the difference, that of their "natures," is basic (4.8 and 12). Under good government the animals are "driven back"; under bad government they return (as in 3.3). They return, says Mencius, partly under the policies of evil kings, with "the increase of hunting parks and fishing grounds" (3.3) when land is withdrawn from cultivation, but they return also in the guise of men like Yang Chu and Micius, who advocate policies found "only among wild animals" (3.3), and Hsü Hsing, whose policy is fit only for earthworms (4.15).

Under venal princes, animals and men change roles (1.23, 3.3), animals getting "governed" while men are "eaten." "Horses and hounds" (see 3.17) provides Mencius with a favourite figure. But a sense of delicacy prevents a True Gentleman from seeing animals suffer (1.5). He "loves all living creatures, but does not treat all with *jen* (Humanity). He treats all human beings with Humanity, but does not treat them all with familial affection" (6.15).

3.3, note 12. It seems to me that Confucius' work on the *Annals*, about which there has been so much discussion, is comparable to Mencius' "work on the *Book of Documents* and the *Songs*," so frequently exemplified throughout the *Works*. It was the sort of exegetical interpretation of these books in which they were made to appear as a protest against the times. It is only thus that I can understand that the sparse archival entries of the *Spring and Autumn Annals* could have struck terror into anyone. To Confucius, they record the story of the unwarrantable assumption of the monarchical rights of the Son of Heaven by the Feudal Lords, a matter which presaged the imminent wrath of Heaven. (see Additional Notes, 6.48, note 51).

3.6, note 19. The words *yung chü* mean, literally, an "ulcer." *Chi* in Chi Huan means "sterile, barren." Whether, as some think, these are proper names, or, as others, punning allusions to names or professions, their names being linked with Confucius' name in spiteful gossip suggests that they were not desirable characters. On this passage, see also the Introduction to 6.73.

3.9, note 33. In these conversations Mencius and Wan Chang are discussing points of interpretation of the texts of the *Book of Documents* (or the *Book of Documents* as it existed in their day). We are never quite sure when they are actually citing the scripture or extemporizing, much, I suppose, as the Bible might be cited without giving chapter and verse between men to whom its very familiarity precludes the necessity for doing so. Certain of Wan Chang's phrases will be found in the present *Book of Documents*.

3.13, note 44. Of whom nothing further is known. Even the location of P'i is disputed. But judging from the presence of the Confucians there it seems likely to be the City of P'i in Lu, at one time the stronghold of the Chi family, which, like other cities at this time, were given in fief with grandiose titles, and hence perhaps the title, Duke, which its incumbents had assumed.

3.14, note 49. Po-li Hsi was the Premier of Duke Mu of Ch'in (7th cent. B.C.). For Mencius he exemplified the wise minister through whom princes achieve lustre (as here), and the minister of humble origin whom Heaven first prepares with suffering (see 6.61). In Mencius' view of history, such men are paragons, and, where history suggests the contrary, history is wrong. Thus Mencius argues, "How could a wise man do such things?" Actually gossip was not too far from the facts.

3.17, note 57. Low on the social scale, but still positions a gentleman might accept if driven by poverty. The environment in which gate-keepers and princes moved is contrasted in 1.10, but in 6.89 such positions are given as examples of the sort of post a gentleman in the delicate position of being pressed by his pocket, but deterred by his scruples, might take.

3.17, note 60. The care with which princes treated their horses and hounds provides Mencius with a favourite figure. In 1.23 and 3.3 (cf. 5.5), princes are accused of "governing animals and eating men"; in 1.8 they treat their ministers like "horses and hounds" (see also 6.91). This gives added point to Mencius' remark in 4.12 where he contrasts the "nature" of animals with that of men (see Additional Notes, 3.3, note 11).

3.19, note 69. A thief takes things to which he has no right. A Feudal Lord has a right to make exactions from the people. When they are excessive he is overasserting his rights, which, though deplorable, is not thieving.

3.19, note 70. *Lieh-chüeh*, "hunt-wrestle," is explained by the Han paraphrist, Chao Ch'i, as a sort of scramble for the game taken after a hunt. Game so secured, he says, was thought a particularly auspicious sacrifice to offer to ancestors.

3.19, note 71. Far better scholars than I have found this passage obscure. I take it (for lack of a better explanation) to mean that Confucius did his best with the situation as he found it, not being over-concerned with what it ought to be.

3.19, note 72. Only a century and a half after the death of the Master, the legend of his worldly success had begun to grow. On the principle of the modern historian, Ku Chieh-kang, of "one Confucius at a time," the reader must understand that biographical details about Confucius in *Mencius* reflect the stage in the growth of legend of his time, and are coloured by the piety of an ardent follower and admirer. For the "Confucius of the *Analects*," see Waley, p. 13 ff. See also the Introduction to 6.73.

3.20, note 75. This passage is a citation from the *Analects* in the version known to Mencius. These citations have to be understood in context, and so I have translated it here. This is not to say that out of such context the terse and sometimes enigmatic "sayings of the Master" are capable of quite other interpretation. Cf., for example, Waley's translation of *Analects*, 13.21.

3.23, note 87. Wen, the Lord of Wei (446-397 B.C.) and a predecessor of King Hui of Liang, is said to have been taught by Tzu-hsia, a disciple of Confucius who set up a School in his state. The prince, on passing Tuan Kan-mu's gate in his carriage, is said always to have bowed. This deference constituted a breach of etiquette (see 1.35 and 2.1 for similar breaches). It was to avoid involving his prince in such a lapse that Tuan jumped over a wall.

3.28, note 104. The Lord of Wei was step-brother, and the Princes Pi Kan and the Lord of Chi, uncles, to the tyrant King Chou of the Shang Dynasty. The King slew Pi Kan and made slaves of his uncles. They became martyrs of the Way in Confucian eyes and are exemplars of *jen* (cf. *Analects*, 18.1). The uncles occur again in 4.11. Chiao Chi, Minister of King Chou, was of humble origin (see 6.61).

3.29, note 105. The key to this long and important passage lies in the fact that the ideal of "remaining unmoved" mentioned in the first question was an ideal of the "knight of fashion." Mencius makes it an ideal of the Knight of the Way. And throughout the passage this comparison and contrast between the "tough knight" and the "True Knight" is sustained. The knight of fashion cultivates imperturbability in the face of danger—he "remains unmoved" (*pu tung hsin*). He cultivates "fearlessness" (*yung*), fearlessness of the consequences of combat as his lord's champion. He cultivates his "physical vigour" (*ch'i*), and exploits it in weight-lifting, wrestling with tigers barehanded, and in prowess in the hunting field. These were knightly ideals and it was things of this sort that no doubt the Prince of Ch'i in 1.9 had in mind when asking Mencius about knighthood. But Mencius turns them to moralistic advantage. A True Knight no less than a tough one can "remain unmoved." A True Knight no less than a tough one can be "fearless" though his fearlessness is of greater order; it is the "greater fearlessness" (*ta yung*) of Confucius. A True Knight no less than a tough one cultivates his "physical vigour" (*ch'i*), but it is the "greater physical vigour" (*Hao-ran chih ch'i*)—the life-force itself—which, permeating the universe, courses mystically through his veins. This the True Knight cultivates.

In turning upon his philosophical opponent, Kao Tzu, Mencius takes *ch'i* in the way that Kao Tzu uses it—as the physical body in contrast to the mind. But, permeating the physical body, Mencius sees "a greater physical vigour"—the mysterious entity behind life itself. Here Mencius comes closest to mysticism. And in making a claim to be adept in the mystical practice of "cultivating the greater physical vigour" his disciple not unnaturally concludes that Mencius has become an Adept—a Divine Sage. This Mencius, of course, disclaims, but modifies his disclaimer by pointing out that Confucius, though a Sage, also disclaimed the title, and that it was only a sense of delicacy that prevented Confucius' disciples from directly naming him as one.

3.29, note 109. Both Tseng Tzu and Tzu-hsia founded "schools" and some of their *dicta* are found in the *Analects*. In comparing two toughs with two of the saints, Mencius is comparing the tough knight of fashion and True Knights of the Way. Both train themselves to be "fearless," but the one has physical courage, while the other's is of a moral order. For Tseng Tzu, see the Introduction to 6.73.

3.29, note 112. The word *ch'i*, which I have translated here as "physical vigour," is the common word for "breath, air" and occurs, for example, in 6.20 ("the night *air*") and in a figurative sense in 1.10 for "the *air* about a man," the prestige and personality he exudes. We say an athlete gets his "second wind," and the connection between breathing and performing physical feats, I take it, is implicit in the use to which Mencius puts the word *ch'i* here. There are techniques of breathing known to the Taoists in inducing the trance state. But it is doubtful if Mencius here is alluding to them. In later Chinese metaphysical speculation, *ch'i* becomes a very important concept indeed, but that is far after Mencius' time.

3.29, note 118. Kung-sun Ch'ou is here taking Mencius up on his statement that a resurrected Sage of antiquity would merely reiterate Mencius' words. It is as though Mencius were claiming for his sayings the same authority as the scriptures of the Sages. Kung-sun Ch'ou cites the reluctance of Confucius to claim such ability. The re-emergence of a Sage was part of the Confucian Messianic hope. But any claim to be the Sage would have produced a sense of shock. One imagines that Kung-sun Ch'ou advanced this suggestion with bated breath, and Mencius certainly received it with horror.

3.30, note 124. This passage is understood quite differently by other translators. I take it that *yi cheng*, "by rectitude," and *yi nu*, "by anger," are in contrast. To teach "by rectitude" I take to mean with a demeanour and attitude proper to a teacher—detached, objective, and the like. Teaching "by anger" I take to mean an excusable outburst when a student has proved idle or wayward. Neither of these feelings, Mencius felt, should govern the attitude of a father to his son.

3.42, note 147. The history of the House of Chou, after a promising beginning, was one of the gradual usurpation of its rights by its Feudatories. Hence Mencius imagines that the Feudatory in its own interest had destroyed records that might incriminate it. Mencius, it must be remembered, had a very rosy view of conditions under early Chou. From all we know from modern epigraphical studies, the picture that he paints of conditions then is largely imaginary. Not all of the inscriptions were destroyed, and those that are extant do not bear out Mencius' view.

CHAPTER IV

Chapter IV, Introduction, note 2. This work has been translated under the title *Yang Chu's Garden of Pleasure* by A. Forke (London, 1912). The text occurs in contemporary editions of *Lieh Tzu* under the title *Yang Chu* and is translated in that guise in A. C. Graham, *The Book of Lieh-tzu* (London, 1960).

Introduction, note 4. *Mo Tzu* has been partly translated by Yi-pao Mei, *The Ethical and Political Works of Motse* (London, 1920).

4.1, note 8. *Chih chung,* "seizing the middle," is here contrasted with *chih yi,* "seizing one side." Mencius says that Tzu-mo affects to favour neither side and to take up a middle position, but, in fact, he takes sides, namely his own.

4.3, note 10. A quotation from the *Book of Documents* (see Karlgren, p. 40). In the passage in which this phrase occurs, however, it follows an injunction to a Feudatory, which if carried out, the writer says, "Just as an infant is held in the arms, so will the people be quiet and under control." Both Mencius and Yi Chih cite this "text from scripture" for their own purposes.

4.3, note 11. I.e., the fault lies with its nurse, who should be nursing it. Mencius' meaning seems to be that the common people, like a helpless child, need to be "held in the arms." If they stray, the fault lies with the ruler who allows them to stray. That the king and not the people is culpable for the crimes of the populace is an early and oft recurring theme in ancient China.

4.3, note 12. It is because we stem from a single stock that we love our own kin. That we should love others in the same degree supposes that we partake in two stocks. This, argues Mencius, seems contrary to common sense.

4.3, note 13. It was not the Mohists' contention that parents should not be buried at all, but that the burial rites in vogue at the time cost a disproportionate amount of time and money. Mencius would argue that, in a matter of such gravity, no expense should be spared.

4.5, note 16. Shen Tzu (Shen Ku-li) has been identified as a pupil and namesake of Ch'in Ku-li the Mohist, and with Shen Tao, who, though well known in his time, has left little trace of either his life or philosophical position. Shen Tao has been variously called a Legalist, a Taoist, and a follower of Yang Chu. His name is included in lists of the members of the Chi-hsia Academy (see 4.17).

   The name Shen Tzu appears in the *Han Catalogue* as the author of a book, but the book presently circulating under his name is a Ming forgery. And neither does this passage in Mencius help us identify Shen Tzu. There are no records of any attempt by Lu to take Nan-yang in an attack on Ch'i, and the notion that Lu might try at this time seems, on the face of it, ludicrous. We must suppose a very big "if" in Mencius' remark. Without much conviction, it seems to me that an obscure pupil of Ch'in Ku-li (who is known to have been prepared to undertake the defence of unlikely cities; see *Mo Tzu* 50) is a more plausible choice as a general for such a hopeless task as an attack on Ch'i by Lu than Shen Tao, a member of the Chi-hsia Academy already profitably employed in Ch'i. The problem is well discussed by Ch'ien Mu, *Hsien-ch'in Chu-tzu Hsi-nien* (Hong Kong, 1956) chapter 137.

4.14, note 33. The stories of Tzu-kung's mourning, and of the attempt to set up Yu-jo as Confucius' substitute, belong to a cycle of legends that are later than the *Analects.* Here the references to Tzu-hsia as a lesser man than Tseng Tzu suggest that these stories emanate from circles of the school of Tseng Tzu (see also 3.29).

CHAPTER V

5.1, note 1. In the west of China at this time, the State of Ch'in under the policies of the Lord of Shang was gathering the strength with which it would ultimately "unite the world." All the princes of the day wanted to do this. Ch'in, however, was to succeed. The Lord of Shang died in c. 338 B.C. (Mencius was about fifty years of age at this time).

In 333 B.C. Kung-sun Yen became Premier of Ch'in. He was succeeded by Chang Yi, who in 323 B.C. managed to summon Ch'i, Ch'u, and Wei to a meeting at Ch'in after the manner of the old Paramountcy. Kung-sun Yen, as a riposte, organized a league of the premiers of five other states and became Premier of Wei. By 317 B.C., however, he was again Premier of Ch'in.

Such men, skilled in diplomacy and statecraft, opportunists unfettered by scruple, were much admired. They became heroes of a school of thought, "the Diplomatists" or the "School of Lateral and Longitudinal Alliances" who collected stories of their heroes' coups and stratagems for the enlightenment of students whose ambitions lay in similar directions.

5.1, note 2. In this unflattering comparison Mencius likens men like Kung-sun Yen and Chang Yi to women for whom the criterion for conduct is to be compliant. The suggestion is that they pandered to the princes, that their power and influence were more those of a persuasive courtesan than those of great men. Almost the only references to women in *Mencius* are to disreputable ones. Even legend has never seriously suggested that Mencius married.

CHAPTER VI

Chapter VI, Introduction, note 1. Translators have dealt with the difficult word *jen* in a variety of ways—"benevolence," "Goodness" (with a capital G), "human-heartedness," and the like—but, however rendered into English, some incongruity will occur. What is needed is a versatile word that provides nouns, verbs, and adjectives indifferently. In picking upon "Humanity," "the Humane man," and "to be Humane or Inhumane," and by using capital letters, I have tried to show the reader that in such contexts the word *jen* appears in the original, and is to be understood in a Mencian sense. Since writing the above I came across the following in Erich Kahler's *Man the Measure* (1961 edition): "to speak of a feature of the human being as humanity may appear to be a tautology. But it is not a tautology because the species man, and so, mankind, unfortunately cannot be identified with the behaviour we call humanity. This behaviour is an exclusively human feature. But it is not a general feature of mankind" (p. 14).

Yi, "Justice," I have capitalized for the same reason. "Righteousness," which appears in some dictionaries, has a fine Old Testament ring, but, it seems to me, has overtones quite foreign to Mencian usage.

P

6, Introduction, note 2. A pun, which Mencius himself uses in 7.2 (and see also 6.39 where *jen* is defined as *jen hsin*, "man's mind"). Another pun which Mencius uses is the word *jen* meaning "to bear, tolerate, endure," particularly in such phrases as *pu jen jen chih hsin*, "a mind that cannot bear to see others suffer" (see 6.1 and cf. 6.2). This leads to *pu jen jen chih cheng*, "government based on the inability to bear to see others suffer," and is comparable to the *jen cheng*, "Humane government," occurring so frequently throughout the Works. Indeed in 6.1 and 6.2, the fact that men "cannot bear to see others suffer" is adduced as the "first sign of Humanity." The pun is carried further in 1.5, where the feeling of being "unable to endure (*pu jen*) to see animals suffer" is said to be *jen shu*, "the way of Humanity," and is attributable to *en*, "natural kindness." For another example of punning, see 5.2.

6.5, note 5. There is a pun here which it is difficult to convey in translation. Arrow-making and the like are crafts (*shu*). *Shu* is a road or way, and thus by extension a "way of doing things, an art." But it is also used in the sense of "a way, a teaching, a doctrine" (*Tao*, "a road, the Way," has a similar etymology). Mencius' point seems to be that doctrines other than the Way are not the less heterodox for being, the one, better than another. These comparisons are pointless. The cowardly soldiers of 1.22 were not less cowardly for only running fifty paces when their fellows ran a hundred.

6.6, note 8. *Songs*, 231. This song describes a bird harried by owls. In the verse quoted here, the bird has built a nest and is defying predators. The poem was interpreted allegorically as a reference to the efforts of the Regent, the Duke of Chou, to protect the child-king Ch'eng.

6.18, note 22. Mencius does not say what the other two are, but the Han paraphrist, Chao Ch'i, says that the second is to concur in the wrong doing of parents, and the third is to fail to provide for parents in their old age. In 3.5 Mencius lists five.

6.25, note 25. To allow *hsing*, "essential nature," its own unimpeded way was a goal of the Hedonists. To attribute everything to *ming*, "Heaven's charge" or fate, is fatalism. Mencius says that in *hsing* there is an element of *ming*, and in *ming* an element of *hsing*.

6.48, note 51. By attempting to read this passage as "their just decisions I ventured to make," later Confucians attempted to support the contention that Confucius himself wrote the *Spring and Autumn Annals* of Lu. But *ch'ü*, "to take from, to deduce," is a meaning too well attested to permit of special interpretation here. See also 3.3.

6.56, note 62. When making warrants of appointment, or making a contract, tallies of jade or bamboo in two parts were placed together and written upon, each party to the transaction then keeping one part. If the contract had to be authenticated, the parts were then placed together again. If they "tallied" exactly, the contract was a "true bill." The word "matching tally" thus came, in metaphorical usage, to mean "part and parcel of the same thing."

6.57, note 63. What Mencius intended by "it" we perhaps shall never know. One suggestion is that "it" is Humanity and Justice. More plausible, it seems to me, is that "it" is the thing they all had in common, namely sovereignty, the contrast lying in the way in which it was acquired. To Yao and Shun as demi-gods it was inherent, to the good kings T'ang and Wu it came as a result of the qualities they cultivated, and to the Paramount Princes it was "borrowed," i.e., usurped, and never returned to its rightful owners, the Sons of Heaven.

6.71, note 103. This passage seems to mean that prosperity enjoyed by the people under the Paramount Princes was more apparent than real. The True King by contrast works silently and without ostentation, and, though apparently unmoved, the people under him move imperceptibly towards the good—though they are not themselves aware of it. This at least is how the Han paraphrist, Chao Ch'i understands the passage. The last line suggests that this passage was an answer to an objector who thought that a True King "would not be much help."

6.81, note 125. The curiously worded phrases, "Heaven's times," "earth's advantages," and "man's accord," refer, as the context makes clear, to obtaining auspicious omens before engaging in a battle, considering the strategic advantage of ground before an attack, and what we should call "civilian morale" respectively. I have retained the words Heaven, earth, and man because they form a sort of trinity in Confucian writing.

CHAPTER VII

7.12, note 3. This passage has been construed variously as "the great man (i.e., the sovereign) does not lose the hearts of his children (i.e., his subjects)" or "does not lose his child's heart (i.e., his early innocence)." *Ch'ih-tzu chih shin* may equally be "the mind of a child" or "the feelings one has for a child."

7.20, note 4. The King of Yen "ceded a large kingdom" in emulation of Yao and of Shun. Mencius, however, says he was a tyrant, suggesting that his "purposes were not pure" and that he was not a man of the order of Yao and Shun. The phrase I have translated "gifts of food" is used of the gifts people living under tyranny offer to their liberators (see 3.15), and, in offering them, they signify their approval of their conqueror. (see 1.15 and 1.16). Here, it seems to me Mencius is deploring any suggestion that the King of Yen had really acted like Yao and Shun. "Tyranny" was written all over his face.

(7B.11)

TEXTS, TRANSLATIONS, AND REFERENCES

The definitive translation of *Mencius* is that of James Legge in the *Chinese Classics*, vol. I, (Oxford, 1893; reprinted by the Hong Kong University Press, 1960). Legge provides a critical apparatus and justifies the textual decisions he makes. He has not yet been replaced. Legge is, however, a difficult translator for those unfamiliar with the original to follow. And, too, since Legge's time a great deal more has been learned not only about *Mencius* but about the language generally of Archaic Chinese. My translation is not intended to supplant Legge, but neither is it a "Legge made easy." It is a new translation made in the light of recent textual and philological research, but with the general reader in mind.

No attempt has been made in annotation to justify departures from Legge, or to provide an apparatus for the expert for interpretations followed. On the whole I have been guided by the readings and notes of Chiao Hsün's *Meng-tzu Cheng-yi*, giving more weight to the Han paraphrist Chao Ch'i (died 201 A.D.) than to the Sung exegete Chu Hsi (1130-1200 A.D.). A number of the problems of syntax in the text of *Mencius* are treated for the specialist in my *Late Archaic Chinese* (1959) and *Early Archaic Chinese* (1962) and in articles in learned journals.

In the matter of dating—a vexed problem for the years prior to the third century B.C.—I have adopted exclusively the chronology of Ch'ien Mu's masterly *Hsien Ch'in Chu-tzu Hsi-nien* (Hong Kong, 1956), preferring to follow a system of reconstruction complete in itself to accepting specific dates that claim to be accurately fixed without being related to a consistent whole.

FINDING LIST

Harvard-Yenching text number	My number
1A.1	1.21
1A.2	1.24
1A.3	1.22
1A.4	1.23
1A.5	1.20
1A.6	1.26
1A.7	1.5
1B.1	1.4
1B.2	1.3
1B.3	1.6
1B.4	1.2
1B.5	1.14
1B.6	1.12
1B.7	1.11
1B.8	1.1
1B.9	1.13
1B.10	1.15
1B.11	1.16
1B.12	1.36
1B.13	1.30
1B.14	1.31
1B.15	1.29
1B.16	1.35
2A.1	3.28
2A.2	3.29
2A.3	6.7
2A.4	6.6
2A.5	6.84
2A.6	6.1
2A.7	6.5
2A.8	6.60
2A.9	6.67
2B.1	6.81
2B.2	2.1
2B.3	2.10

Harvard-Yenching text number	My number
2B.4	2.4
2B.5	2.2
2B.6	2.6
2B.7	2.8
2B.8	1.18
2B.9	1.17
2B.10	2.13
2B.11	2.15
2B.12	2.16
2B.13	2.14
2B.14	2.17
3A.1	1.27
3A.2	1.28
3A.3	1.32
3A.4	4.14
3A.5	4.3
3B.1	3.38
3B.2	5.1
3B.3	3.48
3B.4	3.39
3B.5	3.15
3B.6	1.37
3B.7	3.23
3B.8	1.38
3B.9	3.3
3B.10	4.15
4A.1	6.44
4A.2	6.43
4A.3	6.10
4A.4	6.31
4A.5	7.14
4A.6	5.8
4A.7	6.83
4A.8	6.62
4A.9	5.13

Harvard-Yenching text number	My number	Harvard-Yenching text number	My number
4A.10	6.69	4B.24	6.78
4A.11	5.14	4B.25	6.80
4A.12	6.14	4B.26	4.13
4A.13	6.100	4B.27	2.7
4A.14	6.65	4B.28	6.4
4A.15	5.5	4B.29	6.99
4A.16	7.22	4B.30	3.5
4A.17	5.12	4B.31	6.77
4A.18	4.17	4B.32	2.5
4A.19	3.30	4B.33	5.11
4A.20	6.13		
4A.21	6.8	5A.1	3.12
4A.22	7.9	5A.2	3.11
4A.23	7.10	5A.3	3.9
4A.24	3.32	5A.4	3.41
4A.25	3.33	5A.5	3.10
4A.26	6.18	5A.6	3.8
4A.27	6.12	5A.7	3.7
4A.28	6.52	5A.8	3.6
		5A.9	3.14
4B.1	6.56		
4B.2	6.72	5B.1	6.64
4B.3	1.8	5B.2	3.42
4B.4	7.16	5B.3	3.13
4B.5	6.9	5B.4	3.19
4B.6	7.5	5B.5	6.89
4B.7	7.4	5B.6	3.17
4B.8	7.17	5B.7	3.18
4B.9	7.11	5B.8	3.16
4B.10	7.21	5B.9	1.7
4B.11	7.13		
4B.12	7.12	6A.1	4.6
4B.13	6.17	6A.2	4.7
4B.14	6.40	6A.3	4.8
4B.15	7.1	6A.4	4.9
4B.16	6.101	6A.5	4.10
4B.17	7.8	6A.6	4.11
4B.18	6.73	6A.7	4.12
4B.19	6.19	6A.8	6.20
4B.20	6.59	6A.9	1.19
4B.21	6.48	6A.10	6.21
4B.22	6.50	6A.11	6.39
4B.23	6.90	6A.12	6.33

Harvard-Yenching text number	My number	Harvard-Yenching text number	My number
6A.13	6.32	7A.18	6.41
6A.14	6.29	7A.19	6.92
6A.15	3.4	7A.20	6.16
6A.16	6.96	7A.21	6.93
6A.17	6.95	7A.22	6.66
6A.18	6.11	7A.23	6.86
6A.19	6.3	7A.24	6.74
6A.20	6.79	7A.25	6.54
		7A.26	4.1
6B.1	3.37	7A.27	6.22
6B.2	3.47	7A.28	6.68
6B.3	3.21	7A.29	6.30
6B.4	4.4	7A.30	6.57
6B.5	2.11	7A.31	3.24
6B.6	4.18	7A.32	3.25
6B.7	6.70	7A.33	1.9
6B.8	4.5	7A.34	4.16
6B.9	5.3	7A.35	3.40
6B.10	3.44	7A.36	1.10
6B.11	3.43	7A.37	6.91
6B.12	7.23	7A.38	6.28
6B.13	3.22	7A.39	2.9
6B.14	3.35	7A.40	3.1
6B.15	6.61	7A.41	3.26
6B.16	3.2	7A.42	7.18
		7A.43	1.34
7A.1	6.24	7A.44	7.19
7A.2	6.26	7A.45	6.15
7A.3	6.27	7A.46	6.34
7A.4	6.38		
7A.5	6.36	7B.1	1.25
7A.6	6.37	7B.2	6.47
7A.7	5.4	7B.3	6.46
7A.8	6.88	7B.4	5.2
7A.9	3.46	7B.5	6.45
7A.10	6.63	7B.6	6.55
7A.11	5.10	7B.7	6.98
7A.12	6.87	7B.8	5.6
7A.13	6.71	7B.9	6.82
7A.14	6.35	7B.10	7.15
7A.15	6.14	7B.11	7.20
7A.16	6.53	7B.12	7.6
7A.17	7.24	7B.13	7.3

Harvard-Yenching text number	My number	Harvard-Yenching text number	My number
7B.14	6.94	7B.27	6.85
7B.15	6.51	7B.28	5.9
7B.16	7.2	7B.29	2.3
7B.17	6.75	7B.30	1.33
7B.18	6.76	7B.31	6.2
7B.19	3.45	7B.32	6.97
7B.20	7.7	7B.33	6.58
7B.21	3.35	7B.34	5.7
7B.22	3.34	7B.35	6.23
7B.23	2.12	7B.36	3.27
7B.24	6.25	7B.37	3.20
7B.25	3.31	7B.38	6.49
7B.26	4.2		

My number	Harvard-Yenching text number	My number	Harvard-Yenching text number
1.1	1B.8	1.26	1A.6
1.2	1B.4	1.27	3A.1
1.3	1B.2	1.28	3A.2
1.4	1B.1	1.29	1B.15
1.5	1A.7	1.30	1B.13
1.6	1B.3	1.31	1B.14
1.7	5B.9	1.32	3A.3
1.8	4B.3	1.33	7B.30
1.9	7A.33	1.34	7A.43
1.10	7A.36	1.35	1B.16
1.11	1B.7	1.36	1B.12
1.12	1B.6	1.37	3B.6
1.13	1B.9	1.38	3B.8
1.14	1B.5		
1.15	1B.10	2.1	2B.2
1.16	1B.11	2.2	2B.5
1.17	2B.9	2.3	7B.29
1.18	2B.8	2.4	2B.4
1.19	6A.9	2.5	4B.32
1.20	1A.5	2.6	2B.6
1.21	1A.1	2.7	4B.27
1.22	1A.3	2.8	2B.7
1.23	1A.4	2.9	7A.39
1.24	1A.2	2.10	2B.3
1.25	7B.1	2.11	6B.5

My number	Harvard-Yenching text number	My number	Harvard-Yenching text number
2.12	7B.23	3.37	6B.1
2.13	2B.10	3.38	3B.1
2.14	2B.13	3.39	3B.4
2.15	2B.11	3.40	7A.35
2.16	2B.12	3.41	5A.4
2.17	2B.14	3.42	5B.2
		3.43	6B.11
3.1	7A.40	3.44	6B.10
3.2	6B.16	3.45	7B.19
3.3	3B.9	3.46	7A.9
3.4	6A.15	3.47	6B.2
3.5	4B.30	3.48	3B.3
3.6	5A.8		
3.7	5A.7	4.1	7A.26
3.8	5A.6	4.2	7B.26
3.9	5A.3	4.3	3A.5
3.10	5A.5	4.4	6B.4
3.11	5A.2	4.5	6B.8
3.12	5A.1	4.6	6A.1
3.13	5B.3	4.7	6A.2
3.14	5A.9	4.8	6A.3
3.15	3B.5	4.9	6A.4
3.16	5B.8	4.10	6A.5
3.17	5B.6	4.11	6A.6
3.18	5B.7	4.12	6A.7
3.19	5B.4	4.13	4B.26
3.20	7B.37	4.14	3A.4
3.21	6B.3	4.15	3B.10
3.22	6B.13	4.16	7A.34
3.23	3B.7	4.17	4A.18
3.24	7A.31	4.18	6B.6
3.25	7A.32		
3.26	7A.41	5.1	3B.2
3.27	7B.36	5.2	7B.4
3.28	2A.1	5.3	6B.9
3.29	2A.2	5.4	7A.7
3.30	4A.19	5.5	4A.15
3.31	7B.25	5.6	7B.8
3.32	4A.24	5.7	7B.34
3.33	4A.25	5.8	4A.6
3.34	7B.22	5.9	7B.28
3.35	7B.21	5.10	7A.11
3.36	6B.14	5.11	4B.33

My number	Harvard-Yenching text number	My number	Harvard-Yenching text number
5.12	4A.17	6.40	4B.14
5.13	4A.9	6.41	7A.18
5.14	4A.11	6.42	7A.15
		6.43	4A.2
6.1	2A.6	6.44	4A.1
6.2	7B.31	6.45	7B.5
6.3	6A.19	6.46	7B.3
6.4	4B.28	6.47	7B.2
6.5	2A.7	6.48	4B.21
6.6	2A.4	6.49	7B.38
6.7	2A.3	6.50	4B.22
6.8	4A.21	6.51	7B.15
6.9	4B.5	6.52	4A.28
6.10	4A.3	6.53	7A.16
6.11	6A.18	6.54	7A.25
6.12	4A.27	6.55	7B.6
6.13	4A.20	6.56	4B.1
6.14	4A.12	6.57	7A.30
6.15	7A.45	6.58	7B.33
6.16	7A.20	6.59	4B.20
6.17	4B.13	6.60	2A.8
6.18	4A.26	6.61	6B.15
6.19	4B.19	6.62	4A.8
6.20	6A.8	6.63	7A.10
6.21	6A.10	6.64	5B.1
6.22	7A.27	6.65	4A.14
6.23	7B.35	6.66	7A.22
6.24	7A.1	6.67	2A.9
6.25	7B.24	6.68	7A.28
6.26	7A.2	6.69	4A.10
6.27	7A.3	6.70	6B.7
6.28	7A.38	6.71	7A.13
6.29	6A.14	6.72	4B.2
6.30	7A.29	6.73	4B.18
6.31	4A.4	6.74	7A.24
6.32	6A.13	6.75	7B.17
6.33	6A.12	6.76	7B.18
6.34	7A.46	6.77	4B.31
6.35	7A.14	6.78	4B.24
6.36	7A.5	6.79	6A.20
6.37	7A.6	6.80	4B.25
6.38	7A.4	6.81	2B.1
6.39	6A.11	6.82	7B.9

My number	Harvard-Yenching text number	My number	Harvard-Yenching text number
6.83	4A.7	7.3	7B.13
6.84	2A.5	7.4	4B.7
6.85	7B.27	7.5	4B.6
6.86	7A.23	7.6	7B.12
6.87	7A.12	7.7	7B.20
6.88	7A.8	7.8	4B.17
6.89	5B.5	7.9	4.A22
6.90	4B.23	7.10	4A.23
6.91	7A.37	7.11	4B.9
6.92	7A.19	7.12	4B.12
6.93	7A.21	7.13	4B.11
6.94	7B.14	7.14	4A.5
6.95	6A.17	7.15	7B.10
6.96	6A.16	7.16	4B.4
6.97	7B.32	7.17	4B.8
6.98	7B.7	7.18	7A.42
6.99	4B.29	7.19	7A.44
6.100	4A.13	7.20	7B.11
6.101	4B.16	7.21	4B.10
		7.22	4A.16
7.1	4B.15	7.23	6B.12
7.2	7B.16	7.24	7A.17